Letters from Ladysmith

Eyewitness Accounts from the South African War

Edward M. Spiers

Foreword by Ian Knight

JONATHAN BALL PUBLISHERS
Johannesburg & Cape Town

FRONTLINE
BOOKS

The moral right of the author has been asserted.

Originally published in 2010 in the United Kingdom by
Pen & Sword Books Ltd

This edition published in South Africa in 2010 by
JONATHAN BALL PUBLISHERS (PTY) LTD
P O Box 33977
Jeppestown
2043
ISBN 978–1–86842–415–3

with

Frontline Books
an imprint of
Pen & Sword Books Limited, 47 Church Street,
Barnsley, S. Yorkshire, S70 2AS
www.frontline-books.com

UK ISBN: 978–1–84832–594–4

Typeset by Palindrome
in ITC Galliard 10½/13pt

Printed in Great Britain by MPG Books

Contents

Illustrations

Illustrations may be found between pages 128 and 129

List of Maps

Foreword

The Anglo-Boer War of 1899–1902 was undoubtedly the greatest challenge faced by the British empire during the nineteenth century.

At the very apogee of imperial pomp and pretension, at a time when Britain's reputation as an economic, industrial and military power was still largely unrivalled around the world, the army that had painted great swathes of the map British red, from Canada to Afghanistan and India to New Zealand, appeared suddenly powerless in a series of embarrassing clashes fought in obscure African locations against a relatively small citizen militia of white farmers. The repercussions of the conflict would prove to be enormous, shaping not only the extraordinary twentieth-century history of southern Africa – paving the way for the post-war emergence of Afrikaner nationalism and the rise and fall of the apartheid state – but impacting upon Britain's relations with its European rivals, and offering the British army harsh but valuable lessons on the very eve of the First World War. Indeed, for Britain's professional soldier elite – undeniably experienced as they were – the Anglo-Boer War proved to be something of a final chapter in a complex and often painful evolution that had taken them, within the reign of a single monarch, from an essentially Napoleonic institution, fighting conventional battles in close-order formations and wearing red coats, to a recognisably modern one, groping towards an understanding of all-too contemporary counter-insurgency techniques.

While it is true that the war that broke out at the southern tip of the African continent in October 1899 between the British and the Boer republics of the Orange Free State and Transvaal had much to do with immediate and local tensions – and in particular the conflicts that had arisen between an essentially conservative and inward-looking Transvaal government and British capitalist interests intruding there in the wake of the discovery of gold in large quantities in the Witwatersrand in 1886 – it was in truth part of a much broader contest, a struggle between two very different forms of European colonialism that had emerged in southern Africa across more than two centuries.

In 1652 the Dutch East India Company had established the first European settlement at the Cape of Good Hope. At that time, the Dutch had little interest in the African hinterland – the Company specifically barred its settlers there from travelling beyond its boundaries into the interior – and was primarily concerned with providing a facility to provision and repair its ships on the long maritime haul to the far more profitable Dutch concerns in the Indies. Britain too, of course, relied on its imperial possessions in India and the East as a motor to drive its imperial expansion, and for 150 years Britain's largely amicable relationship with the Netherlands allowed British ships access to the Cape way-station. With the shuffling of long-established alliances in Europe that came first with the Revolutionary and then Napoleonic Wars against France, however, Britain had found that she could no longer take the security of the Cape sea-route for granted, particularly once Napoleon had conquered the Netherlands and established the pro-French Batavian Republic. With Dutch possessions falling under Napoleon's control and raising a very real threat that the sea-route to India around the Cape might be cut, Britain had opted for direct action. In 1806 a British invasion fleet had landed at the Cape and dispersed Batavian forces in a battle fought out on the sand-dunes within sight of Table Mountain. The British took control of the colony – and would remain the dominant regional power for almost exactly a century.

It was not long, however, before the European inhabitants of the Dutch settlement, many of whom were in fact French religious refugees from Europe, came to realise that Britain's interests had little in common with their own. Whereas Britain was a metropolitan power, looking out at the world through networks of economic and political influence of which the Cape was but a link in an extensive chain, the Cape settlers had largely turned their backs on the outside world. Although a common sense of identity and nationhood would elude them until the twentieth century – it came, ironically, as a result of their ultimate defeat in the Anglo-Boer War – they had already come to think of themselves increasingly as a distinct people, not Dutch but Cape Dutch or, latterly, Afrikaners – white Africans. For the most part they were simply known by the Dutch word for a farmer or country person, *boer*. Accustomed to living tough and self-reliant lives on remote farms in a harsh and often unforgiving landscape, buoyed up by a stern religious faith and a sense of racial superiority that kept them aloof from the indigenous inhabitants, they looked instead to find a role for themselves in Africa, and were soon disillusioned with the more liberal approach towards racial interaction and frontier security adopted by the British administration. By the 1830s Boer discontent was sufficient to spur more than 12,000 men, women and children to abandon their farms and livelihoods, to place whatever possessions they could in their ox wagons, and emigrate wholesale beyond the limits of British authority in search of a new life in the interior of southern Africa.

The so-called 'Great Trek' reshaped the political geography of the region. The Trekkers' progress was marked by a series of brutal conflicts with the robust African societies who had occupied the land before them, and while it led ultimately to the creation of the two republics it also framed the parameters of future rivalry with the British. Underpinning initial British concerns that Boer actions should not impact upon their strategic interests in the region, destabilising their borders or encouraging involvement with rival world powers, was a much deeper conflict in which both sides increasingly strove to secure control over the land and its resources – a conflict that saw African groups trapped uncomfortably in between. The British had attempted to reassert their authority in the 1840s, a series of small actions, largely forgotten today, fought out in the Free State and in Natal, and while they had been content, in the end, to relinquish their claims to the interior, they had secured their hold over the eastern coast, leaving the Trekker republics resolutely landlocked.

In the end, however, it was the unexpected realisation that southern Africa possessed immense mineral wealth that had pushed the two groups into a knock-down conflict. With the discovery of diamonds north of the Cape in the 1860s, the British had adopted, for the first time, a forward policy designed to secure their control over the area as a whole. When, in 1877, the Transvaal Republic, beset by conflicts with its African neighbours, had seemed on the verge of bankruptcy, the British had intervened and annexed it; the Boer response was to sit quietly while the British went on to defeat the neighbouring Zulu kingdom and then, in December 1880, to rise in revolt. Stung by a series of defeats in the field – the senior British commander, General Sir George Colley, was killed at the disastrous battle of Majuba on 27 February 1881 – the Liberal administration of Prime Minister Gladstone agreed to abandon the Transvaal once more to the Boers, subject only to vague claims to 'suzerainty'.

The exact extent of that tenuous British influence over Transvaal affairs was thrown into relief by the discovery of gold in 1885. Foreign miners, many of them British, flocked into the Transvaal boom town of Johannesburg, unsettling the conservative Boer government that refused to grant them a franchise. The grumblings of these *uitlanders* ('outsiders')

were taken up by powerful capitalist cliques keen to develop and control
the mining industry. In 1895 Cecil Rhodes, diamond magnate and prime
minister of the Cape, backed an attempt by his lieutenant, Dr Leander
Starr Jameson, to provoke a coup in Johannesburg, but in the event the
uitlanders refused to rise, Jameson was defeated and he and his 'raiders'
captured. The incident highlighted the gulf between British and Boer
interests in the region, however, and many in the Transvaal government
regarded an open conflict as inevitable from that moment. Tension
continued to rise, and in September 1899 Sir Joseph Chamberlain, the
British colonial secretary, issued an ultimatum to the Transvaal government to recognise the rights of the *uitlanders*; Paul Kruger, the Republic's
president, responded with a demand that British troops in southern Africa
be moved away from the Republic's borders. The Free State allied itself
with the Transvaal, and since neither side was prepared to comply with the
other's demands and the war began officially on 11 October 1899.

The fighting that followed was destined to last for more than three
years. It would require by far the greatest commitment from the British
army of the Victorian era − nearly every British regiment would be involved at some point − together with an unprecedented degree of military
support from British colonies in Australia and Canada. In the early stages,
British over-confidence − a fatal under-estimation of the fighting capability
and resolve of the Boer civilian militias − led to a series of defeats that
staggered imperial self-confidence. In the end, the British would achieve a
supremacy of sorts in large-scale conventional contests on the battlefield,
but only after a series of painful and bloody lessons, and only to find
the illusion of victory stripped from them by the refusal of the defeated
Boers to submit. While the British had captured, by the end of 1900, the
capitals of both the Free State and the Transvaal, and secured control of
the arterial railway lines that connected them, they had failed to dominate
the countryside that remained largely in the hands of free-ranging Boer
commando groups. For the British it meant adopting new strategies,
and while it is possible to argue that the army groped its way successfully
towards modern counter-insurgency techniques, dividing the landscape
with fortified lines to restrict the movement of the guerrillas, destroying
farms to deny the enemy re-supply and refuge, and isolating combatants
by removing the civilian population to protected safe centres, it achieved
victory in the end only through an unacceptably high degree of collateral
damage, the deaths of thousands of Boer women and children by disease
in the poorly run 'concentration camps'.

The consequences of the war were immense. Many European powers
− notably Germany − had tacitly supported the Boers, exaggerating

British rivalries internationally, while at the same time encouraging a movement towards greater autonomy among those colonies, like Australia and Canada, who had supported the war. Many British – and, indeed, colonial – soldiers who had learned their craft as middle-ranking officers in southern Africa would find themselves put to the test again under very different conditions on the outbreak of war in 1914. The economies of the two Boer republics were devastated, of course, and in an effort to repair the bitter rifts between the two European groups and placate the defeated commando leaders Britain had agreed to abandon its more liberal attitude towards the African population, revoking the limited franchise that existed, in particular, at the Cape. It was a move that effectively betrayed those black South Africans who had supported the British cause in the hope of winning back some of their old political independence. Although the war did ultimately unite the former British and Boer territories under the Union of South Africa in 1910, it left the population if anything more divided, and not merely along racial grounds. Afrikaner society, in particular, was deeply damaged, leaving some sectors impoverished and bitterly alienated, paving the way for the emergence of an intense Afrikaner nationalism that came to dominate the Union for much of the twentieth-century.

When the war had begun in October 1899, the republics had made pre-emptive strikes against key British-held towns across the borders: at Mafikeng in the west, at the diamond-town of Kimberley in the south, and towards Ladysmith in Natal. Although both Mafikeng and Kimberley commanded a good deal of press attention – owing to the energetic defence of the former by Robert Baden-Powell and the fact that Cecil Rhodes was entrapped in the latter – there is no doubt that Ladysmith was the most important of the three. A garrison town in Natal, at one time nicknamed 'the Aldershot of Natal', Ladysmith was defended by a strong force under Sir George White, and its capture would have been a serious strategic blow to the British, effectively abandoning Natal to the Boers. Yet any attempt to relieve Ladysmith was hampered by a formidable geographical feature, for it lay on the wrong side of the Thukela river, allowing the besieging Boers to occupy a formidable defensive position across the line of any possible British attempts at relief.

The subsequent efforts to defend Ladysmith – and to march to its relief – quickly became the great dramatic saga of the early phase of the Anglo-Boer War, providing the context for a series of dramatic battles that embarrassed the empire and destroyed established reputations. While much has been written about the apparent failings of the British commanders – of the inadvisability of White's decision to occupy

Ladysmith in the first place, and in particular of the failure of Sir Redvers Buller to force a way through to relieve it – it is worth noting that in no other theatre in the war were the practical difficulties so real or the stakes so high.

Professor Spiers is ideally qualified to reassess this crucial campaign: he is Professor of Strategic Studies at the School of History of the University of Leeds and author of dozens of influential and scholarly publications, of which *The Late Victorian Army 1866–1902* and *The Victorian Soldier in Africa* are widely held to be definitive studies. Yet *Letters From Ladysmith* is not so much about the inadequacies of the British high command as about the war as it seemed to those who fought it – both those inside the town cordon, and those battling to cross the Thukela. Many of these eye-witness accounts have not been published since they first appeared in local newspapers more than a century ago. Not only do they add materially to our understanding of the campaign, but they speak with a voice that seems, despite the passage of so much time, remarkably fresh and vivid. In their emphasis on the discomforts of war in south Africa – the smoke, dust, heat, and rain, the poor food, boredom of inactivity and the ghastly sights and sounds of the fighting, conveyed sometimes with a surprising and disturbing honesty – they add an important perspective to the conventional emphasis on the alleged bungles of the high command that is often lacking in other works.

This is Victorian warfare as we seldom encounter it today: 'from the ground up'.

Ian Knight
Chichester

Acknowledgements

I should like to acknowledge the grant from the Scouloudi Foundation which enabled me to complete the research for this work.

Quotations of Crown copyright material in the Public Record Office appear by permission of The National Archives as the custodians of the records. I should also like to acknowledge the assistance of many other individuals who assisted me directly or indirectly in my research: Mr Alastair Massie for the permission to quote from, or refer to, materials held by the National Army Museum, the staffs of the British Library (Newspaper Collection) at Colindale, of the Templar Study Centre of the National Army Museum, of the National Library of Scotland, of the Reference and Local Studies Centres in Liverpool Central Library, Manchester Central Library, Sheffield Central Library and Leeds Central Library and Mr Tony Cox (Devonshire and Dorset Regimental Museum, Exeter).

I should also like to express my thanks to various colleagues who have assisted me in this project, namely Professors John Gooch, Andrew Thompson and Richard Whiting (University of Leeds), Professor Ian F. W. Beckett (University of Kent), Professor Keith Jeffery (Queen's University, Belfast), Professor Fransjohan Pretorius (University of Pretoria), Dr Jeremy A. Crang (University of Edinburgh) and Ian Knight.

I am particularly grateful to David Appleyard for the services of the Graphic Support Unit (University of Leeds) in the preparation of the maps, to Peter Harrington, Anne S. K. Brown Military History Collection, Brown University, Rhode Island for his assistance in finding images for the volume; to the Anne S. K. Brown Military History Collection for permission to use images from their collection, to Mr and Mrs A. M. Cruickshank for kind gift of books from Ladysmith and to Fiona, my wife, and Robert and Amanda, our children, for enduring the preparation of another book.

Edward M. Spiers

Introduction

Ladysmith: the Siege and the Letters

The siege of Ladysmith proved one of the epic events of South African War (1899–1902). Under investment were 12,500 officers and men alongside 5,400 civilians and 2,400 Blacks and Indians in a siege that lasted 118 days from 2 November 1899 to 28 February 1900. Although it may not have lasted as long as the siege of Mafeking (Mafikeng) nor involved a commanding officer as charismatic as Colonel R. S. S. Baden-Powell nor an imperial icon like Cecil Rhodes then trapped in the siege of Kimberley, the strategic and imperial significance of the siege was all too apparent at the time. Had Ladysmith, under the command of Sir George White, VC, fallen to the invaders from the Transvaal and the Orange Free State, the Boers would have seized northern Natal, acquired an abundance of military supplies, and gained the use of a key road and rail junction north of the Tugela (Thukela) River. At the darkest hour in the history of the siege after the defeat of the relief force at Colenso (15 December 1899) when the British commander-in-chief, Sir Redvers Buller, sent defeatist telegrams to Ladysmith and London, stating in the latter: 'I do not consider that I am strong enough to relieve Ladysmith . . . I consider that I ought to let Ladysmith go and to occupy a good position for the defence of southern Natal . . .',[1] the reaction was incandescent. Lord Lansdowne, the secretary of state for war, replied that 'The abandonment of White's force and its consequent surrender is regarded by the Government as a national disaster of the greatest magnitude.'[2] A horrified Queen Victoria declared that she 'thought it was quite impossible to abandon Ladysmith'.[3] From the beleaguered town, Lieutenant Colonel

---

1   The National Archives (TNA), WO 108/399, Buller telegrams of 15 December 1899, nos. 53 and 54.
2   Ibid., Lord Lansdowne to Buller, 16 December 1899, no. 57.
3   G. E. Buckle, *The Letters of Queen Victoria. Third Series. A Selection from Her Majesty's Correspondence and Journal between the Years 1886 and 1901*, 3 vols

Henry Rawlinson, then serving on White's staff as deputy assistant adjutant general, reckoned that the loss of Ladysmith would have been a 'blow not only to England but to the whole British Empire . . . [and] one from which she will not easily recover'.[4] Just as tangible were the feelings of relief when the siege was lifted: 'I thank God', declared White, 'we have kept the flag flying'[5] and massive celebrations convulsed much of Great Britain.

Named after Lady Smith, the wife of a distinguished British officer and former governor of Natal, Sir Harry Smith, the small town located in a deep bend of the Klip river was never intended as a strategic focal point in this war. Indeed, General Sir Redvers Buller, when appointed commander-in-chief of the army corps destined for South Africa, had indicated that he did not wish to garrison towns north of the Tugela River. However, the forces already in the British colony of Natal under the command of Major General Sir William Penn Symons had deployed to Dundee, close to the border with the Transvaal prior to the Boer invasion on 11 October, and some of the first reinforcements, 10,000 soldiers from India under Lieutenant General Sir George White, moved north in support. Ladysmith now assumed a pivotal importance as a supply centre on the main road and rail routes between Durban and the Boer republics. From Ladysmith the railway branched off in a north-westerly direction beyond the Drakensberg Mountains to Harrismith in the Orange Free State and in a northerly direction to Dundee and through Lang's Nek to Volkrust in the Transvaal.

Located in a bowl of hills, Ladysmith was also highly vulnerable and difficult to approach from the south, where the Tugela River and the high hills on its northern bank barred the route northwards. Once the Boers laid siege to Ladysmith, Kimberley and Mafeking, and in the case of Ladysmith entrapping so many troops, it became one of focal points of British strategy. Buller, having arrived at Cape Town on 30 October 1899, abandoned his preconceived plan of marching directly on the Boer capitals, and split his 47,000-man army into separate relief forces to lift these sieges, leading the main force himself in Natal.[6]

This train of events derived from Britain's underestimation of the Boers, often derided by contemporaries as a body of ill-disciplined farmers. Though untrained by European standards, and independent-

(London: 1920–2), vol. 3, p. 435.

4   National Army Museum (NAM), Acc. 1952-01-33-7-1, Rawlinson, diary, 17 December 1899.

5   Quoted in Kenneth Griffith, *Thank God We Kept the Flag Flying: The siege and relief of Ladysmith 1899–1900* (London: Hutchinson, 1974), p. 362.

6   Thomas Pakenham, *The Boer War* (London: Weidenfeld & Nicolson, 1979), p. 158.

minded, the 35,000 Boers mobilised at the outset of the war represented a well-armed, highly mobile and resourceful enemy. For several years prior to the outbreak of war, the Boer republics, desperate to maintain their political autonomy and cultural identity, had resisted the ambitions of Britain's colonial authorities. The latter included the desire of Joseph Chamberlain, the colonial secretary, to pursue his long-term ambition of forging a South African Federation that would encompass Cape Colony, Natal and the two Boer republics. The Europeans, known to the Boers as Uitlanders, who had swept into the Transvaal when gold was discovered in the Witwatersrand in 1886, provided the trigger for the dispute, notably in their demand for political rights that the Boers resisted (requiring residency of fourteen years before they could vote in the Volksraad or parliamentary elections of the Transvaal). Chamberlain exerted pressure, illegally in the support for the abortive raid into the Transvaal by Rhodes's colleague, Dr Leander Starr Jameson and some 500 mounted Rhodesian police in 1895, and later subversively, through the efforts of Sir Alfred Milner, the British high commissioner in South Africa. Milner exploited the demands of the Uitlanders for British intervention on their behalf but the British government proved reluctant to act after the fiasco of the Jameson raid. Following the shooting of a Transvaal mining engineer, Tom Edgar, by the Transvaal police on 23 December 1898, it opened negotiations with the Transvaal in which Milner tried to exert pressure on the Boers. These talks culminated in an abortive conference at Bloemfontein (31 May–5 June 1899) where Milner refused to compromise on his demands for enfranchisement of the Uitlanders, while President Paul Kruger of the Transvaal only offered to halve the fourteen-year residency period.

Throughout these negotiations the British government had not reinforced the garrisons of Cape Colony and Natal lest such action provoke the Boers. By June 1899, the British forces of 10,289 men and 24 artillery pieces hardly constituted a deterrent, and Lieutenant General Sir William F. Butler, the British commander-in-chief in South Africa, who despaired of the prospect of war between the white races, refused to plan for the forward defence of Natal and Cape Colony. Milner pressed for and secured Butler's resignation in August 1899 as well as the despatch of 10,000 reinforcements mainly from India. He also supported the forward deployment of the forces under Major-General Sir William Penn Symons near the Transvaal border. However, Kruger, who had spent several years rearming the Transvaal with latest weaponry, including German Mauser rifles, Krupp 75-mm field guns and French Creusot 155-mm guns, resolved upon a pre-emptive strike, with support from the formerly cautious president of the Orange Free State, Marthinus Steyn.

On 9 October the two republics delivered a joint ultimatum to Britain (only two days after White's reinforcements had landed at Durban), and two days later launched an invasion of northern Natal.[7] In a multipronged advance, the elderly Boer general Piet Joubert had at his disposal some 11,400 Transvaal and 6,000 Free State burghers. He was intent upon cutting the communications between Ladysmith and Dundee at Elandslaagte, crushing Penn Symons's forces at Dundee and then moving on Ladysmith.

In reviewing how British forces responded to the invasion, this work will utilise eyewitness testimony primarily from soldiers but also from civilians, which has not been seen in this form before. The 250 letters were all published in different British newspapers and they provide insights into contemporary perceptions of the battles that preceded the siege, the onset of the siege itself, and the desperate and bloody attempts to relieve the town over the next three months. These letters, reproduced in their original printed form, reflect vividly the feelings of junior officers and other ranks as they struggled to cope with the demands of modern warfare. They contrast with many existing accounts of the siege of Ladysmith that focus upon the personalities, disputes and disagreements between commanding officers and their staffs.[8] They provide first-hand commentary upon the events in Natal that shattered the pre-war confidence in Britain and the widespread under-estimation of an enemy that was often well entrenched, adept at field craft, and, under the skilful command of General Louis Botha, able to exploit the devastating effects of smokeless, flat trajectory, magazine rifle fire.

The letters testify to the way in which Britain, an imperial power, responded to the early reverses by deploying significant military and naval reinforcements by sea and by projecting them rapidly into the theatre by rail. They reflect, too, upon the social consequences of the war, particularly the displacement of large numbers of refugees from the Transvaal,[9] and of citizens from northern Natal, many of whom travelled by rail to Ladysmith and beyond; the medical effects of concentrating a

---

7   On the origins of the war, see Iain R. Smith, *The Origins of the South African War* (London: Longman, 1996) and Andrew N. Porter, *The Origins of the South African War: Joseph Chamberlain and the diplomacy of imperialism* (Manchester: Manchester University Press 1980)

8   Owen Coetzer, *The Anglo-Boer War: The road to infamy 1899–1900. Colenso, Spioenkop, Vaalkrantz, Pieters, Buller and Warren* (London: Arms and Armour, 1996); Ruari Chisholm, *Ladysmith* (London: Osprey Publishing Ltd, 1979).

9   Diana Cammack, *The Rand at War 1899–1902: The Witwatersrand and the Anglo-Boer War* (London: James Currey, 1990).

large number of men in a confined environment; and the vulnerability of transport and communications, which was heavily dependent upon a railway and its accompanying telegraph. In a war shaped fundamentally by rail networks, over-reliance upon the railway could lead the British army, as demonstrated at the battle of Colenso (15 December 1899), into disaster.

In examining these events, the approach will be chronological but as several correspondents wrote at length about many aspects of these events, their letters will be numbered and where more than one reference occurs from the same letter, links with previous passages will be identified by reference to these numbers. As newspapers often published several letters under the same headline (twenty-one in a single issue of the *Blackburn Times*),[10] full references, with subheadings, are given for each letter. Wherever these letters allude to principal individuals or events, or err in their commentary, the letters are annotated and perspectives from enemy sources added. Further points of reference can be found in the maps and illustrations. The afterword will assess the significance of this correspondence – its difference from previous accounts of the siege, the value of the correspondence both at the time and subsequently in understanding how participants responded to the challenge of enduring a siege, and securing its relief.

---

10 'Letters from Local Soldiers at the Front', *Blackburn Times*, 14 April 1900, p. 3.

Chapter 1

Fighting in Northern Natal and the Retreat to Ladysmith

As British reinforcements reached Natal in September and October 1899, with Lieutenant General Sir George White VC, arriving on 7 October to assume command, Major General Sir William Penn Symons had already deployed his brigade in the coalmining town of Dundee in northern Natal. That brigade included the 18th Hussars, a squadron of Natal Carbineers, and a contingent of Natal Police. The eighteen guns were those of the 13th, 67th and 69th batteries and the infantry included the 1st Battalions, Leicesters and King's Royal Rifles, and the 2nd Battalion Royal Dublin Fusiliers. On 16 October the 1st Battalion, Royal Irish Fusiliers joined them. Both the soldiers deployed at Dundee, and those who reinforced them, knew that war was imminent, that the previous war with the Transvaal in 1881 had proved disastrous, and that a swift, decisive victory was expected on this occasion. They would see the social consequences of war as hundreds of displaced persons fled through their ranks. They would also engage the Boers in the first set-piece battles of the war and experience the effects of crossing fire zones swept by smokeless magazine rifles.

Anticipating War

1

On the eve of war, 21 September 1899, Corporal G. H. Spence, 1st Battalion, Leicestershire Regiment, wrote from Ladysmith:

> We go to the front about Wednesday, Sept. 27th . . . It is our proud boast that we are to redeem England's fallen flower and Mr. Gladstone's one mistake[1] – God bless his name! . . . We are all in

---

1   The signing of the peace at the Pretoria Convention (1881).

grand condition, and hope to wipe all the troubles out, and we have the men to do it; so don't worry . . .

'Leicester Man's Letter from the Front', *Leicester Chronicle*,
28 October 1899, p. 5

2

Having arrived in Ladysmith from India, an officer of the 2nd Battalion, Gordon Highlanders, wrote:

We are here in the meantime, but for how long I don't know. It is quite the most God-forsaken spot I was ever in, nothing but hills covered with rocks and dust. We arrived here on Tuesday morning, having started from Durban about 10.30 a.m. on Monday . . . We had a fairly comfortable journey up country, for we got plenty to eat. The men suffered from the cold rather, as they were in open trucks. It is a narrow gauge railway, and the gradients are very steep. We got in about 3 a.m. and had great difficulty in finding the camp, which is over two miles [3.2 km] from the station . . . The next night I was in officers' quarters, but it is only a galvanised iron shanty, into which all the wind comes, and I was colder than I have ever been for ages . . . We are about 5,000 feet [1.5 km] above the sea here, so it is naturally rather cold at night. It was very warm yesterday, but it is cold and wet again today. The first day we arrived we had a very bad dust storm, which was far worse than an Indian one, as the dust is larger and grittier. . .

We had a most enthusiastic reception at Durban, and at every station all along the line. There are a lot of people who remember the regiment in 1881.[2] We don't know when we leave here, but when we do we go with 35 lb of kit and no tents, so we won't be very luxurious. It is rather a bad time of year to start operations, for although it is getting warmer every day, it is the beginning of the rainy season.

There are piquets out day and night on the hills all round the camp, and cavalry patrols always out, so we are fairly well protected from surprise. There is one of our companies out on a new post which was started yesterday, and which we have called 'The Gordons' Post'. I don't know whether they intend to keep it on always. It is a great treat to get back to the land of good bread and butter again. The food here is quite like the food at home, and not like the Indian abominations.

---

2   Three companies of Gordons (then the 92nd Highlanders) served in the defeat of British forces at Majuba Hill (27 February 1881).

Sunday, 15th October . . . According to the Natal papers, the first shot was fired yesterday . . . If the Boers had any sense at all they would do something now before we have more troops out here. They won't have much of a look in after our Army Corps comes out from home. I hope we don't wait till then, for it is getting tiresome living more or less under service conditions without any actual fighting going on.

'The Gordons at Ladysmith', *Free Press (Aberdeen)*,
15 November 1899, p. 6

3

Writing from Dundee on 17 October, Lance Corporal Alfred Bishop, 1st Battalion, Leicestershire Regiment, stated that

We are in camp here waiting for troops to arrive from home. I shall be glad when we make a start and get it finished . . . Old Kruger's troops are flying all over the show here. The civilian people are all turned out of house and home, and are flying to us for protection. It is shameful to see the way they have been served. Women and children turned out in the road to starve in the rain. Some came into our camp yesterday that had walked over thirty-six miles in the heat of the day, which was about 110 in the shade. So it was awful to see them. One young woman, about twenty-five, was thrown out of a passenger-train into a coal truck, and gave birth to a child in the truck with about one hundred more people crammed in. I don't think the Boers in the Transvaal will receive any mercy or pity from our men when we start.

'Leicestershire Men at the Front', *Leicester Chronicle*,
25 November 1899, p. 7

4

Meanwhile in Ladysmith Camp, a Gloucester officer wrote a letter on 19 October, describing how his men, after their arrival from Durban,

stayed two days in the camp, and the next two days and nights were dotted about the hills on picket duty. Those two nights I slept out in the open in my overcoat with my half-company under arms, all rifles loaded with ten rounds, and my revolver loaded. We had four sentries out, and sent out patrols at intervals. The other companies did similar work on other hills. I slept alternately with a sergeant and a corporal the first night, and with a sergeant the second, each of us taking it in turns to sleep and visit the sentries . . . The remaining troops of the

Gloucestershire regiment are scattered about on different hills, and
our work is to secure any part of Ladysmith from surprise. Cavalry
go out every day and night to patrol, and two shots were fired at
them by the enemy's artillery a couple of nights ago. The rest of the
troops are round in the camp and different places, quite close. The
Gloucestershire Regiment are what are called divisional troops, and do
not belong to any brigade, but we are independent, and consequently
have an awful lot to do.

It is warm in the daytime here, and the sun very hot, but the weather
is cold at night. I have been sleeping on the ground (when I could get
any sleep) up to now, but at last I have got my tent here, though, of
course, I must leave it here with the others, and only take my luck at
getting a bit of sheltered ground to lie on whenever I go out again. . .

There is nothing to be seen all around but rocky hills, which you
have to clamber over with great difficulty. There is no grass to be seen.
The place is nothing but small and large rocks and stones. A compass
cannot be used owing to the iron in the ground.

'With the Gloucesters at Ladysmith', *Gloucestershire Echo*, 14 November 1899, p. 3
and in *Gloucestershire Chronicle*, 18 November 1899, p. 7

5

Henry Burgess, formerly of Mexborough, near Sheffield, was a fireman
on one of the armoured trains. In a letter dated 27 October, he observed
that

General White is well liked by the men. You need not have the
slightest fear about us, Ladysmith is so well protected and guarded
against all emergencies, and is the strongest garrison town in South
Africa. Our troops are unanimous in their declaration of colouring the
whole map of South Africa red . . .

While I was working the Ladysmith to Charlestown section of
the Johannesburg mail, just before war was declared, the sights were
sufficient to make one's blood boil. People came to our engines
to beg hot water in order to prepare food for babies and invalids.
They could not even get a drink of water while coming through the
Transvaal. Food was refused them simply because they were British.
Women and children were packed, almost to suffocation, in coal
trucks, while the brave 'God-fearing Boers' were leisurely riding in
coaches. At every station the poor women were jeered at, and rifles
shoved in their faces, and some of the cowards even flung stones.
How different the poor people fare when under the Union Jack.

Food was then given them, and tea or coffee, and they were made as comfortable as possible. Six births occurred in one train of coal trucks, in which men and women and youngsters were crowded together.

'A Letter from Ladysmith', *Free Press* (*Aberdeen*),
4 December 1899, p. 6

The Battle of Talana Hill (20 October 1899)

Having occupied the summits of Talana and Lennox Hills, about two miles [3.2 km] east of Dundee, General Lukas Meyer deployed some 4,000 Boers with artillery and a Maxim-Nordenfelt pom-pom gun. He began shelling the British camp at 5.30 a.m. on 20 October 1899, where Penn Symons had concentrated his 3,700 men and eighteen 15-pounder guns.

6

Lieutenant Reginald Stirling, 1st Battalion, King's Royal Rifles Corps, recalled:

We paraded as usual in the morning at 4.30. We had dismissed the men, and went back for a cup of tea, when one of our fellows said, 'There they are.' Of course, we all laughed, went and got our glasses, and saw them all on two hills two or three miles away. We were so amazed we must have stood there for nearly a quarter of an hour, when suddenly a shell brought us to our senses . . . We started to attack the hill at a quarter to six o'clock. The Dublins first, or firing line, we the support . . . Beyond the river was a bit of open ground about a quarter of a mile, then came a wood, then a bit more open. When we got the order to advance my heart was rather in my mouth . . . However up I had to get, and give my men a lead. They all behaved splendidly . . . In the wood there were plenty of ditches, and at the end of the wood was a wall. We lay there to get breath. Poor Hambro[3] was shot through the jaw, but would take no notice. Then came a bad part. There was a bramble hedge on top of the wall, so no one could get over, but there was a gateway, and through this we all had to go, and it was a hot time . . . When we got under the wall some heavy firing took place, lasting nearly two hours . . . Then we crossed the road to take the hill. That was the worst place . . . We lay down under the rocks as the firing was very heavy. We saw lots of men

---

3   Lieutenant Norman J. Hambro (King's Royal Rifles) was killed by British shrapnel, Lewis Childs, *Ladysmith: The siege* (Barnsley: Leo Cooper, 1999), p. 45.

shot as they crossed the wall . . . When I went up the hill a second
time . . . We must have been there for an hour, bullets whistling over
us. Colonel Sherston[4] was dying; his groans were awful. Then an awful
part happened – our artillery taking us for Boers, began firing on us.
Colonel Gunning,[5] who was just below me stood up and yelled out
'Stop that firing.' These were the last words I heard him speak . . . By
this time our artillery had stopped. We again ascended the hill, and
got to the top to see the veldt [open, unforested country] black with
retreating Boers. A good many Boers were dead on the top . . . The
Rifles consisted of three very junior officers – Marsden, Reade (joined
six days) and myself.

'The Battle of Talana Hill', *Northern Whig (Belfast)*,
28 December 1899, p. 6

7

Sergeant Pearce, 18th Hussars, indicated that

the 18th Hussars was the only Cavalry regiment there, and we were
in the first engagement in the Boer war. We had our colonel, adjutant,
and a major, taken prisoners with 76 men[6] . . . It was a warm fight I
can assure you . . . when, to our joy, we saw the enemy retiring. We at
once got orders to gallop round the flank and cut off their retreat but
they saw what we were on and went in another direction over the hills
where we could not get our horses. Then we got orders to dismount
and go up the hill to try and check them that way, but they were too
strong for us so we had to retire under a heavy fire.

'A Holybourne Man's Experience in Ladysmith', *Hampshire Observer*,
14 April 1900, p. 6

---

4   Lieutenant Colonel J. Sherston DSO, a nephew of Lord Roberts, was a special
service officer.
5   Lieutenant Colonel 'Bobby' Gunning, King's Royal Rifles, who led the final
assault, was killed on the crest of the hill. Childs, *Ladysmith*, p. 44.
6   Of the British casualties at Talana Hill, 9 officers and 237 men were taken prisoner,
the vast majority of them, including 85 officers and men of the 87th Hussars, were under
the command of Colonel Bernhard D. Möller. Having split his mixed force of cavalry
and mounted infantry, he mistakenly led the main body away from the Boers' line of
retreat and encountered another large force of Boers under General D. J. E. Erasmus,
taking up position on Impati Hill. Vastly outnumbered, Möller surrendered. Marquess
of Anglesey, *A History of the British Cavalry 1816–1919* (London: Leo Cooper, 1986)
IV, pp. 38–45. Deneys Reitz recalled how Möller looked 'pretty crestfallen, but the
private soldiers seemed to take the turn of events more cheerfully', Deneys Reitz,
Commando: A Boer journal of the Boer War (London: Faber & Faber, 1929), p. 30.

8

'After the battle of Dundee', wrote a Dublin Fusilier,

> we saw some wounded on the hill who were Irishmen, and told us
> that they had to fight for the Boers. It is hard times when we have to
> fight against our own countrymen,[7] as we had to do that day.
>
> 'Letter from a Dublin Fusilier', *The Irish Times*,
> 13 December 1899, p. 6

9

Private E. Francis, 1st Battalion, Leicestershire Regiment, observed that

> On Saturday we were out early watching Glencoe Station and Imparta
> [*sic* for Imparti] heights amid rain and a strong mist. About five
> we returned to camp, and just as tea came up we were in the same
> predicament as the day before. The Boers started shelling our camp
> with some heavy 40-pounders.
>
> 'Leicester Soldiers' Letters from Ladysmith', *Leicester Chronicle*,
> 2 December 1899, p. 3

'Our field batteries were unable to reply', added a Royal Irish Fusilier,

> so there we lay until 2 a.m. with shells bursting every minute or so
> among us . . . At 2 a.m. we commenced a further retreat on to a hill
> just out of range of that beastly 40 pdr., which we playfully named
> 'Long Tom'.[8]
>
> 'Letter from an Armagh Soldier', *Armagh Guardian*,
> 29 December 1899, p. 3

---

7   With Irish Nationalists supporting the Boers, and Maud Gonne leading anti-recruiting drives in Dublin, Irish involvement in the war aroused great controversy. In fact less than 300 Irish and Irish-Americans served in the two Irish Brigades compared with 30,000 Irish soldiers for the Crown. Donal P. McCracken, *MacBride's Brigade: Irish Commandos in the Anglo-Boer War* (Dublin: Four Courts Press, 1999), p. 31 and David Fitzpatrick, 'Militarism in Ireland, 1900–1922' in Thomas Bartlett and Keith Jeffery (eds), *A Military History of Ireland* (Cambridge: Cambridge University Press, 1996), pp. 379–406 at pp. 379–80.

8   This was the first appearance of the 155-mm Creusot BL 40-pounder guns that far outranged Royal Artillery 15-pounder guns. With a normal range of 9,880 m (and a maximum range of 11,000 m), it fired a common shell (43 kg or 94 lb) and a shrapnel shell (41 kg or 89 lb). Pakenham, *The Boer War*, pp. 142–3 and Louis Changuion, *Silence of the Guns: The History of the Long Toms of the Anglo-Boer War* (Pretoria: Protea Book House, 2001), pp. 18–19.

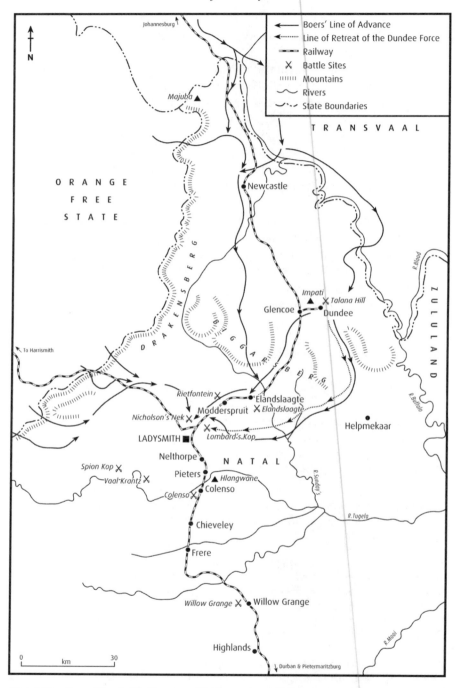

Map 1 Northern Natal, 20 October–15 December 1899

10

'The order came on Sunday night', recalled an Oakham gunner,

> that we must shift at once, or they would murder us the next morning,
> being so many of them, and we losing our general. So General Yule[9]
> took command. He had just come from India, and did not know the
> country. But, anyway, he said, we must go that night, so we started
> about eight o'clock. We had nothing to eat all day, but we did not
> care about that . . . we started on our terrible journey the same night,
> and marched all night round the enemy's position . . . We had to leave
> everything, canvas tents, and tons of food and forage. The next day
> they followed us up, and we had just got through a dreaded pass when
> they lined guns on the top. So we had to keep on marching, day and
> night, until we arrived at Ladysmith. It rained and hailed three nights
> in succession. I shall never forget the morning we landed in Ladysmith.
> They did give us a reception, everything we wanted. I believe the
> Queen sent a message to the officers and men, congratulating us on
> the way we got away. We keep having a go at them. I did not think I
> should have the heart to kill a white man, but I have had to roll a good
> many over before breakfast. I am quite used to it now. After them
> firing on our hospital I would show them no mercy.
>
> 'Oakham Man's Interesting Letter', *Leicester Daily Mercury*,
> 2 December 1899, p. 3

11

Sergeant Thomas Robinson, 2nd Battalion, West Yorkshire Regiment,
had a quite distinctive experience. Writing from Ladysmith to his parents
in Leeds, he commented:

> I took a very active part on that memorable occasion [the battle of
> Talana], being up in the fighting line nearly all the day, administering
> First Aid to the wounded, and pulled through without a scratch . . .
> I fancy it was one of the hardest fights it will be my lot to see. The
> behaviour of the troops engaged was simply magnificent, and those
> who are won't to speak disparagingly or sneeringly of our 'Boy army'
> should have been there to see. I was, as you know, attached to the 18th
> British Field Hospital, and was left behind when the troops departed

---

9   Brigadier General James Yule, who replaced the mortally wounded Symons, was
awarded the CB in 1900 but never advanced his career. He died in 1920 as Colonel
Yule.

for Ladysmith. We were taken prisoners next day by the Boers, who, with one or two exceptions, I must say, treated us very well indeed. Being non-combatants, we were handed over on the 4th November to the British authorities here, and have been besieged ever since.

'A Yorkshire Soldier's Experiences at Ladysmith', *Leeds Mercury*, 27 March 1900, p. 5

Battle of Elandslaagte (21 October 1899)

After General Johannes H. M. Kock, with some 1,000 Transvalers had cut the railway at Elandslaagte to the south of Dundee, and only 12 miles (20 km) north of Ladysmith, Major General J. D. P. French with five squadrons of Imperial Light Horse[10] and the Natal Field Battery advanced to reconnoitre. Coming under fire from two 75mm Krupp guns, French called for reinforcements. While the 5th Lancers and 5th Dragoon Guards with the Natal Mounted Rifles and two batteries of Royal Field Artillery came up by road, seven companies of 1st Battalion, Devonshire Regiment, four of the 1st Battalion, Manchester Regiment and five of the 2nd Battalion, Gordon Highlanders came up by train on the 21st, bringing French's force up to 3,500 men and 18 guns.

12

Private J. Isaac, 1st Battalion, Devonshire Regiment, recalled that

Our troops here are divided into Brigades and stationed in chief places to protect the people and property. We had orders on the 21st about 1 o'clock to proceed to a place called Elandslaagte. We got ready in field service order, and 150 rounds of ball ammunition, and carried with us field service rations. We went about 16 miles by train and were not long before we got into action. The infantry were composed of the Devons, Manchesters, and the Gordon Highlanders. There were also Field Batteries of Artillery, Lancers and Hussars. The Boers opened fire as soon as they spotted us. They started firing with their big guns, and then they opened rifle fire upon us as soon as we were within range of their rifles. We were advancing in single rank, about 15 paces interval from one another, so we could not form a big target

---

10   Ben Viljoen, then vice-commandant of the Johannesburg Commando, described the Imperial Light Horse as 'a corps principally composed of Johannesburgers, who were politically and racially our bitter enemies', General Ben Viljoen, *My Reminiscences of The Anglo-Boer War* (London: Hood, Douglas & Howard, 1903), p. 32.

for them.[11] We were advancing by Companies – A Company and so on. Their bullets were bursting around us like a lot of peas. We were under fire for four hours. Their position was on a high hill, and our troops were advancing on the plain as well as they could. We got to the bottom of the hill before sunset. We had the order to fix bayonets and charge the enemy out of their position. We got up to the top, and our gallant Devons took their two big guns. We took their camp, for they ran for their lives out of our way. Our regiment took seventy prisoners. There are about 16 Torrington lads here fighting for Honour and Glory. I am in splendid fighting trim, and you need not be in the least trouble about me.

'A Torrington Soldier's Letter', *Devon Weekly Times*,
24 November 1899, p. 5

13
'After a halt of about an hour', observed an Imperial Light Horseman,

we were ordered round to flank the Boers, and after about three hours of manoeuvring we hemmed them in, and along with the Gordon Highlanders, Manchesters, and Devons we stormed the Boer camp, we having dismounted. The advance was about three-quarters of a mile [1.2 km], and the whole time we were pelted with a prefect storm of bullets.

'Letter from Ladysmith', *Inverness Courier*,
9 February 1900, p. 3

14
Lieutenant Walter W. Macgregor, 2nd Battalion, Gordon Highlanders, stated that

We advanced by short rushes, one lot covering the advance of the others, and all the words of command were 'Cease fire' and 'Advance'. We seemed to get over the 'fire beaten zone' somehow. No one seemed to think of not going on . . . The enemy's position . . . afforded natural cover, as the ground was strewn with stones and

---

11   Colonel Ian S. M. Hamilton (1853–1947), an officer experienced in the hill fighting of India, required the Devons to advance in extended order, so reducing their casualties, a deployment that contrasted completely with the compact formation ordered by Major General Hart that proved so disastrous for the Irish Brigade at the battle of Colenso. John Lee, *A Soldier's Life: General Sir Ian Hamilton 1853–1947* (London: Pan Books, 2001), pp. 49–50.

rocks. We could see nothing of the enemy until we got to within 100 yards [91.4 m], when they retired over the skyline . . . We assaulted the left of the enemy's position, mixed up with the Manchesters and the Devons on the left. When we advanced to the attack the guns were on our left and they only shelled the enemy's right. I think that was one reason why we lost so heavily and our kilts are a good mark, too.[12] You'll see in the papers 'position carried at the point of the bayonet', but really they had all gone before we were anything like there, and we only walked in . . . The enemy played that old, low-down game of theirs and showed the white flag. Colonel Ian Hamilton (who was in command of the infantry) had the 'cease fire' and 'retire' sounded at once, and the men who were swarming down the slope (in pursuit of the enemy) began slowly to retire up the hill. At once the Boers opened fire on us and our men 'legged it back'. . . we lost a lot of officers[13] when that 'retire' went and we went back up the hill' . . . I must say that the Boers behaved very bravely and fought well. Some of them didn't leave their position till the last minute. Report says that they were specially ordered to fire at the kilts. We took a lot of prisoners. They all speak English perfectly. A good many gave themselves up, and some said they were glad to be taken, as they would not have to fight any more; they were sick. Very few had beards, which surprised me as I thought they all had them. Sir George White, who was watching, is reported to have said, 'Look at my boys; nothing will stop them.' He commanded the regiment once.[14]

'The Battle of Elandslaagte', *Tamworth Herald*,

9 December 1899, p. 5

---

12   The heavy losses suffered by the Gordon Highlanders in this battle would lead to the injunction that aprons should be worn over kilts in this war.

13   The Gordons lost five officers killed and eight wounded (70 per cent of those engaged), and this would lead to injunctions against officers wearing distinctive insignias and carrying claymores, which caught the light and became a target for the Boers. Lieutenant Colonel A. D. Greenhill Gardyne, *The Life of a Regiment: The history of the Gordon Highlanders*, 3 vols (London: The Medici Society, 1939) vol. 3, pp. 25–6.

14   Sir George Stuart White (1835–1912) was an Ulsterman who was commissioned into the 27th (Inniskilling) Regiment and saw service initially in the Indian Mutiny. He transferred to the 92nd (Gordon) Highlanders and fought in the Second Anglo-Afghan War as second-in-command where he won his Victoria Cross in leading an attack on a strongly fortified hill fort at Charasiah (6 October 1879). He became the commanding officer of the 92nd in 1881, was knighted in 1886 for his military service in Burma, and became commander-in-chief, India in 1893. As commander of the forces in Natal, he commanded the garrison at Ladysmith through the 118-day siege. Criticised for his largely passive defence of Ladysmith, he later served as governor of Gibraltar (1900–4), became a field marshal in 1903 and died in Chelsea Hospital on 24 June 1912.

15

An officer of the 5th Lancers added:

The fight at Elandslaagte was a very good show, only it began too late in the afternoon, and there was not sufficient daylight for the cavalry to finish off the affair in a really workmanlike manner. Only one squadron of ours got amongst them, but they did a fearful damage. The Boers own to 70 having been speared.[15] We lost only one man . . . The night at Elandslaagte was cold and wet, and most people walked about to keep warm. I thought my horse would have died of the cold but he's none the worse. . .

'An Officer's Impressions', *Liverpool Mercury*,
29 November 1899, p. 8

16

Although Ben Viljoen escaped from the Lancers on his 'sturdy little Boer pony', he recalled 'the snorting of their unwieldy horses, the clattering of their swords. These unpleasant combinations were enough to strike terror into the heart of any ordinary man.'[16] Another witness to the charge was Walter Herald, a Mancunian chemist then serving with the Boer ambulance force. He described how the first British shrapnel

went through the shed. The next shot struck one of our mules and took half its head away. The third shell burst close by, and part of it went through wagon in which I was dressing . . . In the afternoon the British turned up in great numbers and the battle began in earnest. For two hours the firing was incessant, artillery and rifles going the whole time, and in the middle of it we had our photograph taken, with the shells bursting all around. After about two hours the Boers began to give way, and retreated right on the hospital, and while I was dressing my first wounded man, the famous Lancer charge took place within six yards from us. Luckily we came through all right.

'Elandslaagte from the Boer Standpoint', *Western Times*,
5 December 1899, p. 6

---

15 The Boers, their allies and contemporary South African historians regarded this form of killing as peculiarly gruesome, Fransjohan Pretorius, *The Anglo-Boer War 1899–1902* (Cape Town: Struik Publishers, 1985), p. 14; Colonel John Y. F. Blake, *A West Pointer with the Boers* (Boston: Angel Guardian Press, 1903), pp. 71–3.
16 Viljoen, *My Reminiscences*, p. 35.

17

'We have a terrible hard job here', wrote Colour Sergeant Lee, 1st Battalion, Devonshire Regiment:

Since my last letter we have been through some terrible work on the battlefield. On Saturday last, the 21st (October) we fought with the enemy at Elandslaagte and my Regiment was in the front line all the time, including myself. What passed that day is too horrible for my feeling to express. We commenced fighting at 2.30 p.m. and never ceased until half-past six, when we managed to drive them out of the strong position they held. God only knows how I am still alive to write to you, for I expected every minute to be the last. No one can imagine what a battlefield is like, only those who have been on one. No sooner had we come in sight than shells from the enemy's artillery were falling all around us and plenty of poor fellows were killed . . . Having got to about 600 yards [548.6 m] from the position it simply hailed bullets on us, but never fearing, we fixed bayonets and charged the position and won. Yes, won, but at what cost is too horrible to think of. We had 327 casualties on the English side, but we estimate the Boers had over a thousand.[17] The sights to behold would turn one cold, headless bodies, others disfigured, limbs lying about in all places, for our artillery made great work on the enemy. I found one poor fellow badly wounded and talking about his poor mother at home and it touched my heart, although he was one of the enemy, I can assure you, for they are white people like ourselves . . . We returned here on Sunday but not to rest in peace for long again, for yesterday, the 24th inst., we were off again at 4 o'clock in the morning to fight another battle (Rietfontein). We were fighting all day until half-past four in the evening, and not quite as bad as the battle of Elandslaagte for my Regiment only had one killed and five wounded, one in my Company only . . . It's rough times I can assure you, some days no food all day when fighting. Yesterday all we had was water from three in the morning until seven at night, when we returned to our camp drenched to the skin, as it often rains here . . . This won't be over I am sure for about another four months, as we have got no troops from England yet, and waiting for them badly.

'The Devons at Elandslaagte. A Colour Sergeant's Experiences', *Totnes Times*,
30 December 1899, p. 8

---

17 These claims are not accurate: the official British casualties were 50 killed and 213 wounded while the Boers lost 38 killed, 113 wounded (of whom 8 died), and 185 taken prisoner, Fransjohan Pretorius, *Historical Dictionary of the Anglo-Boer War* (Lanham, Maryland: The Scarecrow Press, 2009), p. 138.

18

On the effects upon the Devons, who fought in an open-order formation, Private S. Ansley, 1st Battalion, Devonshire Regiment, commented:

> It was very strange, but not one of our regiment was killed, and we were in the thickest of the fight, and only 34 were wounded. The Gordons lost 24 and 76 wounded, the Manchesters' loss was 10 killed and 31 wounded, while there were other casualties in other regiments. The Devons who captured the colours, were received with great enthusiasm on arriving at Ladysmith.
>
> 'A Topsham Man's Elandslaagte Experience', *Western Morning News*,
> 22 November 1899, p. 8

19

Sergeant Lawrence Forbes, 2nd Battalion, Gordon Highlanders, described one of the more distressing injuries:

> When I had got about half way across I saw the Colonel [William Henry Dick-Cunyngham VC][18] lying. Sergeant McArthur, who was kneeling beside him, called to me to help to bind the old chief up, which I did. It is a wonder McArthur and I were not both wiped out there. We were exposed to the Boers' fire for almost five minutes. Then we carried the Colonel in behind a boulder for shelter . . . he lay and cheered on the men, and after he had a bit of a rest he managed to go a bit further. He tried to be up at the charge but couldn't manage it.
>
> 'Battle of Elandslaagte', *Leeds Mercury*,
> 22 November 1899, p. 8

20

An officer of the 1st Battalion, Manchester Regiment, wrote from the Wesleyan Chapel, Temporary Hospital, Ladysmith, on 24 October:

> My chief regret is that I got knocked over just before getting into position. I had just got my sword and revolver out, and had started on

---

18   Lieutenant Colonel William Henry Dick-Cunyngham VC (1851–1900) was the fifth son of the eighth baronet and joined the 92nd in 1872. Awarded the VC for conspicuous gallantry in the attack on Sherpur Pass on 12 December 1879 during the Second Anglo-Afghan War, he served in the Anglo-Transvaal War (1880–1) and commanded the 2nd Battalion, Gordon Highlanders in Natal. Having recovered from this wound, he was mortally wounded at Wagon Hill (6 January 1900). Greenhill Gardyne, *Life of a Regiment*, vol. 3, pp. 58–60.

the charge with a crowd of my boys behind me when I was suddenly knocked clean off my legs . . . I jumped up again, but only to go down head over heels, for my right leg was powerless. I had no idea I had been shot till I saw the blood all over my trousers . . .

I am glad my Tommy – a private in my own company stayed with me, for he wrapped me in his own greatcoat and lay down with his arms around me all the night to try and keep me warm. If he hadn't, I am afraid I should have pegged out, for it was bitterly cold and I couldn't move at all. Search parties were out all night, of course, looking for us, and four men tried to carry me in their arms, but it was too frightful, as they kept falling amongst the rocks and dropping me till I had to cry off. About 6.30 a.m. I was put on a stretcher and carried about three miles to the railway, where our regiment was drawn up to cover the entrainment of the wounded. They were all gloriously happy, having captured three big guns, two of the enemy's flags, and as many rifles, pistols, bandoliers, stores, blankets, provisions, etc., as they could carry. They gave me a hearty greeting as I was carried past them, for I had been reported dead.

When we arrived at Ladysmith,[19] I was carried to the head hospital and was dressed by Major David Bruce. He was awfully nice and kind, though frightfully busy, and up to his eyes in blood. The bullet was still in my leg, and he decided to have me under the X rays next day and see if he could find it . . . Yesterday I had a bit of a doing, being lifted from my bed on to a stretcher and carried to the Town Hall, lifted from the stretcher, and placed under the X rays, where I was for about an hour. While there I discovered the bullet in my hip, and as it was not very deep in I was put on the stretcher and carried off to the operating theatre. I had had breakfast, so could not have chloroform, and Major Bruce cut it out. It did hurt a bit, I must confess, but I was jolly glad to have it out . . . I am feeling a good deal better now, and really the treatment here is quite wonderful. The nurses in this ward are perfect dears, and nothing is too much trouble for them, though they are most frightfully hard worked. There are 22 beds in this ward, and on Sunday and Monday they were all occupied by men who could do next to nothing for themselves. There are only

---

19 Nurse Kate Driver described how the platform and station yard 'were crowded with rows and rows of stretchers, d'Hoolies, as we called them in Natal. As we threaded our way through them we heard moans of agony coming from under the green covers.' Nurse Kate Driver, *Experience of a Siege: A nurse looks back on Ladysmith* (Ladysmith: Ladysmith Historical Society, 'Diary The Siege of Ladysmith', No. 6, revised edition, 1994), p. 4.

two nurses and two orderlies for the ward, and so you may guess the work is pretty hard.

'A Soldier's Letter', *Liverpool Mercury*, 14 December 1899, p. 8.
This letter or extracts from it were republished in the *Bristol Times and Mirror*,
14 December 1899, p. 3, and the *Crediton Chronicle and
North Devon Gazette*, 16 December 1899, p. 8

21

Though hit three times, including a bullet through his left wrist, Private John Henderson of the Gordon Highlanders reckoned that he 'had never enjoyed anything so much in my life'. Having claimed five victims himself, he was 'pretty well satisfied', especially as he and a Perthshire friend from the Imperial Light Horse found a case of John Dewar's whisky in the Boer camp:

Never was 'Scotch' hailed with so much pleasure, as after the heavy fight, and the night cold and wet, we were all in a sorry state . . . We along with other I.L.H., Gordons, Devons, etc., drank to Elandslaagte and Dewar, and for once forgot our wounds. Part of the case we retained for those more heavily wounded and near at hand.

'Whisky in the Boer Camp. A Lively Letter', *Inverness Courier*,
1 December 1899, p. 5

22

Some of the wounded from Talana Hill and Elandslaagte were moved by railway to Wynberg Hospital near Cape Town. One of the inmates, Private Satby of the Devonshire Regiment, forwarded a copy of a report by visitors to his father in Bristol:

Two things struck the visitors very forcibly, and these were the marvellous escapes some of the men must have had and the healing qualities of Tommy Atkins . . . As illustrating the rapidity with which many of these brave fellows have recovered, some of the Gordons and Devons who had been shot through the shoulder, arms, wrists, hands, calves, and thighs showed their wounds so far as advisable, and proudly exercised their muscles, showing that it would not be long ere they could again use their limbs if duty required. Amongst the more marvellous escapes may be mentioned one poor fellow who . . . was shot through the head, the bullet entering on one side, about level with the eye, and coming out at exactly the same position on the other. He was given up as dead, but on being taken into camp,

and after three days' unconsciousness, began to pull through . . . All
the men agreed that they felt no pain when wounded beyond a sharp
sting, and some had doubled a distance of some 600 yards [548.6 km]
before the loss of blood and the numbness brought them to a halt.
The marks on the wound where the bullets entered were not much
larger than a threepenny piece, while where the exit was made it is
surprising how anything larger than a pea could have had so small a
trace of injury.

'The Wounded. Many Wonderful Escapes', *Bristol Observer*,
2 December 1899, p. 1

Battle of Rietfontein (24 October 1899)

To cover the retreating force from Dundee, Lieutenant General Sir
George White VC moved north from Ladysmith with a substantial
force, comprising 5th Lancers, 19th Hussars, the Imperial Light Horse,
Natal Mounted Rifles, 42nd and 53rd batteries, Royal Field Artillery,
No. 10 Mountain Battery, Royal Garrison Artillery and 1st Battalions,
Gloucestershire, Devonshire and King's Liverpool Regiments, and 2nd
Battalion, King's Royal Rifles Corps. At Rietfontein, they came under
fire from leading elements of the Orange Free State forces under General
Marthinus Prinsloo, including the Heilbron commando under the
temporary command of Vice-Commandant Christiaan De Wet.

23

A Gloucester soldier, whose knee was shattered by a Boer bullet in the
battle, described how:

We had moved out from Ladysmith on the Newcastle road to cover
the right flank of a column coming in from Dundee, and when
about seven miles [11.3 km] out the Boers opened on us with their
guns from a hill on the left of the road. Our left half battalion was
ordered to advance in echelon of sections, supported by the right
half. After climbing a hill we were advancing over a plateau, when
my half company, which was then on the left of the advanced line,
spotted the enemy on our flank, and only a short distance. We
changed front as sharp as we could but before we could open fire
the Boers started on us. The Artillery in the rear then began shelling
the heights the Boers occupied, and we were ordered to lie still
. . . My company lost three killed and 18 wounded, the regiment
altogether losing eight killed and 55 wounded. The killed included

the colonel,[20] who was struck on the face by a richochet [*sic*] just before the finish.

'The Spirit of the Gloucesters', *Gloucestershire Chronicle*,
23 December 1899, p. 7

24

'Under cover of our artillery fire', wrote Private Thompson, 1st Battalion, King's Liverpool Regiment,

the infantry advanced, the Gloucester regiment forming the firing line, and Liverpool regiment the supports . . . On arriving at the crest of the hill the sight that met my gaze I shall never forget. The dead were lying in heaps, literally blown to pieces by the artillery . . . As we advanced the cavalry protected the flanks. It was when the firing line had advanced to about 1,500 yards [1,371 m] that the fire was most effective. The stretchers were being continually requisitioned, but I am pleased to say that the majority of cases the men were only wounded. . .When we retired about three in the afternoon, the country round the position was one blinding mass of flames where the shells had set fire to the grass. Our casualties were very light . . . I do not know the official number of casualties but do not think our loss will exceed 15 killed (including the colonel of the Gloucester regiment) and about 40 wounded.[21] On arriving in barracks we were out on outpost duty all night, so can assure you campaigning is not a very agreeable occupation.

'His First Battle', *Liverpool Mercury*,
29 November 1899, p. 8

25

While Christiaan De Wet recalled that the morale of his corps was high after keeping the British at least 200 paces from their lines at a cost of eleven men killed and 21 wounded, of whom two died subsequently,[22] the British had still managed to cover effectively the retreating column under Brigadier Yule. As an officer of the 5th Lancers observed:

---

20   Lieutenant Colonel Edmund Percival Wilford (1846–99).
21   Official British casualties at Rietfontein were 1 officer and 13 men killed, 6 officers and 92 wounded and two missing, F. M. Maurice and M. H. Grant, *The History of the War in South Africa, 1899–1902*, 4 vols. (London: HMSO, 1906–10), vol. 1, p. 463.
22   Christiaan R. De Wet, *Three Years War (October 1899–June 1902)*, (London: Archibald Constable & Co. Ltd, 1903), pp. 16–17.

Wednesday we went out to meet the troops coming from Dundee, was one of the wettest I've seen, but we had a few things with us that time. I got into a sort of waterproof bag, and was as snug as possible. The troops we went to meet were in a bad way after their long march over muddy roads, but they were in good spirits, and arrived without losing a man. This town is fairly full of troops now, but the country is rather fuller of enemies. I fancy we are going to-morrow to try and give them another hammering. There's plenty of beer and port wine, and lots of food, thank goodness. The only things one goes short of are sleep and washing. But I've never been fitter, and the same with the men – you feel as if you couldn't tire.

'An Officer's Impressions', *Liverpool Mercury*,
29 November 1899, p. 8

'Mournful Monday' '30 October 1899)

As 14,000 Boers approached Ladysmith, and a 155 mm Creusot gun was installed on Pepworth Hill about four miles (6.5 km) north-east of the town, White deployed his forces for attack on Sunday night. Colonel G. G. Grimwood, commanding the 8th brigade (1st and 2nd King's Royal Rifles, 2nd Royal Dublin Fusiliers, 1st King's Liverpool and 1st Leicestershire) was to seize Long Hill to the east of the railway and road to Newcastle, and enable Sir Ian Hamilton with the 7th Brigade (1st Devonshire, 1st Manchester, 2nd Gordon Highlanders, 2nd Rifle Brigade, 5th Dragoon Guards, 18th Hussars and the Imperial Light Horse) to seize Pepworth Hill. Six field batteries were left in support, with the left flank covered by a force of six companies of the 1st Royal Irish Fusiliers, five-and-a-half companies of 1st Battalion, Gloucestershire Regiment and the 10th Mountain battery under Lieutenant Colonel F. R. C. Carelton. This unit was supposed to cut off any Boer retreat through Nicholson's Nek. A Cavalry Brigade under the command of French was expected to protect the right flank. Blunders in the deployments during the night, however, left Grimwood with only half of his force. In the ensuing action at Lombard's Kop, Grimwood was forced to retire, compelling Hamilton to abandon the assault on Pepworth Hill.

Battle of Lombard's Kop

26

'I shall never forget Lombard's Kop as long as I live', recalled Private R. Cross, 1st Battalion, Leicestershire Regiment:

It is one thing to read about a battle, but nobody can realise the real thing until they see it for themselves. We were fired at from three different directions,[23] and only got one way out of it, so it was a lucky thing we retired in time . . .

'Letters from the Front', *Leicester Daily Mercury*,
2 April 1900, p. 3

27

In a letter of 10 November, 3294 Private H. E. Williams, signaller, 2nd Battalion, Rifle Brigade, described how

We were ordered to the front on the 29th, and reached our destination at 3.30 a.m. next day. After having breakfast we went on the battlefield, arriving just in time to see the first shot go off from Long Tom, one of the Boers' big 40-pounder guns. We gave him that name because he has such a long range and all the shells from it go into the ground before exploding, so they do little or no damage. We were at it till 1.30 in the afternoon, and then we had orders to retire to Ladysmith, my regiment being left behind to cover the retreat, and we did not get back into camp till 5.30 p.m. We had tea and then moved around the hills to take up a position the following morning. We slept in the open air that night with only our great coats. Next day we had two blankets and a waterproof sheet issued out to each man. We took up a position all around the hills of Ladysmith and entrenched ourselves. We built a few fortifications, and have been there ever since.

'Whitchurch Man Describes the Siege of Ladysmith', *The Hampshire Observer*,
31 March 1900, p. 6

28

Sapper E. C. Matthews, of the 23rd Company, Royal Engineers, added that

on the Monday following, we took part in the battle of Lombard's Kop, being part of the moveable reserves. We were under rifle fire, as well as shell fire, the greater part of this day, although our casualty list[24] was not stated.

---

23   French failed to move sufficiently forward before daybreak and deployed his cavalry on Lombard's Kop some two miles [3.2 km] in the rear of Grimwood's force. While the cavalry endured heavy fire, the Boers attacked Grimwood's force from three sides.
24   At Lombard's Kop and Nicholson's Nek, the British lost 70 killed, 249 wounded and 954 men as prisoners, Maurice and Grant, *War in South Africa*, vol. 1, p. 465.

'With the Royal Engineers in South Africa', *West Briton and Cornwall Advertiser*, 2 August 1900, p. 2

29

Writing to his brother in Devonport, a non-commissioned officer recalled:

we have had here three battles, the last being on Monday, 30th October. The fighting on each occasion was terrific, this probably being due to the artillery on both sides with explosive shells, the Boers firing shells right into the midst of our camp. Fortunately for us, the Naval Brigade from HMS *Powerful* at Durban came on the scene with their big guns[25] and turned the battle in our favour. The sailors fought splendidly, and they richly deserve the credit of silencing and disabling the Boers' big gun, which we all call Long Tom.

'A Devonport Man at Ladysmith', *Western Morning News*, 29 November 1899, p. 8

30

'Heaps of wounded here after the battles of Glencoe [Talana Hill] and Elandslaagte', wrote Sergeant C. Figg (Royal Army Medical Corps) to his mother from No. 12 Field Hospital, Ladysmith, on 2 November,

Fighting commenced about two miles [3.2 km] from our camp the morning after our arrival . . . It was terrible on both sides, the artillery doing so much damage. It is heartrending to see some of the wounded and dead so shattered by the shells, and the heat has been intense, which makes it worse. Very little water to be had, and like gutter-mud. We had 24 hours' armistice yesterday to collect the wounded and dead. I was on night duty the night before last, and it was awful to hear the groans of the wounded. We have been under fire ever since our arrival here. All the people, of course, have left the town.[26] In fact, firing is going on all around us at this present minute, but I thought I would scribble these few lines to you while awaiting the next batch of wounded. We are

---

25 The Naval Brigade, having arrived in Ladysmith at 8.30 a.m. on 30 October, brought three 12-pounders to Limit Hill. Although a shell from the Long Tom overturned one gun, the other two guns with their range of 6,500 yards [5.9 km] were able to silence the Long Tom and cover the retreat. The upset gun was recovered.
26 It may have appeared from the confines of a field hospital that all civilians had left Ladysmith but some 5,400 civilians and 2,400 Blacks and Indians endured the siege, Childs, *Ladysmith*, p. 75.

longing for the Army Corps to get out here. The Boers, no doubt, are
terrible fellows and can fight, too. They treat the wounded very well.

'Doverite in Ladysmith's Neutral Camp', *Dover Telegraph*,
28 March 1900, p. 5

31

Although the experiences of patients varied considerably, a nurse, writing
on 28 October, described

A touching little scene happened yesterday. One of the Gordons had
his arm amputated. A Boer in the next bed had his arm taken off
exactly in the same place. I took charge of the Boer as he was brought
from the theatre, and on his becoming conscious the two poor fellows
eyed each other very much till our good-natured Tommy could stand
it no longer.

'Sister,' he called, 'give him two cigarettes out of my box and tell
him I sent them. Here is a match. Light one for him.' I took the
cigarettes and the message to the Boer, and he turned and looked
at Tommy in amazement, and then quite overcome he burst into
tears. Tommy did the same, and I was on the point of joining in the
chorus but time would not permit. We have a splendid staff of skilled
surgeons who are kept constantly at work, and our nursing staff is all
that could be desired.

'Ladysmith Nurse', *Morning Leader*,
20 November 1899, p. 8

The Battle of Nicholson's Nek

32

An officer of the Gloucesters commented:

We were ordered out with six companies of Royal Irish Fusiliers and
No. 10 Mountain Battery Royal Artillery to make a night march
through the Boer lines and hold a hill behind their right flank . . .
We started at half past eight p.m., and got to the foot of the hill
about two a.m . . . The Royal Irish Fusiliers had got part way up the
hill – a very steep one – when three mounted Boers galloped down
amid clouds of dust, rolling stones, etc. They started off the battery
and S.A.A. [small arms ammunition] mules, the Boers firing as they
passed. The mules cut right through the regiment, and all was chaos

for a time . . . We were ordered – as soon as we got on the hill[27]– to put up sangers [*sic*], which we worked at by the light of a very small moon until daylight.

'Nicholson's Nek Described by a Gloucestershire Officer', *Gloucestershire Chronicle*, 16 December 1899, p. 7

33

After the mules bolted, 'We were unable to get a complete gun together', recalled an officer of the 10th Mountain battery, then a prisoner in Pretoria,

We went all over the valley but could not find a chase mule. This was in the middle of the enemy's line. We got ten boxes of small arm ammunition, however . . . The enemy's fire was hot and extremely good.[28] We had little ammunition, and could not keep up a continuous fire . . . I was twice hit by splinters of rocks,[29] and by a spent bullet (ricochet off a rock); they did not even penetrate my jacket. The last rush to cover, 80 yards [73.1 km] across the open, was a miracle. It was swept by both frontal and flank fires. The men on my right and left fell. How anyone crossed alive beats me. The Boers have treated us very well indeed, on the railway journey up giving us not only coffee, bully beef, and bread, but also cigars and cigarettes . . . We were marched to the Boer camp; from there taken to Elandslaagte, where we spent the night, driving next day to Glencoe, from which place we were brought by train here. Our captors have been most kind and considerate, giving us water and rations. On the way up we were given coffee three times, also provisions. At Volkrust, the commissariat officer (Boer) got two bottles of whisky – all that was obtainable – and gave it to us. The people at the stations were most curious to see us.

'Letter from Pretoria', *Cheltenham Chronicle*, 16 December 1899, p. 5

---

27 Tchrengula Hill.

28 De Wet admitted that 'It was very lucky for us that the English were deprived of their guns, for it placed them on the same footing as ourselves, it compelled them to rely entirely on their rifles. Still they had the advantage of position, not to mention the fact that they outnumbered us by four to one.' De Wet, *Three Years War*, p. 24.

29 Lacking good entrenching tools, soldiers built sangars (stone breastworks) as a means of improvising defensive protection but, as at Majuba Hill, they merely provided a target for the Boers and men were injured by rock splinters. Leo Amery, *The Times History of the War in South Africa 1899–1902*, 7 vols (London: Sampson Low, Marston and Co. Ltd, 1900–9) vol. 2, p. 254.

34

Father L. Matthews, chaplain to the Royal Irish Fusiliers, recounted how

The mules knocked me down. It was pitch dark. We had one hour's
sleep. Firing began just after day light. It was slack for some time, but
the Boers crept round. The firing became furious. Our men made
a breastwork of stones. After 12 o'clock there was a general cry of
'Cease fire' in that direction. Our fellows would not stop firing, Major
Adye came up and confirmed the order to cease fire . . . In our sangar
there was a rumour that the white flag was raised by a young officer,
who thought that his batch of ten men were the sole survivors.[30] We
were nine hundred alive, having started perhaps a thousand. I think
many of the battery men escaped. Our men and officers were furious
at surrendering. The Boers did not appear to be in great numbers on
the spot, but I heard that the main body had galloped off. . .[31] The
officers were taken away from the men, and sent to General Joubert.[32]
On the same day the officers went in mule wagons, and slept at
some store en route, and the next day took the train to Pretoria. The
officers are very well treated, and so I heard are the men. There has
been no unpleasantness in Pretoria. The officers are in the Model
School,[33] and are allowed to walk as they please in the grounds.

'Why the Gloucesters Surrendered', *Gloucestershire Chronicle*,
18 November 1899, p. 7

35

Writing to his wife from Pretoria on 9 November, Colour-Sergeant
Marsden, 1st Battalion, Royal Irish Fusiliers, observed that

---

30   This appears to have been the case. A small advanced, and isolated, party of
Gloucesters raised the white flag without any authorisation. As the Boers accepted the
surrender, Carleton felt obliged to honour this and surrendered his 37 officers and
917 men. Maurice and Grant, *History of the War in South Africa*, vol. 1, p. 195.
31   As the Royal Irish Fusiliers still had plenty of ammunition, and had suffered few
casualties, there was bad blood between the two regiments after the surrender. 'The
Surrender of the Gloucesters', *Gloucester Journal*, 22 September 1900, p. 3.
32   Commandant General Petrus (Piet) Jacobus Joubert (1831–1900) had commanded the Boers successfully in the Anglo-Transvaal War and led the invasion of Natal.
33   A subsequent inmate at this Model School was Winston Churchill after the
armoured train in which he was travelling between Frere and Chieveley was ambushed
on 15 November 1899. On 14 January 1900, Churchill escaped and, with assistance,
made his way to Durban. Winston S. Churchill, *My Early Life: A Roving Commission*
(London: Odhams Press, 1930), pp. 258, 264–94.

Six companies of the regiment are prisoners here. We were sent out on Sunday night, the 30th October, and were out of Ladysmith, and after 7½ hours' fighting we had to surrender. We had a lot of casualties. I could not tell you all of them; but, thank God, I came out safely, although I had some very narrow escapes . . . I cannot say very much, as our letters are read before they are sent.

'Nicholson's Nek', *Irish Times*,
30 December 1899, p. 5

Onset of the siege

36

In an interview, Seaman Louis Smith, Royal Naval Brigade, described how

We took part in the fight on Lombard's Kop – we had a great duel there that day, and we had all through a pretty rough time, but still we managed to get along. We were there, and had to put up with it and had nothing to do but to rest our minds content . . .

'A Newton Man in the Naval Brigade which saved Ladysmith',
Mid Devon and Newton Times, 16 June 1900, p. 8

37

Many Boers were less phlegmatic, chafing at the failure of Joubert to pursue the retreating British after Lombard's Kop,[34] but in a council of war on 1 November they decided to lay siege to Ladysmith. 'On 2 November', wrote Sapper Ernest A. Payne of the Telegraph Section of the Royal Engineers,

firing commenced early and sharp practice took place. Several were killed and wounded in the afternoon. The Boers had been trying to hit the balloon[35] all day, and were unsuccessful until it was coming down, and a piece of shell disabled it thus preventing its ascension

---

34   Reitz quoted Joubert as explaining his reticence by saying, 'When God holds out a finger, don't take the whole hand', Reitz, *Commando*, p. 44; see also Viljoen, *My Reminiscences*, pp. 48–9.

35   The Royal Engineers used observation balloons, tethered to the ground to make maps. On 18 November 1899, Captain G. M. Heath, RE, made a map of the Boer gun emplacements round Ladysmith from a balloon. Although the balloon became an iconic image of the siege, symbolising British defiance, its value appears to have been marginal, Martin Marix Evans, *Encyclopedia of the Boer War 1899–1902* (Santa Barbara, CA: ABC-Clio, 2000), p. 15.

again for a few days. Another was, however, rigged up to take its place, which appeared to worry the Boers very much . . . In the night of this day (2nd November) the railway and telegraphs were cut or destroyed by the enemy, who surrounded us. The siege started on the 3rd. The chief gunner of the Naval Brigade[36] was killed. The fourth shot fired by this gun (Naval) smashed Long Tom, but not for long.

'Our County's Share in the War', *Somerset County Gazette*,
4 August 1900, p. 7

38

'The day after our fight at Lombard's Kop', wrote Lieutenant Merriman, 1st Battalion, Manchester Regiment,

the Boers began shelling the town and we got orders to move our camp and go up on a hill, Caesar's Camp, overlooking Ladysmith, about three miles [4.8 km] out. We are told to hold it at all costs. The Boers, who have their big guns on every hill around, shell us whenever they like. Our chief duty is outpost duty round the hill. We can see the Boers plainly, looking at us.

'Lieutenant Merriman's Experiences at Ladysmith', *Essex County Standard,
West Suffolk Gazette and Eastern Counties Advertiser*, 31 March 1900, p. 5

39

Writing on 7 November 1899, Lieutenant Guy Reynolds, 5th Dragoon Guards, noted that

The railway is in the possession of the Boers, and we are in a state of siege, and shall be until we are relieved by the Army Corps, which cannot be for some time yet, we are not having a good time by any means. Shells are pouring into the town all day, and every day, and though they not do much damage their moral effect is pretty strong. It is not at all a pleasant sensation to hear a shell whistling towards you not knowing where it will land or whether it will burst or not . . . their big guns are all around the town and they keep us lively. I am very fit and well in spite of very hard work and very little sleep. We are often out for 24 hours together, and always nearly in our clothes. I

---

36   Lieutenant Frederick G. Egerton was hit in the legs by a shell that passed through the earthworks on 2 November and he died the same night. G. Sharp, *The Siege of Ladysmith* (Cape Town: Purnell, 1976), p. 42.

feel very dirty, a bath being an unknown luxury. The drinking water is about the colour of Mersey water. It is a very healthy place, and there is little or no sickness.

'Letters from the War', *Warrington Guardian*,
31 March 1900, p. 2

40

'I am on outpost duty', stated Corporal Lowes, 2nd Battalion, King's Royal Rifles Corps, in his letter of 1 November 1899,

and have been since Sunday, and goodness knows when I shall be relieved, and you never know when you are going to get a bite to eat, and when you get it it is composed of one hard biscuit and a drink of water. Occasionally you get hold of a bit of fresh bread, and that is a luxury . . . At the present time we are surrounded . . . They started shelling our camp yesterday, but did no damage. I can assure you they are a better lot than they were made out to be. They do not carry any sword, just their rifle and bandolier, dressed in their ordinary civilian garb, and they can move about those hills. . .We had a terrible wetting yesterday. We got wet through to the skin and had to remain so through the night, for we have got nothing at all but just what we stand up in, viz. One shirt, one pair of socks, one suit of khaki, and a greatcoat, with a blanket and a waterproof sheet to lie down on where best we can on the ground, with just the sky above us, so you can guess what it is like.

'Liverpool Man's Experience in Ladysmith', *Liverpool Courier*,
27 March 1900, p. 7

41

On 3 November 1899, Captain the Honourable Hedworth Lambton, RN, reported an outrage to Sir George White:

about 2.15 p.m., the Boer large calibre gun having been struck by one of my small 12-pounders, a man jumped onto the parapet of the gun and vigorously waved a white flag, which he kept displayed for at least 15 minutes. My gun immediately ceased fire. To my astonishment this Boer gun had the wickedness to recommence firing, and as I write is throwing shells with great accuracy into the cavalry camp. I desire that you will communicate this cowardly breach of warlike etiquette to that noble and high-minded officer, General Joubert. By all the rules of civilized warfare this Boer gun and the officers and men working it are my prize; the gun should be dismantled, and the officers and men sent into Ladysmith as prisoners of war.

'An Indignant Naval Officer', *Yorkshire Post*,
20 December 1899, p. 6

42

Writing on 11 November 1899, Captain Neil Gordon, Royal Artillery, recorded that

This is the 12th day of our bombardment, and considering they have fired several hundred if not more shell of 94 lbs each into the town and camp, the damage done is wonderfully small both to person and property. We ought to be relieved in a week from now. I live up in a little camp under the hills by myself with all the reserve ammunition, and we get a good many shells plugged specially at us, with not much effect luckily so far. It is pretty lonesome, and the day is awfully long, as tents are struck at daybreak, and they fire on us at intervals, from 5 a.m. till 7 p.m., when they stop, so far thank goodness, they have not fired at night . . . They are making a good fight for it, but outnumber us by 30,000 to 9,000[37] – so folks judge.

'The Siege of Ladysmith', *Inverness Courier*,
30 March 1900, p. 3

43

A nurse, writing to her mother from Durban on 11 November admitted:

I cannot describe to you the horrors of war! To see our brave, loyal soldiers smashed, and yet so patient and good! . . . During Monday's skirmishing, we lost so many men, and the Gloucesters and Irish Fusiliers were taken prisoners. We had twenty-six men brought in to us who had been wounded on the Monday, and lay out in the open veldt all that day and night, and discovered by the ambulance wagon on Tuesday. Never, never can I forget their intense thirst and their joy at having their wounds attended to. We were operating, amputating all Tuesday night, and they were dying all around us . . . Last Friday I had orders from the principal medical officer to accompany the ambulance train, with ten officers and 200 regulars, to Durban and then return. We got nearly to Colenso, where the Boers were firing; but they dared not fire on the Red Cross, so I, with other nurses

---

37   The British actually retained some 12,500 officers and men in Ladysmith.

and orderlies, brought the wounded down to Durban . . . Of course neither I nor the ambulance train could return to Ladysmith, as the Boers have torn up the rail, and we are quite cut off from Ladysmith.

'Experiences of a Nurse', *Leicester Chronicle*,
23 December 1899, p. 4

Chapter 2

Besieged in Ladysmith and the Battle of Colenso

Sir George White established his headquarters in the centre of the town. At the outset of the siege he commanded approximately 12,500 men and retained a reserve force, mainly mounted men nearby, intended to reinforce any part of the perimeter if required. The perimeter defences stretched some 14 miles [22.5 km] round the town and enclosed an area with a diameter of about 4 miles [6.4 km]. The perimeter included four principal sections, A, B, C and D, each of which was connected by telephone with White's headquarters. Colonel W. G. Knox, CB, commanded section 'A' that ran from Junction Hill facing north, through Tunnel Hill, Cemetery Hill to Helpmekaar Ridge. This included some of the most vulnerable low-lying sections of the defences overlooked by the Boer guns on Lombard's Kop and Umbulwana Hill. Major General F. Howard, CB, CMG, ADC, commanded section 'B' that ran from Gordon Hill due north of the town in a westerly direction encompassing Cove Redoubt, Leicester Post, Observation Hill and King's Post and then southward through Ration Post to Rifleman's Post. Colonel Ian Hamilton CB, DSO commanded section 'C' that stretched from Flagstone Spruit through Range Post and included Maiden Castle and the entire southern defences from Wagon Hill to Caesar's Camp in the south-eastern corner. Finally Colonel Royston and the Natal Mounted Volunteers held section 'D', stretching from the south-east corner to due east of Ladysmith, joining section 'A' at the Klip River.[1]

Some of the Boer commandos moved south and ultimately manned defences north of the Tugela River. They left nearly 9,900 men with 22 guns and five machine guns to mount the siege. These commandos held positions on the encircling hills, stretching over 30 miles [48.2 km]

---

1   Griffith, *Thank God We Kept the Flag Flying*, pp.102–3.

in length, including several dominating positions: Umbulwana Hill, 7,400 m south-east of Ladysmith (and only 4,800 m from the nearest defensive position) was a flat-topped hill 152 m above the town that commanded most the British defensive positions; Lombard's Kop and Gun Hill, 6,100 m due east of the town (and 3,300 m from the nearest British position); Pepworth Hill, 6,300 m north-east of the town (and 5,500 m from the nearest British position); and Middle Hill, 7,900 m south-west from the town (but only 2,700 m from the nearest British position). On each of these hills the Boers deployed a Long Tom with a range of 9,880 m. Boers also held Long Hill to the north-east; Surprise Hill and Thornhill Kop to the north-west; Telegraph Ridge, Star Hill and Rifleman's Ridge to the west; Mounted Infantry Hill, Middle Hill and End Hill to the south. On the more distant hills they deployed 12-pounder guns, 9-pounders and machine guns to the south, a 4.7-inch howitzer to the north and south, and a 37 mm pom-pom due east of the town. There were movements of guns during the siege and a howitzer was later deployed on Gun Hill. As the standard 15-pounder guns of the Royal Artillery had a range of only 3,750 m, and so were outranged by the Long Toms, the two 4.7-inch (120-mm) naval guns and four 12-pounders were a valuable addition to the defences of Ladysmith.[2]

44

Sapper E. C. Matthews, in continuing his letter **28**, recalled that after the withdrawal from Lombard's Kop

> We heard with practically not a thought of what was before us of the cutting of our communications, and afterwards of our being surrounded. Well, we didn't mind this at first, as the food was good, and we were told it would only last ten days, but we have lived to find that the ten was multiplied by twelve. We were worked very hard for the first month of the siege night and day on gun emplacements, laager [a defensive position], etc., and this, no doubt, told on the men later in the siege. We have most of us seen the inside of a hospital, but I was pleased to say both my brother and myself have no serious illness.
>
> 'With the Royal Engineers in South Africa', *West Briton and Cornwall Advertiser*,
> 2 August 1900, p. 2

---

2   Ibid., pp. 103–4; Changuion, *Silence of the Guns*, pp. 20–1, 24, 29–30, 53; Pretorius, *Historical Dictionary*, p. 236.

45

In his letter of 18 December 1899, Private L. M. Chamberlain, B Company, 1st Battalion, Leicestershire Regiment, described how outpost duty evolved during the siege:

Our duties now consist of forming a huge circle round the town and camp. Each corps in the garrison has its own area of the circle to defend. When it is your turn to be actually out in the front line of outposts, you are there for three days and four nights, during which period you only get brief snatches of sleep, the remainder of your period on duty is to be continually watching any movement of the enemy. After your three days' duty, you are relieved by a like force. Then you return into the shelter of the hills close to the town and camp, for two days and one night, during which you can sleep all day if you like, unless you are called upon to resist any attack.[3] Occasionally a small force of our garrison will go out at dark with fixed bayonets, and smash up one of their big guns, rendering it useless,[4] or perhaps we will go to a farm, and drive in any loose cattle, right from under the Boers' noses. I am enjoying the best of health up to present, and although I have been in hot places now and then, I have so far escaped from any wound.

'Letters from Ladysmith', *Leicester Daily Mercury*,
26 March 1900, p. 3

---

3   There was an attack by Boers from three directions on 9 November, inflicting four deaths and 27 casualties on the British: the 5th Lancers and two companies of the King's Royal Rifle Corps repulsed the attack on Observation Hill; the Manchesters, Imperial Light Horse and the 42nd Battery, RFA defended Caesar's Camp from an assault by the Vryheid burghers; and the Devons and Liverpools held Helpmekaar Ridge. Griffith, *Thank God We Kept the Flag Flying*, p. 105; Childs, *Ladysmith*, p. 92.
4   Major General Archibald Hunter led 400 Natal Carbineers, 100 Imperial Light Horsemen, eighteen of the Corps of Guides and detachments of Royal Engineers and No. 10 Mountain Battery in an attack upon the Boer gun emplacements on Gun Hill on the night of 7–8 December. They disabled a 4.7-inch howitzer and a Long Tom, removing its breechblock. Another attack on Surprise Hill three days later was less successful. It destroyed a 4.7-inch howitzer but 11 Boers led a counter-attack, killing one officer and 16 men, another three men died of their wounds, and a further four officers and 34 men were wounded, with six men missing. Archie Hunter, *Kitchener's Sword-arm: The Life and Campaigns of General Sir Archibald Hunter* (Staplehurst: Spellmount, 1996), pp. 131–2; Reitz, *Commando*, pp. 54–9; Maurice and Grant, *History of the War in South Africa*, vol. 2, p. 549.

Intombi Field Hospital

On 4 November 1899 an armistice was arranged when White asked
Joubert if he would allow the transfer of all the civilians and wounded
out of Ladysmith. Joubert only agreed to the creation of a neutral field
hospital at Intombi, with a train going back and forth daily, moving
the sick, wounded and any civilians who had not been involved in the
fighting. Initially there were approximately 300 patients, mostly wounded
from the battles of Elandslaagte, Rietfontein and Lombard's Kop, treated
by 30 doctors and 120 trained staff. On 4 November there were only
twelve cases of dysentery in the hospital, and two weeks later, the first
two patients with enteric (typhoid fever) joined 21 patients suffering from
dysentery. The numbers of sick climbed steadily thereafter, peaking on 27
January 1900 when there were 842 patients with enteric and 472 with
dysentery, and when the relief force arrived after 118 days the numbers of
sick from these diseases were 708 and 341 respectively. During the course
of the siege, the hospital had to bury some 600 patients, 510 from enteric
or dysentery and only 59 from wounds.[5]

46

Sergeant Figg, writing on 28 November (in a continuation of his letter
30), explained how the hospital arrangements had been handled:

> The day after I wrote Ladysmith was literally bombarded with shells
> by the Boer artillery. They fell in and around our hospital: in fact, it
> got too lively for us. One shell fell without bursting just beside me
> and threw up a tremendous lump of earth which just missed me,
> otherwise I should have been flattened out . . . The firing got so
> thick, and we had so many wounded, that at last an officer of ours
> went out under a flag of truce to the Boers to inform them that the
> hospitals were copping it with their shells, with the result that we were
> allowed to a place four miles [6.4 km] out, where they made a piece
> of ground to remain neutral, to form a hospital camp; and it is this
> particular spot, viz., 'Intombi Spruit' and that we have been here ever
> since. The wounded are sent by rail (we lay just along the line) every
> day. Of course the line is all cut off below us still, so we don't get any
> news whatever. We are just simply working, hoping and waiting for

5   Maurice and Grant, *History of the War in South Africa*, vol. 2, pp. 577, 600,
655; Childs, *Ladysmith*, pp. 90–1, 136–7. On the formation of the hospital, see Alan
Chalmers, *Bombardment of Ladysmith Anticipated: The diary of a siege* (Weltevreden
Park: Covos-Day, 2000), pp. 52–4.

the reinforcements to come up. Although we are in this neutral camp we are surrounded by Boers on the hills and firing goes on over our heads, but we are getting quite indifferent to their actions or presence either . . . We had their doctors down to visit our hospitals the other day to see how their patients were being treated at our hands. In spite of plenty of work, etc., here, it's getting very monotonous, and I shall be glad if we go farther up to the front again when the reinforcements come up. If the line could only be opened up we could transfer our sick down country, as at present we are getting hampered with so many, and there is plenty of enteric fever and dysentery, which plays the deuce and has caused a good many deaths. Of course we have to do our own funeral work. The water is very bad here; you could almost cut it with a knife, it is so thick. We had several fearful heavy thunderstorms since being here, and nearly swamped out with the rain. You may be sure it is pleasant at such times, being under canvas, and again, especially at night time, it is extremely lively with scorpions, tarantulas and all sorts of moving things crawling over you. One way or another, I am properly enjoying myself in this rough life.

'Doverite in Ladysmith's Neutral Camp', *Dover Telegraph*,
28 March 1900, p. 5

47

The Rev. Thomas Murray, a military chaplain connected with the Free Church, reflected on his experiences at the Intombi camp:

An arrangement was made between General Sir George White and General Joubert for the removal of the hospitals and hospital staff to Mtombi [*sic*], a place on the veldt, 3½ miles [5.6 km] south of the town. The cross fire of the opposing forces constantly went over the camp. The chaplains received orders to accompany the hospitals; so, from 5th November till after the end of the siege, I remained at Mtombi, where I found very ample occupation. My position has been that of Presbyterian chaplain to the Natal Field Force, which includes not only the Gordon Highlanders but details in other regiments, in the artillery and engineers and cavalry, and in the various corps of the Natal Colonial troops. In the latter especially there were many Scotsmen. Circumstances led to my having charge of such Wesleyans also in these different corps as were brought sick or wounded to Mtombi. Very soon enteric fever and dysentery appeared among the troops and the daily morning train from Ladysmith brought over fresh batches of patients. The hospital camp grew rapidly. The maximum number was nearly 1,900, but for many weeks the daily average was 1,700. Unhappily, of the four Church of England chaplains, three were at an early stage laid aside by sickness, and for more than months the whole of the work fell to one Church of England chaplain and myself. We worked hand-in-hand. It was not a question of 'religion', but wherever spiritual help was needed, there one of us was found. Our first work each day was the burial of the dead. Daily, for three long months, one or both of us might be seen heading the dismal procession of six, or ten, or fifteen, and on one occasion of nineteen dead, whom we were conducting to their last resting place. That duty over, the remainder of the day was busily employed in ministering to the sick and dying in the numerous hospital marquees. On Sunday we did what we could to hold services in these marquees, but it was impossible on any one day to overtake all. There was, however, each Sunday afternoon an open-air service at which convalescent patients could be present.

Besides this work I have just described, I had another piece of work unexpectedly cut out for me, which was full of interest and rich in good fruits.

Close by our hospital camp was a civilian camp, where dwelt in tents or in rude, shanties several hundreds of refugees. There were well-to-do farmers and their families, driven from their homes in Upper Natal, railway people, stationmasters, guards, clerks, etc.; miners from Glencoe and Dundee; and not a few people from Ladysmith itself. The greater number of these were [*sic*] Scotch, and it was natural that I should take spiritual charge of them, for they were out in the wilderness, sheep without a shepherd. Every Sunday morning at ten o'clock, and Sunday evening at seven o'clock, I had an open-air service for them, the convalescents from the military camp attending likewise. It was a sight I shall never forget, to see these homeless ones sitting round me up the veldt, listening to the preaching of the Gospel, making welcome as perhaps some of them had never done before, the precious promises of Divine consolation of which their souls stood so much in need. Many were devout and earnest Christian men and women; and the weekly fellowship, in song and supplication, with God and with one another, did much, I do not doubt, to enable them to endure the tribulations which were their appointed lot.

'A Presbyterian Chaplain at Ladysmith. An Interesting Letter', *Inverness Courier*, 8 May 1900, p. 3

Siege conditions at the outset

Although siege conditions would deteriorate over the course of the 118-day siege, at first when no one knew how long the investment would last, spirits were high and provisions relatively plentiful.

48

Corporal J. Roberts, 2nd Battalion, Gordon Highlanders, recalled that

We fared very well at the start as regards food. The military authorities commandeered (famous word that now) everything in the town, and for a week or two we had bacon for breakfast one day and then jam and cheese the others, with mealie made into porridge.

'Lively Epistle from a Gordon Highlander', *Manchester Evening News*,
12 April 1900, p. 5

49

Mr Butt, a resident of Ladysmith, agreed that

After being cut off from outer communications for more than a week, he had no fault to find with the supply of provisions, and looked for an early release . . . [later when in front of the Royal Hotel he] saw a shell go through the roof and out the front door. This was the shell that killed Dr Stark of Torquay.[6] Having become acquainted with Mr Turnbull, a photographer, he usually went round with him with the camera. One day they were showing some photos to the officers of the Medical Corps, when a shell came through the shop and burst amongst them. It killed a coolie standing on his left and within touching distance. He says 'We took no more photos that day.' On November 27th rations were reduced to ½ lb meat a day.

' "Yeovil Villa" in Ladysmith', *Devon and Somerset Weekly News*,
19 April 1900, p. 6

---

6   On 18 November Dr A. C. Stark, a Devonian doctor of medicine and an ornithologist, was killed by a shell, which passed through the floor of his bedroom without detonating, before passing out onto the street where it struck him. The shell removed one of his legs while smashing the other. He died quickly and a plate in the pavement, with the base of the shell embedded, now commemorates the spot where he was hit. Ken Gillings, *Battles of KwaZulu-Natal* (Durban: Art Publishers, n.d.), p. 37.

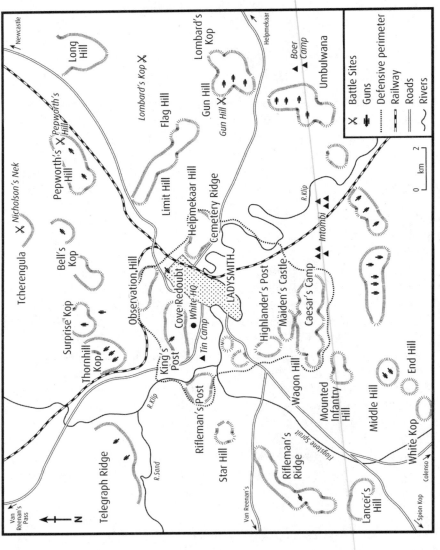

Map 2 The defence of Ladysmith

50

'It was very well for a start, whilst we got plenty to eat,' remembered Private F. Moore, 1st Battalion, Leicestershire Regiment,

> For nearly two months we were getting bacon, cheese, and jam for breakfast, and were able to buy plenty. A few shells also came when we had our meals. We were doing duty on Cove Hill and Gordon's Post then, but have been on Leicesters' Post, and now Observation Hill, and here in the sangar.
>
> 'Letters from the Front', Leicester Chronicle,
14 April 1900, p. 4

Shelling

The shelling of the town was the immediate manifestation of the siege, affecting soldiers and civilians alike. Apart from Sundays it became a regular occurrence, varying in intensity. Civilians sought refuge by hiding in shelters dug into the river bank, and the military prepared trenches in which they could take cover, relying upon a system of warning signals, including whistles and the waving of flags. From their proximity to the Long Tom, nicknamed 'Puffing Bill' on Umbulwana hill, the Gordon Highlanders reckoned that they had about 23 seconds from the puff of white smoke to the shell burst.[7] The besieged gradually got used to the shelling, which sometimes failed to burst and which had very limited effects upon people or property within a sparsely populated area.[8]

51

Seaman Smith, in his letter number **36**, proffered a naval perspective on the incoming fire:

> they pitched plenty of shells into the town, but on account of the charge being bad many of them never burst, otherwise there would have been hundreds more killed than there were. In the first part of

---

7   Greenhill Gardyne, *Life of a Regiment*, vol. 3, p. 39. As De Wet explained in *Three Years War*, p. 30, the shelling and counter-shelling reflected the inability of either side to storm the defences of their adversary.

8   As R. J. McHugh, the correspondent of the *Daily Telegraph* wrote on 9 November 1899, 'When one considers the great number of projectiles, including common shell, ring shell, and shrapnel, which have been fired into the town since October 30, and compares it with the casualties, the proportion of effective hits is infinitesimal.' R. J. McHugh, *The Siege of Ladysmith* (London: Chapman & Hall, 1900), p. 12.

the siege this was particularly the case but latterly they appeared to have obtained a better supply. Of course nothing pleased us better than to see their shells pitch and not burst; we used to enjoy the fun. We could see our shells burst all right, as when they pitched we could see them throw up a tremendous cloud of smoke . . . we were up on a hill by ourselves, whilst the Boers were on still higher hills further away . . . We never expected an attack from our side, because if the Boers had come that way they would not have had a ghost of a chance. We had a 12-pounder, 8 cwt gun, a Maxim, and 4.7 gun on Junction Hill; on another hill there were three Maxims, and a 12-pounder; on Cove Redoubt Hill there was a 4.7 and a 12-pounder; and on Wagon Hill there was only a 12-pounder belonging to the naval brigade . . . We didn't use our Maxims much, because the Boers did not come close enough; we only wished they did. We believed they had spies in the town who gave them the tip not to attack on that side. If they had done so, we should have mowed them down like grass before a sickle. Their ammunition never seemed to run short, and that no doubt was because their communications were intact. They were firing away pretty well all the week long at us, and as we replied with a few rounds at intervals, it probably gave them the impression that we must have plenty of ammunition left yet.'

'A Newton Man in the Naval Brigade which saved Ladysmith', *Mid Devon and Newton Times*, 16 June 1900, p. 8

52

The Reverend Charles Thomson, minister of the Congregational Church at Ladysmith, described how:

We have had shells flying around every day more or less, but none of us have been hit so far, and I trust we may come out of it safely. One shell from "Long Tom" fell at the large gate . . . and with earth falling on the roof, I thought the house was down, but not a window was broken. A piece of another shell went through the roof, and made a hole about three inches wide, but did not come through the ceiling. Another piece struck a branch of the peach tree at the Kaffir [African native] House door, and sent flying over one hundred peaches. The Congregational Church has not yet suffered. The Townhall has had two shells, and one killed a patient in bed and wounded several others, but all have been removed from there now.

'Life at Ladysmith', *North Devon Herald*, 8 February 1900, p. 2

53

In a further section of his letter, number **37**, Sapper Payne of the Telegraph Section recalled that

On the 7th [November] the shells from the Boers continued to pour in nearly all day, but doing little damage. Seven shells pitched into our camp, smashing a waggon [*sic*] and killing two bullocks and one horse. The latter we made use of. A shrapnel burst over our camp, but luckily the men were taking cover, or no doubt many would have been killed . . . It was at this lively time I was ordered off to Rifleman's Post, to assist a party to put up a line, where I stayed as an operator at sunset.

On the 9th sharp shooting took place all round my post,[9] the K.R.R.'s doing duty there, although the position was a most dangerous one, and still under fire at noon we all stood up and gave three cheers for the Prince of Wales, that day, as you were aware, being his birthday. His health was also toasted in rum by each man in the evening. I may mention that I think this was the first occasion on which a Royal Salute had been fired with 21 shells in action, 17 of which were effective. This is an example of our daily life in Ladysmith during the siege with little variation. It was very fortunate that the whole of the shells did not burst, or I'm afraid there would have been very few left to tell the tale. We suffered very considerably from rain and cold at night. On the 19th the Boers began very early, but did little damage. We replied with a few shells closing their fire . . . On the 23rd the Boers were shelling us all afternoon in all directions: 11 shells pitched very close to where I was occupied. They thought evidently they had smashed us up, as their fire ceased on the 24th. We had a very lively time of it. Some cattle, numbering about 170 to 180, were driven out too far by the Kaffirs: the Boers opened fire on them, and they quickly ran away, coming into camp saying the Boers were trying to capture them. About 200 mounted infantry and a few of the K.R.R.s were ordered out, and sharp fighting took place. We managed

---

9   This abortive assault convinced Joubert that further attacks upon Ladysmith would be too costly in the loss of Boer lives, so he relied upon attrition to wear the defenders down while yielding to the pleas of more vigorous commandants, such as Louis Botha, to launch an expeditionary force south of the Tugela. While leaving the elderly Vice-President Schalk Burger to oversee the siege, Joubert accompanied Botha's expeditionary force of some 2,000 burghers. Rayne Kruger, *Goodbye Dolly Gray: The history of the Boer War* (London: New English Library, 1964), p. 106; Field Marshal Lord Carver, *The National Army Museum Book of The Boer War* (London: Pan Books, 2000), pp. 24–5.

to save 70 or 80, the Boers capturing the rest. Only one of our horses
was killed and one wounded on that occasion. On that night the
lightning and thunder were very terrific, and the rain exceedingly
heavy. Later in the night some men went out and captured a few
goats, and we were glad to have them for dinner. On the 27th we had
a few shells at us, which we commenced to get used to. Of course we
had shells every day . . . Nov. 29th – Few shells this morning: only
four at my post. They stopped shelling us about 11.30. At about
four p.m. the Naval gun, which had been fixing up during the night,
commenced to fire a few shells at this gentleman. They did not fire
again from this hill, so they made away with this gun to another hill,
and then sent a few more chums into us. We soon found the gun,
and the Howitzer Battery had a few words with it, and five men were
wounded.

'Our County's Share in the War', *Somerset County Gazette*,
4 August 1900, p. 7

54

Sergeant F. W. Green, 1st Battalion, Devonshire Regiment, served at
Helpmekaar Hill for the first two months of the siege, where:

We had to live in trenches, and keep our ammunition and everything
on. Whilst there I didn't get a wash for three weeks, so you can guess
what sort of a state we were in. We can get a wash every day where
we are now. The way we pass the day is to stop behind a high wall
we have built of stones to protect us from the big guns. Every time a
Long Tom fires the sentry blows a whistle, and then everybody runs
under cover. The Glosters are with us here. Their wall wasn't thick
enough, and one of Long Tom's shells (95 lbs) went through, killed
9, and wounded 8, one went into our Officers' Mess killing 2 officers
and wounding 8. There is no fear of them coming through our wall,
as it is about 16 feet [4.87 m] thick.

'A Colchester Man at Ladysmith', *Essex County Standard*,
21 March 1900, p. 5

55

Children proved irrepressible amid the shelling. As one young girl recalled
after a Long Tom shell landed in a nearby paddock:

I saw some soldiers running to see where it struck, so I said I would
run over and get a piece of the shell as a memento. No sooner said

than done. Off I scampered. Spoke to the first soldier I came to. He said, 'Come with me; I can warn you in time before another shell comes.' So I went gaily on, talking away. Another soldier said, 'Here comes another,' and before we had time to think the awful booming and shrieking came . . . I just shut my eyes and clung to a barbed wire fence, and whispered, 'Good God'. It exploded about 20 ft [6.1 m] away, perhaps not so much, and the earth shook under me . . . After it was over I wanted to get a piece of that shell, and then fled home with three lumps. How I carried them home I can't think now, for they are awfully heavy. At the time they felt as light as feathers . . . When I got back I got such a wigging. They had all watched it from the verandah. Also a lot of soldiers and Carabineers [*sic*] saw from the road. I smelt all over of the shell stuff, and, of course, the shell was quite hot when I got it . . . Somehow you don't care what you do in war time.

'A Girl's Experience', *Sunderland Herald and Daily Post*,
18 December 1899, p. 3

Sorties

Although the conduct of the siege was largely passive on both sides, with only limited and localised attacks by the Boers on Observation Hill and Caesar's Camp on 9 November, the British mounted two sorties in December. The first, launched under Major General Archibald Hunter[10] on the evening of 7/8 December, aimed to relieve the pressure from Gun Hill, which overlooked the lowest sector in the Ladysmith defences. The inactivity of the siege had eroded discipline among the Boers, and Reitz admitted that at night, 'we did not take our watches very seriously'.[11] This enabled Hunter's team to take the Boers by surprise and to disable a Long Tom and a 4.7-inch howitzer and bring back the Long Tom's breechblock, a gun sight and a Maxim machine gun.[12] This certainly boosted morale among the besieged but a second sortie, launched at Surprise Hill to the north of Ladysmith on 10 December, failed to catch

---

10   Major General Archibald Hunter (1856–1936), an Ayrshire Scot, who was commissioned into the King's Own, had seen active service with the Egyptian Army in several campaigns in the Sudan. He had been earmarked as the chief of staff for Sir Redvers Buller but, when trapped in Ladysmith, served in this capacity for Sir George White. Regarded as one of the successes of the siege, he continued to serve with distinction throughout the war. He rose in rank to become full general (1905) and also received the GCB and GCVO.

11   Reitz, *Commando*, p. 52; De Wet, *Three Years War*, p. 31.

12   Hunter, *Kitchener's Sword-arm*, p. 1.

the Boers unawares. As the Boers counter-attacked, the sortie proved much more costly in loss of life (see note 4 above, p. 39) and White never sanctioned another sortie.

56

Sergeant Pearce, 18th Hussars, continuing his letter 7, informed his mother that

> On the 8th December we went out to reconnoitre for the enemy, for a report came in that there was not a Boer to be seen within six miles [9.6 km] of Ladysmith, but we soon found out that they were not three miles [4.8 km] out. We lost two men killed and several wounded, so we had to retire back to our respective camps. We had to come across a plain and the bullets fell around us fast and thick. We had to gallop to get out of their range.
>
> 'A Holybourne Man's Experience in Ladysmith', *Hampshire Observer*,
> 14 April 1900, p. 6

57

Sapper W. Bland, writing to his wife in Blackburn and his parents in Darwen before his death in the battle of Wagon Hill, commented that

> We have had a fearful time of it here at Ladysmith up till now. Shot and shell are flying about the town every day and night. Poor Ladysmith is nearly in ruins now, but I don't think the siege will last much longer. The Boers are getting fed up with trying to get in here. If they had any fighting in them at all they would have got in here long ago. Their force is nearly forty thousand strong, and we are only ten thousand; so that is four to one. The Boers haven't the pluck to come out into the open and fight like men, but they get in among the rocks. The other night 250 of us went out and blew up three of their big guns, and also captured one Maxim. They did not know what to make of it when we rushed into their midst with fixed bayonets. They fired a few shots, and then they ran over the hill as though the devil was after them with 200 of us following them, while the other 50 blew up the guns. We killed about 150 Boers while our loss only amounted to one killed and one wounded. We saw them next morning taking away the three guns, but they are now no good . . . [13] It is just nine weeks to-morrow since we were shut off from the

---

13 Just as Sapper Bland exaggerates the number of Boers committed and their losses

outside world. We are expecting the relief force here soon, and then won't the Boers get a lively time of it.

'Letters from Local Soldiers at the Front', *Blackburn Times*,
14 April 1900, p. 3

58

In his lengthy letter **37** and **53**, Sapper Payne noted that

On Sunday, the 10th of December, the R.E. and R.B.'s [*sic*] had a go at Surprise Hill and destroyed two guns and a lot of ammunition. Our loss was rather heavy, being five killed and between 50 and 60 wounded. One gun was ready loaded. This attack was made during the night. We could hear the guns of the relief column, and also see shells bursting but at a distance daily.

'Sapper Payne's Experiences of the Ladysmith Siege', *Somerset County Gazette*,
4 August 1900, p. 7

Relief Force and the action at Willow Grange

With White's forces beleaguered in Ladysmith, Joubert pressed southwards with his expeditionary force of 2,000 burghers seeking defensible positions from which to thwart the advance of the British reinforcements. By the evening of 14 November they had reached Chieveley, 20 miles (32.2 km) north of Estcourt, where most of the 2,300 British soldiers in southern Natal were located. Next day, despite the proximity of the Boers whose advance patrols were detected only a few miles north of Estcourt, the British sent their armoured train northwards to Colenso. Manned by a company each of Royal Dublin Fusiliers and Durham Light Infantry, about 150 men, with six men of HMS *Tartar* to man the naval 7-pounder and some plate-layers to repair any broken line, the train was ambushed by the Boers. After a brief firefight, the Boers captured 56 prisoners, including Winston Churchill, then the highly paid war correspondent of the *Morning Post*. Having complimented Churchill for his gallantry in leading a party that decoupled the engine from the derailed carriages,

---

– only about 7,000 burghers were committed to the siege, and they lost only a handful of men in this action – his belief that the Long Tom had been damaged beyond repair proved mistaken. Although the muzzle was damaged and the breechblock removed, the gun was removed to Pretoria where it was repaired within a month. Changuion, *Silence of the Guns*, pp. 51–5; Bridget Theron, *Pretoria at War* (Pretoria: Protea Book House, 2000), p. 57.

and enabled it to return with the wounded to Frere, the Boers sent the prisoners, including Churchill, off to Pretoria.[14] They now moved round Estcourt, cutting the railway line at Highlands, and concentrating on the high ground near Willow Grange, 10 miles (16.1 km) south of Estcourt. On the 22/23 November the leading British brigade under Major General H. J. T. Hildyard counter-attacked at night in a thunderstorm and in the following morning. Despite losing only one man and six horses killed (while the British suffered 86 casualties), the Boers were unable to hold a position between the Estcourt garrison and the British forces assembling on the Mooi River. They decided to retreat, taking their 2,000 looted horses and cattle, and to defend the northern bank of the Tugela at Colenso.

59

After the ambush of the armoured train the railway employees who had escaped asked a Reuters correspondent to inform their general manager of

> their admiration of the coolness and pluck displayed by Mr Winston Churchill, the war correspondent who accompanied the train, and to whose efforts, backed up those of the driver, Wagner, is due to the fact the armoured engine and tender were brought successfully out after being hampered by the derailed trucks in front, and that it became possible to bring the wounded in here.
> The whole of our men are loud in their praise of Mr Churchill, who, I regret to say, has been taken prisoner. I respectfully ask you to convey their admiration to a brave man.
>
> 'Tribute to Churchill', *Morning Leader*,
> 18 November 1899, p. 7

60

Writing from Mooi River on 25 November, Private T. Finch, 2nd Battalion, Royal Scots Fusiliers, who would later die at Colenso, commented:

> We intended to go to Estcourt, but could not get there as the Boers had turned up the railway, three miles [4.8 km] from where we are at present (14 miles [22.5 km] off Estcourt). The Boers shelled this camp about three days ago, but did no damage – one man killed and several

---

14   Maurice and Grant, *History of the War in South Africa*, vol. 1, p. 268.

wounded . . . It is a grand piece of country where we are stationed. Several spies have been caught from the Boer side, and they were shot at once. We are expecting this place to be attacked at every hour, but we are well prepared . . . Our food at present is very good; plenty of supplies in stock. Everybody has a healthy appearance, and all in good spirits.

'Bolton Soldier Killed at Colenso', *Bolton Evening News*,
21 December 1899, p. 3

61

Part of the Estcourt garrison, Private James Gant, 1st Battalion, Border Regiment, participated in the action near Willow Grange, fighting on

Beacon's Hill. We advanced during the night about five or six miles [8 or 9.7 km] and had a rest, and as soon as daylight came we extended in skirmishing order and advanced upon the enemy's position about four miles [6.4 km] from us. The naval gun opened the ball by a plugged shell from about 5,000 yards [4.6 km], covering our advance. We got up within 800 yards [731.5 m] of the enemy, and took shelter behind a wall from the heavy fire the enemy poured into us, but we took pot shots at them, and some of our men went round and charged their position and captured a lot of their stores, such as blankets, ammunition, and eatables, but they poured in such a hail of bullets and shell we retired on to our own position and waited for them, but they were too cunning. They did not come any nearer, so we went back and enjoyed a good sleep at Estcourt. A few days afterwards we went up to a small place called Chieveley on the way to relieve Ladysmith.

'Letters from the Front', *Carlisle Journal*,
19 January 1900, p. 6

62

As reinforcements arrived in Natal, Private W. J. Steele, 1st Battalion, Royal Inniskilling Fusiliers, described his journey to Frere camp, south of Chieveley:

We reached Capetown on 30th November, and left for Durban 1st December, reaching there on the 5th. We got into open trucks, packed so that some of us had to stand, and amid shouting and cheering, we started for this place. We met with the greatest

enthusiasm all along the line, kind ladies giving us fruit, tea, bread
and butter, tobacco, pipes, and matches; in fact, offering to write
home for us if we would only give them our addresses. It was grand
to us tired chaps to meet with so much kindness. Everyone, old and
young, showed it in many ways. I heard lads and girls not more than
eight years shouting 'Kill the Boers, kill the Boers' repeatedly until
we were out of hearing.

'A Belfastman at Frere', *Northern Whig (Belfast)*,
13 January 1900, p. 6

63

The relief force, under General Sir Redvers Buller VC, then numbering some
21,000 men with 46 guns, assembled at Frere camp, prompting Private
Willis, 2nd Battalion, Devonshire Regiment, to write on 13 December:

Our force is about 20,000 strong, a very tidy army on paper. We
are expecting to advance to-morrow (the 13th) towards Ladysmith,
but half way there is a Boer force of about 22,000, and they have a
splendid position.[15] We have the advantage one way in having more
big guns, which are generally expected to do the biggest part of the
fighting. There are two naval guns that will carry ten miles [16.1 km],
but we are expecting a big battle and a bloody one before we can
relieve Ladysmith . . .

It's no use trying to shirk it now; we have to face it, and are
looking forward to showing the whole world what we are made of.
It's the first time the British Army has been under such a fire, all the
latest weapons, but the Boers have some bad shells . . .

I expect we shall be in Ladysmith by Christmas, it is only about 30
miles [48.3 km] from here. We have the Commander-in-Chief here
with us, General Buller.[16] He thinks there is no one like his 'Devon

---

15   Once again the British soldiers exaggerated the numbers of the enemy – only
4,500 Transvaal Boers and five guns blocked the route to Ladysmith north of Colenso
– but they held a strong defensive position. Some 3,000 of their number would be
engaged in the battle of Colenso while another 2,000 Free State Boers were deployed
along the Upper Tugela. Pretorius, *The Anglo-Boer War*, p. 17.

16   General Sir Redvers Buller VC (1839–1908) was the scion of Devonian gentry
and retained strong bonds of affection within the county. Having joined the 60th
Rifles in 1858, he served in numerous small colonial campaigns. Conspicuously brave,
he earned his Victoria Cross in the Anglo-Zulu War (1879) and rose as part of Lord
Wolseley's 'Asante ring' to the rank of adjutant general. Although commander of the
Aldershot District when the South African War erupted, he had never held field command when he was appointed as the commander-in-chief of the Army Corps, South

Boys' as he calls us, and won't have anyone except our Regiment to keep guard over him; he is a fine fellow. There won't be much fear of our being left on the battlefield to die of our wounds because about 1,000 refugees have joined us as an ambulance company, and we have the biggest leading doctors of the day. This is the biggest force in South Africa, and we expect this will be the biggest battle fought as they seem to think out here after this there won't be much more left to do. Let's hope not at any rate.

'Experiences of a Barum Reservist at the Front', North Devon Herald,
11 January 1900, p. 5

The Battle of Colenso (15 December 1899)

Initially Buller envisaged crossing the Tugela River by a wide flanking operation at Potgieter's Drift [ford], some 29 km upstream of Colenso, but the news of heavy British defeats at Stormberg (10 December) and Magersfontein (11 December) convinced him that he dared not leave the railway. Lacking both accurate maps and specific intelligence about the Boer positions (his reconnaissance parties were driven back by mounted patrols), he failed to detect the Boer entrenchments in the front of the hills. Botha, who had assumed command of the Boers after Joubert fell from his horse and retired to Pretoria, deployed the bulk of his 4,500 burghers along the northern bank of the Tugela. He anticipated that Buller would attack along the railway and across the open veld, and so concentrated 3,000 burghers to cover this approach, siting his trenches to maximise the effects of their flat-trajectory magazine rifles. Botha also ordered the construction of dummy trenches and gun pits on the high ground to the north of the river, and occupied Hlwangwane, a 544-foot [165.8 m] hill on the southern side of the river, located just north of the river's bend, from which riflemen could enfilade an advancing enemy. By not engaging in the preliminary artillery bombardment launched by Buller on 13 and 14 December, and by withholding fire for as long as possible, Botha sought to maximise the surprise effects of his firepower.

Oblivious of these plans, Buller prepared for a three-pronged frontal

---

Africa. On arriving in Cape Town just after 'Mournful Monday', he split his relief force to raise the sieges of Kimberley, Ladysmith and Mafeking. He would be lampooned in the British press, particularly by Leo Amery of *The Times* over his various defeats in Natal. The publication of his poorly phrased telegrams after Colenso, and a subsequent speech at Aldershot, damaged his reputation irreparably, but not in the west country, where funds were raised to erect a memorial to him in Exeter. Geoffrey Powell, *Buller: A Scapegoat?* (London: Leo Cooper, 1994).

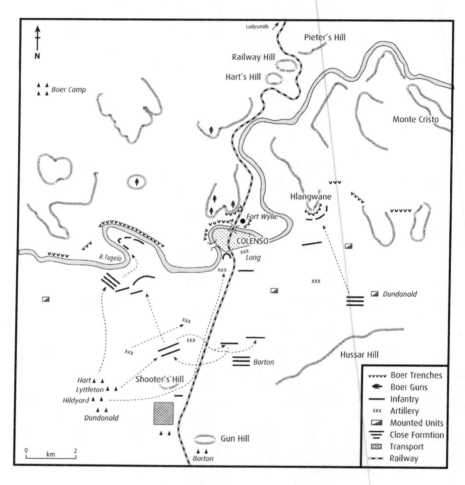

N

Boer Camp

Ladysmith

Pieter's Hill

Railway Hill

Hart's Hill

Monte Cristo

Hlangwane

Fort Wylie

COLENSO

R. Tugela

Long

xxx

xxx

Dundonald

Hussar Hill

Barton

Hart

Lyttleton

Hildyard

Dundonald

Shooter's Hill

Gun Hill

Barton

0 km 2

ᵛᵛᵛᵛᵛ Boer Trenches
       Boer Guns
────   Infantry
xxx   Artillery
       Mounted Units
       Close Formtion
       Transport
━·━·━ Railway

Map 3 The Battle of Colenso, 15 December 1899

advance, with Major General A. Fitzroy Hart's Irish Brigade (1st Battalions of the Royal Inniskilling Fusiliers, Connaught Rangers and Border Regiment and the 2nd Battalion, Royal Dublin Fusiliers) to cross the Tugela by a ford and engage the enemy's right; Major General H. J. T. Hildyard's Brigade (2nd battalions of the Devonshire, Queens, East Surrey and West Yorkshire) to seize the village of Colenso and cross the river by the 'iron bridge'; and Colonel Charles J. Long to bring his artillery (14th and 66th Field batteries) to bear from east of the railway in support. While the 1st Royal Dragoons were to guard the left flank, two batteries of 15-pounders under Lieutenant Colonel L. W. Parsons were to support Hart, backed by two longer-range naval 4.7-inch guns, and Colonel Lord Dundonald, with his mounted infantry, were expected to protect the extreme right and, if possible, occupy Hlangwane.[17] Two other brigades, those of Major Generals Neville G. Lyttelton (the rifle regiments) and Geoffrey Barton (the other fusilier regiments), were deployed in reserve.

64

After advancing in Hart's Brigade, Lance Corporal J. Jones, 1st Battalion, Border Regiment, recalled that

> Our guns had been shelling Colenso for three days, but not one of their shots were returned, and our scouts reported only a few Boers visible. We marched up in mass of quarter columns, Dublin Fusiliers first, Connaught Rangers second, Border Regiment third, and Inniskilling Fusiliers fourth. We had got about 200 yards [182.8 m] from the Tugela River and about 1,400 yards [1.3 km] from the enemy's fort (Fort Wylie), and everything seemed deserted – our naval guns were shelling from our right flank and firing over our heads right in the trenches – and all of a sudden a puff of white smoke came from Fort Wylie . . . a shot dropped about ten yards in front of the Dublin Fusiliers . . .
>
> 'Interesting Letters from Soldiers at the Front', *Liverpool Courier*,
> 26 January 1900, p. 7

65

After the first shell, added Sergeant A. J. Windrum, 1st Battalion, Royal Inniskilling Fusiliers:

---

17 W. Baring Pemberton, *Battles of the Boer War* (London: Pan Books, 1964), pp. 125–7.

This was followed by a second, which burst in the rear of us (the Inniskillings), doing no harm. We immediately deployed, under a very heavy enemy fire, and I dare say the company doubled about a mile [1.6 km] before they got their place in the line. Then commenced the advance. Company after company advanced on their position. The men dropping like leaves, managed to get as far as the river, but could not cross, as it was too deep, and the enemy's advanced trench was only two hundred yards [182.8 m] off. They could concentrate too heavy a fire on us to allow a bridge being thrown across it. A section of the Dublins – about fifteen men – jumped into the river, and were instantly drowned, the weight of their equipment, etc., being too heavy for them. Our fellows had nothing else to do but retire, and, by George! Didn't they suffer then? Some men got as far as five or six bullets in them; one fellow actually strolled into camp in the evening with three bullets in his leg . . . We got out of range at last, about 12 noon, after being in action seven hours, and I wasn't sorry either . . . To tell you the truth, I never want to experience the same again, for while it lasted it was terrible. It's all very well when you can see something to shoot at, but the beggars never show themselves . . . We had about one hundred casualties in the Inniskillings and over eight hundred in the brigade. I will give you an idea of how cool our fellows were, when they were smoking away[18] with the shells and bullets dropping all around them.

'The Bravery of the Irish Brigade', *Northern Whig (Belfast)*, 29 January 1900, p. 6

66

Among those who suffered severely, argued Sergeant H. Holt, 3rd Battalion, King's Royal Rifles, were the

Connaughts, who formed our extreme left guard. By some oversight they were left unprotected by artillery, and the Boers managed to get a Maxim gun trained upon them. Instead of the Colonel [L. G. Brooke] retiring he went forward at a run, and got within 500 yards [457.2m] of the position. He could get no nearer because the River Tugela lay between, and the men were shot down like dogs. Out of 1,200 officers, non-commissioned officers and men who went like

18   This is confirmed by Private Frederick Tucker, 1st Rifle Brigade, in his diary, 15 December 1899, Pamela Todd and David Fordham, *Private Tucker's Boer War Diary: The Transvaal War of 1899, 1900, 1901 & 1902 with the Natal Field Forces* (London: Elm Tree Books, 1980), p. 32.

lambs to the slaughter, only 430 returned . . .

'A Warrington Sergeant at the Battle of Colenso', *Warrington Guardian*,
20 January 1900, p. 2

67

An Inniskilling, Private J. Speer was understandably critical of the formation:

We had a great battle at Colenso, where by mistake we were marched up to within 500 yards [457.2 m] of the enemy's position in the trenches before we were extended, and were for nine hours on an open plain under fire. I had a narrow escape. There were five of us in a group, and I was the only one who escaped, but very shortly afterwards my helmet was knocked off with a piece of shell.

'The Battle of Colenso', *Northern Whig (Belfast)*,
23 January 1900, p. 6

68

A Cameronian witnessed the debacle from a vantage point in the rear:

Our position enabled us to overlook the battlefield, and we could see General Fitzroy Hart march his brigade down almost close to the river in close mass of columns, and he appeared to be about to dress them on markers when the Boers from lines of trenches and rifle pits close to the river opened a tremendous fusillade upon them. The Dublin Fusiliers and Connaught Rangers quietly extended and advanced to the river, which proved too deep to ford, and was found to be filled with barbed wire, which entangled many of those who attempted to swim across. A few managed to cross, but found it impossible to advance further in face of the tremendous hail of bullets which was poured upon them from the Boer lines, and about 10.30 Hart's brigade was ordered to retire. Almost two-thirds of the casualties occurred during the retirement.

'A Scottish Riflemen's Experience at Colenso', *Glasgow Evening News*,
25 January 1900, p. 3

69

In the centre the Devons comprised the firing line where, as Private W. Willis recalled:

We had to advance amidst a perfect hail of bullets and shells, but the brutes did not fire until we were close to them: it is an old trick of theirs . . . Bullets were flying around me for fully five hours, while just on the right of us were two batteries of artillery. Of course the guns and the horses made a good target to fire at. The gunners were mowed down like grass; in fact, there were not enough men to man the guns, and they had to be abandoned.

'Letter from the Front', *North Devon Herald*,
18 January 1900, p. 5

70

Those in reserve lines sometimes had a better overall view. As Private Martin, 1st Rifle Brigade, commented:

we got within 600 yards [548.6 m] of the Boer entrenchments. We met with a terribly heavy shell fire, and as we got up to the firing line, the Mausers [Mauser bullets] fell thick among us. A shell fell and burst into our section and knocked us all down. My mouth and eyes and ears were full of dust and small stones, I was smoking a short clay pipe and that disappeared for ever. The shell, luckily for us, only partially exploded . . . The enemy concentrated their fire on the battery which we were supporting, killing one officer, and several of the horses were disembowelled. To hear the shrieks of those animals, the groans of the dying and wounded Inniskilling and Dublin Fusiliers were pitiful . . . you will not get the truth through the press, as it is under Government censorship, but that frontal attack was human butchery.

'Letters from South Africa', *Nairnshire Telegraph*,
24 January 1900, p. 3

71

Despite the carnage, Colonel Harington-Stuart of Torrance paused for reflection after he

came across General Lyttelton, commanding the brigade of rifle regiments, and who at once pointed out the old 1st Battalion to me. I was soon alongside Colonel Norcott, who was quite pleased to see me . . . The situation did seem strange, indeed. More than 45 years ago I had served as a subaltern under his father in the Crimea, in 1855; now, in December 1899, I was riding alongside the son on another battlefield, who was commanding the same battalion which his father led at Alma and Inkermann, and of which he was so long the beloved and popular commanding officer. Truth, indeed, seems sometimes stranger than fiction.

'Colonel Harington-Stuart on the Battle of Colenso', *Hamilton Advertiser*,
27 January 1900, p. 3

72

Meanwhile Long's artillery suffered severely. Gunner Albert H. Butler, a survivor of the 66th Battery, Royal Field Artillery, explained how

We were advancing towards some hills, Colonel Long[19] in command, but there were no scouts out at all. The Boers were all hid between the hills and trenches, and when we got within 700 yards [640.1 m] of them they opened fire on us. The bullets came among us like hailstones, killing both men and horses. The horses came off worse. When all our ammunition was out we could not get any more, for the teams got shot . . .

'Leicester Artilleryman at Colenso', *Leicester Chronicle*,
27 January 1900, p. 2

73

'The gunners kept up a fire for as long as possible,' recalled Lance Corporal J. Vaughan, Royal Welch Fusiliers,

but could not go on because the enemy kept up a terrible fire between the guns and the ammunition wagons, which tried to get to the guns, and, of course, the guns were silenced, all the gunners being killed or wounded.

'Letters from the Front', *Midland Counties Express*,
27 January 1900, p. 6

74

Jimmy, serving with the 1st Division, Ammunition Column, recalled that

Our Column was ordered to carry ammunition to one of the Batteries . . . [but] directly we got close enough they let fly. The shells were dropping all around us, but strange to say only one driver was hit and three horses killed. It will give you some idea of the escape I had when I tell you that the leading horse (there are six to each ammunition

---

19   Colonel Charles J. Long (1849–1933) had seen active service in the Afghan War and at Omdurman. Although he deployed his batteries in accordance with the conventions of service, his men were so exposed that the subsequent loss of ten guns ruined his career. Buller removed him from command of the artillery in the Natal Field Force.

cart) had his head shot clean off, and the driver wounded. We made
three attempts to get to the Battery but it was no good, we had to
retire.

'A Terrible Experience', *Hampshire Independent*,
20 January 1900, p. 1

75

However, the right flank stalled as well. Major M. A. Close, 13th Hussars,
described how

Our regiment was on the right flank, which we were protecting.
We found two different parties of Boers in our front – one of 200
about, holding a kraal [corral for animals], and the other of about
1,000 or more holding a high knoll.[20] Two mounted infantry colonial
regiments were with us, and they were told off to attack the kraal and
knoll, while we remained in support. They suffered severely, but our
regiment had only two men wounded. We only came in for unaimed
fire, and a few bullets and shells came round us. Whenever that
happened we changed our position of course, and were all day behind
rising ground, from whence we could not see the main attack of our
infantry; but we saw shell after shell bursting in the Boer trenches,
from which they must have suffered fearfully. Our losses were also
very great . . . The battle raged for ten hours, but we were not
successful. The Boers fight wonderfully They conceal themselves so
well that they can't be seen till they open fire, and even then it is hard
to know how many there are. Our infantry advanced against a very
severe fire with the greatest valour.

'Letter from Major Close, 18th Hussars', *Northern Whig (Belfast)*,
23 January 1900, p. 6

76

Gunner H. G. Young, who would win a Distinguished Service Medal for
his gallantry in this battle, recalled the reaction when Buller called for
volunteers to save the twelve guns:

We sat half-stunned for a minute, and then Corporal Nurse got up,
and as soon as we saw him we volunteered at once to fetch them.
We had two officers to take us up to do so. Lord Roberts's son was

---

20 Hlangwane. A knoll is a round hillock.

shot, and the other Captain Schofield, got safe away.[21] We faced a few thousand rifles and went like madmen, and saved two guns out of the six without getting hurt.

'Saving the Guns at Colenso', *Western Morning News,*
8 February 1900, p. 8

77

Captain Walter Norris Congreve, Rifle Brigade, who would win the Victoria Cross, tended the badly wounded Roberts while under fire and wounded himself, and arranged for Roberts to be carried into a nullah [watercourse] where Lieutenant Colonel George Mackworth Bullock and some Devonians provided protection:

About half-past four the Boers rode up and asked us to surrender, or they would shoot us all. Colonel Bullock was our senior unwounded officer, and had perhaps 20 rifles all told. He refused, and the Boers at once began a fusillade from 50 yards [45.7 m] distance, and our people returned it. It was unpleasant, and only a question of minutes before they enfiladed our trench and bagged the lot. Bullock's men knocked over two, and then they put up a white flag and parleyed, said we might remove our wounded, and the remainder either be taken prisoners or fight it out. However, while we were talking 100 or so crept round us. We found loaded rifles at every man's head, and we were forced to give in.

'The Guns at Colenso', *Hampshire Independent,*
10 February 1900, p. 7

78

How this denouement happened was explained in more detail by a Sheffield cavalryman on the headquarters staff of the Cavalry Brigade. 'The battle was practically over', he wrote,

by about one o'clock, all of ours who remained in the front line by that hour being the Devons and officers and men of the artillery in the donga [gulley]. It was hopeless for those to look for succour unless the whole division came to their relief, as the whole of the enemy's guns, and the Boer riflemen in the entrenched kopje in the immediate

---

21 Lieutenant Frederick H. S. Roberts (1872–99), the only son of Lord Roberts, was wounded fatally in trying to recover the guns. He was awarded a posthumous Victoria Cross. Captain Harry N. Schofield (1865–1931) also received the Victoria Cross.

front, not to speak of the various Maxim, automatic and Hotchkiss guns on the left, were ready to pour a withering fire the moment any living thing showed itself within range.

The end came about 5 p.m., when the Boers seeing that the field was clear, and the naval guns on the far ridge could not shell them for fear of hitting our own men, rode out and demanded the party surrender, along with the guns, taking our men prisoner. They subsequently drew the 10 captured guns to the river and threw them in.

The sun went down on Friday night to the boom of the big naval guns, giving a last intimation, ere twilight came, that the British troops would take their revenge before long for the repulse of Colenso.

'The Colenso Failure. A Sheffield Cavalryman's Graphic Description',

Sheffield Daily Telegraph, 26 January 1900, p. 6

Immediate reflections on the battle

79

The outcome, asserted Private R. Banks, was

only the fault of one man, that was Colonel Long, I presume, in charge of our Brigade of Artillery, three Batteries and two Ammunition Columns, of which he got two cut up to mince-meat, which I am sorry to say, or else we should have relieved the poor fellows in Ladysmith. . .

'A Creech St. Michael Man at Chieveley', *Somerset County Gazette*,

14 April 1900, p. 11

80

Trooper Luke Tait of the Imperial Light Horse, like several others,[22] agreed:

The most regrettable incident of the day was the losing of ten of the Royal Artillery's guns. Colonel Long went forward to within 800 yards [731.5 m] of the Boer riflemen, without any shelter on an open plain, and the horses and men were shot down as they got forward. Colonel Long himself was shot down in two or three places . . . This was a sad mistake, which, I believe, lost us the battle; otherwise

---

22 Private Alfred Tillotson, 3rd Battalion, King's Royal Rifles, in 'Colenso A Ruse of General Buller's', *Blackburn Times*, 27 January 1900, p. 3; 'A Glasgow Reservist at Colenso Battle', *Glasgow Herald*, 9 February 1900, p. 8; and an officer, in 'Sidelights on the War', *Northern Whig (Belfast)*, 22 January 1900, p. 5.

we would have cleared the Boers out of their positions, if the two batteries could have been effectively used.

> 'The Battle of Colenso', *Newcastle Daily Chronicle*,
> 19 January 1900, p. 5

81

The effectiveness of British artillery fire remained a matter of dispute. While several shared the sentiments of Private Flanagan, 2nd Battalion, West Yorkshire Regiment, that

> Our artillery and naval fire was splendid. Hundreds of shells burst fairly in the trenches, and must have wrought tremendous havoc amongst the Boers.
>
> 'Letters from the Front', *Liverpool Courier*,
> 22 January 1900, p. 7

Private S. Preston of the same regiment prudently observed:

> Our naval guns were shelling the trenches end to end, but we could not tell whether they were doing any good or not.[23]
>
> 'No Note of Grumbling Heard', *Leeds Mercury*,
> 19 January 1900, p. 6

82

For many soldiers, the abiding memory of Colenso was their inability to see the enemy. 'They were down in trenches on the hills in front,' wrote Private Charlie Wright, 2nd Battalion, Devonshire Regiment,

> They were down in the trench, and we could not see them, and then they started firing on us. . .
>
> 'A Molland Man at the Tugela Battle', *Western Times*,
> 26 January 1900, p. 2

83

Frustration mounted accordingly, as a bandsman with the 1st Battalion, Border Regiment, recalled,

---

23 Boers had only 38 casualties. Pretorius, *Anglo-Boer War*, p. 17. For an account of the naval shelling, see Lieutenant C. Burne RN, *With the Naval Brigade in Natal 1899–1900* (London: Edward Arnold, 1902), pp. 16–18.

We being on the open plain and having no cover whatever had to
fall on our faces. You could see men of ours actually crying with rage
because they could not see what they were firing at. Had it not been
for the Navy guns we should certainly all be massacred.

'The Border Regiment Weeping with Rage', *Carlisle Journal*,
26 January 1900, p. 5

84

Physical stresses had compounded the impact of the Boer firepower, as
acknowledged by a sergeant of the Royal Scots Fusiliers:

We were not ordered to retire until 4.30 p.m., having been in a broiling
sun, with no food or water, for ten hours. There were many miraculous
escapes. One man got a bullet in his water bottle, and another had his
rifle butt shattered. The physical endurance and bravery of all arms was
admirable, and made one feel proud of his countrymen.

'Ayr Soldiers at the Front', *Ayr Observer and Galloway Chronicle*,
23 January 1900, p. 6

85

For veterans, this was a new and more demanding form of warfare. Private
H. Worth, 2nd Battalion, Devonshire Regiment, admitted that

It was awful to see our poor fellows dropping down by hundreds by
the side of us. It was cruel to be in the battlefield for 12 hours and
in the burning sun and to face so many thousands of them and they
in trenches for miles and miles around. Tell about the last one I was
in in Tirah – it was nothing compared to this.

'Newton Soldier's letter', *Devon Weekly Times*,
9 March 1900, p. 7

86

Another Devonian Reservist, Private George Brealey grasped that smokeless, flat-trajectory, magazine rifles had changed the nature of war:

You see they had every range from their position; they simply have to
lie in their trenches and shoot at us directly we got into rifle range.
There is a lot of difference in attacking and defending, but I consider
I am very lucky in only having one wound, because every time we
made a run towards their trenches we could hear hundreds of bullets
rattling pass in the air.

'Letter from the Front', *Western Times*,
16 February 1900, p. 8

87

Towards the end of the battle, observed Sergeant J. Tomlins of the Royal
Army Medical Corps,

> it was a sight I don't want to see again, for there were dead and
> wounded all over the field, and while we were picking them up the
> Boers were firing at us . . . When the Boers were told about it they
> said they did not see the Red Cross. It was sickening to see the men
> that were not wounded lying about the field for want of water, for it
> was very hot and the men were done up.

'Boers Fire on the Bearer Corps', *Lichfield Mercury*,
26 January 1900, p. 8

88

Another member of the ambulance corps, Peter Skirving confirmed that
the Boers had fired on them but then ceased when 'the Red Cross flag
[was] flying before them. Our men', he reported,

> were badly cut up, mostly Irishmen, of the Dublin Fusiliers and
> Connaught Rangers. The Boers took all the rifles off the dead men
> and everything else they could lay their hands on. I may tell you that
> we had to fall back on Estcourt again. We were fairly beaten.

'Letters from the Front', *Kinross-shire Advertiser*,
27 January 1900, p. 3

89

Burial details, as described by Private Charles Wilcock of the Royal Welch
Fusiliers, were even more gruesome:

> It was a sight, though, men shot in the face, eyes, arms, some had their
> bowels ripped open. They have been burying our dead all day long, and
> we have hundreds wounded. Trainloads have been taken to the base,
> where the hospital is,[24] all day long. To make matters worse we were
> beaten off, and had to retire, which is rather a bad start for Buller.

'Swindonians at the Front', *Evening Swindon Advertiser*,
20 January 1900, p. 3

---

24 Chieveley.

90

Although officers and men realised the scale of the defeat, they often consoled themselves with the belief (which was quite erroneous) that the Boers must have fared even worse. 'Our casualties', wrote Corporal Cecil Cooke, A Squadron, 1st Royal Dragoons, 'were very heavy, not so many killed, but there were 1,400 odd killed and wounded to some 2,000 or over of the Boers (the devils!)'[25] Private Joseph Bailey, 2nd Battalion, West Yorkshire Regiment, reported similar losses, 'about 1,147 killed, wounded, and taken prisoners, and the Boer losses were over 2,000,[26] so I think we had the best of the scrimmage'.[27]

91

Casualties were particularly severe within certain sections and companies. 'I expect you would see the number of our killed and wounded', wrote Private Jonathan Haining, 2nd Battalion, Royal Scots Fusiliers, to his brother,

> We lost 44 altogether out of 86, so you can have an idea how my company suffered – that is, B Company and A Company had about the same. The plain fact of the matter is, we got a surprise, as they hid in their trenches until we came near them, and then every rifle and cannon they had fired on us.

'Letters from Ayrshire Men', *Ayr Advertiser or West Country and Galloway Journal*, 25 January 1900, p. 4

92

Confidence in Buller, nonetheless, seemed barely dented. A Balham reservist with the 2nd Battalion, East Surrey Regiment noticed that the general shared their grief: 'General Buller cried when we returned from the day's slaughter at Colenso.'[28] Private George Burgess, a Cameronian, commended the tactical withdrawal: 'We had to retire as General Buller would not sacrifice any more lives.'[29]

---

25 'Letters from the Front', *Gloucester Journal*, 20 January 1900, p. 7.
26 This was another huge exaggeration: the official British casualties included 143 deaths, 756 wounded and 240 missing, that is, 1,139 or vastly in excess of the 7 Boers killed, one drowned and 30 wounded. Maurice and Grant, *History of the War in South Africa*, vol. 1, p. 470 and Pretorius, *Historical Dictionary*, p. 92.
27 A Bayonet Charge', *Leeds Mercury*, 19 January 1900, p. 6.
28 'Another Letter from the Front', *Dover Telegraph*, 28 February 1900, p. 4.
29 'A Marple Man at the Tugela Disaster', *Manchester Evening News*, 25 January 1900, p. 5.

And Private J. Richardson, Royal Army Medical Corps, affirmed that

General Buller . . . is a brave and steady man, as steady as a rock
under fire. He stood watching the artillery fire while bullets and shells
dropped all about him, and when he was hit in his side with one, the
doctor, Captain Hughes, who has since been killed, rode up to him
and asked him if he could do anything for him. He calmly replied that
it had only just taken his wind a bit. If he is not worth following, I
don't know who is. He is as brave as a lion.

'General Buller's Bravery', *Blackburn Times*,
27 January 1900, p. 3

Further Reactions to Buller's Defeat

93

Within Ladysmith the sense of anti-climax was palpable. Writing on 28
December Private Edward Lightfoot, Natal Carbineers, admitted that

I don't know what Buller is doing; we hear his guns sometimes.
We get no news, and we have been cut out of the world since the
beginning of November[30] . . . We are all heartily sick of this. We don't
have much to do, and that is one good thing, for we are not strong
enough to do it if we had.

'Interesting Letters from Soldiers at the Front', *Liverpool Courier*,
30 January 1900, p. 3

94

In fact, messages were passed between Ladysmith and the relief force. As
a member of Buller's signalling staff at Estcourt, Corporal John Thomas,
2nd Battalion, Somerset Light Infantry, confirmed:

We are in communication with Ladysmith through a place called
Weenen. We receive scores of messages every day from Ladysmith,
most of them being private to friends all over the world. They are
all right and quite confident of being relieved shortly. It seemed to
surprise them when they had news that General Buller's attack at

---

30   Some civilians were also perplexed by the lack of news initially, and then found it
hard to believe the reports of a defeat and guns lost at Colenso. William Watson, *The
Siege Diary of William Watson Oct. 1899–Feb. 1900* (Ladysmith: Ladysmith Historical
Society, 'Diary The Siege of Ladysmith', No. 7, 1989), pp. 14–16.

Colenso failed. They could hear the firing quite plainly, but they could not make out how the fight was proceeding. All the messages between Buller and White are in figure cipher, and it is impossible for anyone to know the content unless they have the key, and that is the last thing anyone could expect to get. It puzzles the Boers to see the signals going on between us and Ladysmith, and it makes them wild to think that they can't stop us communicating.

'Signalling to Ladysmith', *Liverpool Courier*,
30 January 1900, p. 3

95

Writing on Christmas Eve Sergeant Greenwood, 2nd Battalion, Gordon Highlanders, conceded that they were

playing the waiting game until General Buller, General Clery or Lord Methuen[31] relieves us, for we are only 10,000 strong, and we are keeping 20,000 Boers at bay[32] . . . They have not much pluck or they would make a bold attempt to take Ladysmith. They come within one and a half miles [2,414 m], and no further, for they are funky. They are also under the impression that they are starving us out, but we can exist for another six months. You would be sorry for the cavalry and artillery horses; they are all on half rations, for corn is scarce . . . Now about us, well the principal thing we are living on is Indian corn ground down like flour to make porridge of it. I have not seen butter for ages, we have dry bread for breakfast, and Indian corn and rice for dinner, and dry bread for tea . . . we are going to make a pudding tomorrow with Indian corn for flour, we are going to steal the currants, and beg the raisins from the officers.

'Letters from the Scene of the War', *Manchester Evening News*,
30 March 1900, p. 5

96

Sergeant Farrier J. Cresswell, 69th Battery, informed his mother that he had passed Christmas Day

---

31 Lieutenant General Sir Francis Clery (1838–1926) commanded the 2nd Division in Natal, while Lieutenant General Lord Methuen (1854–1932) commanded the 1st Division, which advanced towards Kimberley but was defeated at Magersfontein on 11 December 1899.

32 This is yet another exaggeration of the Boer numbers, although Reitz confirmed that these numbers varied over the course of the siege, Reitz, *Commando*, pp. 47–9.

not relieved yet, but are expecting it soon. I know you must have thought a good deal about us on Christmas Day. I will tell you of what our meals consisted, on that day – one pound of bread for the day, pint of tea for breakfast, and a pint of tea, half pound of meat and four ounces of rice, and a little flour with a few raisins in for dinner. You can guess how we were situated. Matches are four shillings [20 p] a dozen, and sugar nine pence [3.5 p] a pound, and that is all we can buy until the line is open. I have had no letters from any of you since I left India, but I expect there are some somewhere, which I shall get when we are relieved.

'Letters from the Front', *Hampshire Observer*,
12 May 1900, p. 2

97

Meanwhile at Estcourt, Christmas dinner was not much better. 'We had four biscuits and half a pound of corned beef for our Christmas dinner', wrote Private J. McNamara, 2nd Battalion, South Lancashire Regiment,

but never mind that. We are hard, but I am sorry for the young soldiers. They are a bit frightened, never having been abroad before, and things are strange to them.

'A Cheerful Lancashire Private', *Liverpool Courier*,
30 January 1900, p. 3

98

Lance Corporal H. White, East Surrey Regiment, noted that

by the papers we are going to get a lot of things from different people for Christmas, but we have not seen anything of them. This is what we had for our Christmas dinner: fresh meat boiled with potatoes, and one pint of beer, and a piece of pineapple. Of course we are expecting more to come, such as Christmas puddings and the chocolate which the Queen is sending us out. I think this is the best Christmas I have spent up to now.

'With the East Surrey', *Dover Express*,
26 January 1900, p. 5

99

As criticisms of Buller became known, most soldiers in the relief force rallied round their embattled commander. Writing to his father in Leeds,

Colour Sergeant Craven, who had just been promoted to sergeant major, disapproved of the

> criticism directed against, and pays a high compliment to, the Generals, who have found the Boers in the strongest possible positions, from which it was almost impossible for any infantry in the world to dislodge them . . . To see the high hills and kopjes [small hill] in which the Boers were sheltered was nearly enough to break the heart of the soldiers, 'but when once our men get at them with the bayonet, as they were eager to do, they would be severely punished.' Personally, he had had a lot of work to do, and his company assisted in covering the retreat from Colenso, where they had only one man killed and a few wounded.

'Promotion for a Leeds Man', *Leeds Mercury*,
19 January 1900, p. 6

100

At Frere Camp, there was both reorganisation and reflection in the wake of defeat. As Sergeant Walter Appleyard of the Royal Dublin Fusiliers explained in a letter dated 26 December 1899:

> Ever since the battle of Colenso we have been encamped here behind a spur of hills in front of the Tugela, at the other side of which the enemy are in position. After the battle it was found that our three companies of the first battalion had lost so heavily that it was considered advisable to dissolve them, and they have consequently been dissolved, and the men in them posted to the 2nd battalion. Thus I now belong to the 'A' Company, 2nd Royal Dublin Fusiliers ...
>
> It is very exasperating for us to remain here in sight of the enemy's position, with the consciousness that it is practically impregnable. This is owing to the fact that the Boer artillery is immeasurably superior to our own, both in range and weight, in fact, our field guns here appear to be of no use at all, and if it were not for our Naval Brigade we should be hopelessly outclassed.
>
> The enemy still remain behind their entrenchments on the other side of the river, and cannot be persuaded to show themselves, although our naval guns shell their position regularly every day. What effect our fire has upon them cannot be seen as their earthworks are cunningly concealed, but I think our lyddite must be doing some

damage.[33] The infantry remains inactive, as it is evidently impossible to carry the position by assault. The campaign is likely to last much longer than was at first supposed, as, in point of armament, our enemies are very superior to us; they have some excellent artillery and evidently know how to use it, contrary to the opinion of some newspaper correspondents.

'In Camp at Frere', *Sheffield Daily Telegraph*,
30 January 1900, p. 6

101

Fittingly perhaps the last word should go to the Senior Service. George Crowe, master-at-arms on HMS *Terrible*, maintained that the Naval Brigade had come through Colenso with

only three wounded, and yet we were occupying a central position with our guns the whole of the battle . . . the enemy had every advantage on their side, and the manner in which they defended the place would do honour to any European troops . . . It is quite a fallacy to imagine we have an untrained army to deal with. The firing is very accurate from their guns. . .

'A Naval Man at Tugela', *Sheffield Daily Telegraph*,
24 January 1900, p. 7

---

33 Named after an artillery range in Kent, lyddite was a compound of picric acid used in high-explosive shells. These exploded with a huge flash and emitted clouds of yellow smoke, but the visual effects, as Churchill observed, greatly exceeded their tactical impact. Winston S. Churchill, *London to Ladysmith via Pretoria* (London: Longmans Green, 1900), pp. 242–3; Pretorius, *Historical Dictionary*, p. 251.

Chapter 3

Fighting for Ladysmith

If Colenso was the third and heaviest of the defeats after Stormberg and Magersfontein known collectively as 'Black Week', it was only a foretaste of the severe and bloody fighting that would occur in Natal before Ladysmith was relieved. Both in the siege itself, where the Boers launched their fiercest assault upon Caesar's Camp and Wagon Hill on 6 January 1900, known to them as the battle of Platrand, and in the relief operation, the biggest battle of the war occurred at Spion Kop (Spioenkop), the culmination of a seven-day period from 17 January when British forces under Lieutenant General Sir Charles Warren[1] crossed the Tugela. As battles they may not have proved decisive, with the latter prompting Buller to make another abortive attempt to relieve Ladysmith through the battle of Vaal Krantz (Vaalkrans), 5–7 February 1900, but they reflected the increasing intensity of the fighting in this crucial theatre.

Initially, though, Buller allowed his forces time to recover while he waited for further reinforcements.

102

Writing to his mother from the camp at Estcourt on 27 December Private Jack Jones, 1st Battalion, South Lancashire Regiment, assured her that

They are feeding us like fighting cocks – more meat than we can eat

---

1   Sir Charles Warren (1840–1927) was better known as the former Commissioner of the Metropolitan Police when his force failed to apprehend Jack the Ripper. Although he had served in South Africa, including the bloodless Bechuanaland campaign (1884–5), he had derisory combat experience, and had only commanded the Diamond Fields Horse in the north-western Cape campaign of 1877, when he was given independent command of Buller's forces in the flanking operation to cross the Upper Tugela.

and plenty of white bread extras with every meal. We are only 15 miles [24.1 km] from the front. We have close on 5,000 head of cattle in camp taken last week from the Boers. Buller has them hemmed in at Colenso on every side.

'Letters from the War', *Warrington Guardian*,
27 January 1900, p. 2

103

Morale was high in Estcourt as Sergeant J. Hartley, 2nd Battalion, Lancashire Fusiliers, observed:

I am now in communication with Ladysmith by heliograph and the situation up to now is just the same. We had messages from Buller and White, sending Christmas greetings to the staff here. All the troops are in excellent health. I myself never felt better in my life. It is very hot during the day, and cold at night, but we are used to it and don't mind it one jot.

'A Wigan Policeman in Natal. "England Might Well Sacrifice So Many Lives"',
Warrington Guardian, 27 January 1900, p. 2

104

Like the previous British forces, the reinforcements received hearty welcomes in Natal. The 2nd Battalion, Somerset Light Infantry received a 'good reception in Durban', wrote Private Lionel Graham, and moved up country by train to Estcourt, where

there are all kinds of regiments, and all the wounded come down from the front here to the hospitals. We have nothing much to do here. It reminds me of the manoeuvres. We go bathing and playing football every day. You would not think we are on active service. We live a lot better here than on the Majestic [the troop ship that brought them to South Africa]. There were forty Boer prisoners brought here yesterday.

'Interesting Letters from a Somerset in South Africa', *Somerset County Gazette*,
10 March 1900, p. 2

105

Life was somewhat different in Ladysmith. When he wrote to his mother on New Year's Day – a letter that arrived after she received intimation of his death from enteric fever – Lance Corporal A. Matheson, 2nd Battalion, Gordon Highlanders, observed:

When I wrote you three weeks ago I thought we were getting relieved that week . . . We are lying out every night in the cold and wet, and never have our clothes off. We had to leave everything behind us, nothing but what we have on our backs . . . We have fearful wet weather. Some mornings I waken up and find myself wet to the skin, and have to let my clothes dry on my back. There is an awful lot of the troops sick owing to the bad food, and especially owing to the bad water. It is seldom we get our faces washed, the water is very scarce and very bad, and we are fearfully thirsty after being out all day . . .

'Letters from the Front', *Highland News*,
21 April 1900, p. 6

Battle of Wagon Hill or Platrand (6 January 1900)

The Platrand is a long hill, about 300 feet [91.4 m] high, south-east of Ladysmith that the British held throughout the siege. The principal defensive positions were Wagon Hill to the west and Caesar's Camp to the east. Apart from some stone walls or forts and gun emplacements, with the latter still under construction on Wagon Hill, it was not heavily fortified when the Boers launched an attack at 2 a.m. on the morning of 6 January. While 900 Transvaal men under the command of Schalk Burger attacked Caesar's Camp, 400 Free Staters under Commandant C. J. de Villiers attacked Wagon Hill and Wagon Point in the west. In the centre another 600 men from the Vryheid and Winburg commandos and the German Corps were supposed to complete the assault, but only a small minority of them took part. An artillery barrage from nearby hills proffered support.

106

As Lieutenant Merriman wrote in letter **38**, the 1st Battalion, Manchester Regiment bore the brunt of the assault. 'The Boers', he declared,

did not mean to be idle much longer. The great day came on January 6. I happened to be on one of the picquets on the hill, at about 2.30 a.m. I heard firing on Waggon [*sic*] Hill, neighbouring this one, and at once stood to. I thought there was something up. At dawn a heavy fire was opened under our very noses in the valley below,[2] and up the slope,

2   This was about 3.45 a.m. and the Manchesters lost heavily on the south-east corner of Caesar's Camp, Major A. W. Marden and Capt. and Adjt. W. P. E. Newbigging, *Rough Diary of the Doings of the 1st Battn. Manchester Regt. During the South African War, 1899-1902* (London: John Heywood, 1904), p. 33.

these beggars having crept up under darkness and under cover as the valley is full of trees, during the night. Soon both sides were loosing off heavily, Boer guns playing on the crest of the hill with effect. Soon the whole Regiment was engaged also the Gordons and Rifles, who had come up from below during the previous afternoon. The Boers actually got on top, but were soon bayoneted off. Our guns did good work. The fight at Waggon Hill was still raging, and the Boers practically occupied it, but were driven off again. On the hill above we lost 70 killed and 80 wounded. The Regiment lost 45 killed and 34 wounded, including four officers; one was taken prisoner but escaped during the scrimmage. Our fellows fought like tigers. Waggon Hill lost heavily. The Boers lost about 500.[3] A terrible thunderstorm came on in the middle of the show, when the fire was at its worst I could not see for the rain. The Boers did not retire till dark, after 16 hours fighting.

'Lieutenant Merriman's Experiences at Ladysmith', *Essex County Standard, West Suffolk Gazette and Eastern Counties Advertiser*, 31 March 1900, p. 5

107

In another letter **105** to his mother, written on the 8 January, Corporal Matheson described how

On Saturday last, 6th January, we had to turn out at three o'clock in the morning. My Company and other two were on watch upon a big hill, and there was another Company of an English regiment out in front of us, nearer the enemy. Our companies lay down to rest, but were awakened by heavy fire, so we marched up to the very top of the hill, and the General[4] met us and took two of our Companies to the right, and he left my Company to go to the left to help the English Company, but we only got a few yards when it got daylight, and we were in the open plain, and the enemy began to fire their big guns on us. Half of the Company were in front, and I was with it. When we got to the corner of the hill the enemy was within 50 yards [45.7 m] of us in strong force. Our Captain gave us orders to open fire and

---

3   The British suffered 424 casualties, 175 of which were either killed or died of their wounds (more than at Colenso), Maurice and Grant, *History of the South African War*, vol. 2, p. 570, while 'the Boer casualties were between 62 and 68 killed or died of wounds, and between 119 and 135 wounded. Nearly two-thirds of the losses occurred among the Transvalers on Caesar's Camp. . .' Pretorius, *Historical Dictionary*, p. 335.
4   Sir Ian Hamilton, whose 'dash and gallantry', and that of 'some other officers', in the battle frustrated the Boers in Rawlinson's opinion. NAM Acc. No. 1952-01-33-7-1, Rawlinson diary, 7 January 1900.

to fix bayonets; but there was some of our men wounded, and they began to get a bit frightened, and no wonder, as the enemy were ten times stronger than us . . . We were unable to chase them off it, so we had to hold the position we were in at all cost. This was about 5 a.m., and we sent back for more men, but we had to stay in that position till about 4 p.m., when we got some help from the Rifle Brigade, and all that time under heavy fire. The only shelter I had was behind a little stone you could lift easily. I lay behind it, and was crouched like a rabbit. The company of the Rifle Brigade that came up to where we were had their three officers wounded and a lot of their men before they got up to us. At 4 p.m. the rain came on in torrents, and we had to advance and get the enemy off the hill at all costs before dark. We advanced under heavy fire . . . Our Company had three killed and ten wounded. The Colour-Sergeant is severely wounded, and not expected to get over it.[5] Next morning what a sight there was on the field with dead bodies, both our own men and those of the enemy. I do not want to see the like again, but thank the Lord, I got through it without a scratch.

'Letters from the Front', *Highland News*,
21 April 1900, p. 6

108

Corporal John Murphy, F Company, 2nd Battalion, Rifle Brigade, recalled how his company

was told off to reinforce the Manchester Regiment. We got about 30 yards from them, and the Boers put a hot fire into us. There were 20 killed and 26 wounded out of my Company. Some more of our regiment came across to help us drive them down the hill again with our swords . . . It was a hard fight. It is a horrible thing to see your comrades killed and wounded on the ground.

'The Siege and Relief of Ladysmith', *Devon Weekly Times*,
12 April 1900, p. 7

109

On Wagon Hill, the Imperial Light Horse met the first assault: 'I had two

---

5 Colour Sergeant W. Pryce survived on account of his pocket watch; as he informed his watchmakers, the watch despite 'being struck by several splintered bullets . . . is still going and keeping good time', *West Briton and Cornwall Advertiser*, 26 April 1900, p. 3.

great friends killed on Waggon [*sic*] Hill on January 6th', wrote Trooper
A. T. Case, Imperial Light Horse,

> They were shot dead not far from me. Out of 30 in my squadron we
> had ten killed and eight wounded that day, but the Boers did not get
> the hill for all that. It was the hardest fight we have had. We fought
> for sixteen hours without a drop of water or food. The rain came
> down in torrents . . .
>
> 'In the Siege of Ladysmith', *Somerset County Gazette*,
> 21 April 1900, p. 3

110

On both positions the fighting was desperate as Private J. Boyd, Gordon
Highlanders, recalled:

> The enemy very nearly managed on top of us on the early morning
> of the 6th January, as we all had our jackets and equipments lying
> on the ground about fifty yards [47.5 m] from us when they came in
> great numbers, at two o'clock in the morning. As it was pitch dark,
> we could not see them, but we heard the different low whispers of
> language. We dashed for our rifles, got them, and a terrible battle
> raged for seventeen hours at close quarters, both sides being on
> the one hill all that time. They outnumbered us by thousands [*sic*],
> but there was nothing left for us but to win the day, or the dreadful
> thought of the fall of Ladysmith.
>
> 'Letter from a Blantyre Man in Ladysmith', *Hamilton Advertiser*,
> 21 April 1900, p. 3

111

With the alarm sounded by telephone,[6] White sent reinforcements,
including the 18th Hussars of whom Sergeant Pearce, continuing his
letter 7 and **56**, explained how

> we were called on to go to Waggon Hill [*sic*] to protect a big gun. We
> were on the flank of the hill waiting for them to come round the corner,
> but they never came that way. Then it came on to rain in torrents, and
> then the Boers thought they would make another rush up the hill. So
> up they came. A few of them got on the top, but they never went down

---

6   H. Watkins-Pitchford, *Besieged in Ladysmith: A letter to his wife written in
Ladysmith during the siege* (Pietermaritzburg: Shuter & Shooter, 1964), p. 50.

again until they were carried down during the rain. The men on top were getting overpowered so they shouted for us to rush up the hill. We went just in time to save it, with only one killed and four wounded. That was in the 18th Hussars,[7] the Imperial Light Horse suffered most that day as they were on duty up there at the time.

A Holybourne Man's Experience in Ladysmith', *Hampshire Observer*,
14 April 1900, p. 6

112
Sergeant W. Duncan, Gordon Highlanders, reckoned that

if Mr Boer had been plucky enough he would have taken Ladysmith from us, as we had not sufficient men to keep him out, and owing to the want of food we were in a very bad condition. We were all right after we got the Royal Field Artillery in action. They fairly wiped them out . . . It took them three days to bury their dead. We had the pleasure of seeing them burying their dead on Sunday January 7th, and it was Tuesday night before they finished.

'Letter from the Front', *Ayr Advertiser or West Country and Galloway Journal*,
16 August 1900, p. 4

113
Corporal F. Greinslade, 1st Battalion, Devonshire Regiment, thought more highly of the enemy after the attack on 6 January:

The Boers are a plucky lot of fellows, and they fight bravely. They have kept us pretty well shelled in here with their big guns.

'Ladysmith After the Siege', *Morning Leader*,
12 April 1900, p. 2

114
Nevertheless, Corporal J. Roberts, Gordon Highlanders, continuing his letter **48**, claimed that

We were 'licked beat', but like the usual British bulldog didn't know it, or rather didn't see it. Put any other troops in our position and Ladysmith was lost. It was hard hand to hand bayoneting, throttling,

---

7   For the official report, see Major Charles Burnett, *18th Hussars in South Africa: The records of a cavalry regiment during the Boer War 1899–1902* (Winchester: Warren & Son, 1905), pp. 69–70.

kicking, anything and the Boers held a position on Wagon Hill for
over twelve hours. They greatly outnumbered us[8] but we knew what
we were fighting for and stuck like glue. On the 7th it was a dreadful
sight, I never wish to see the like of it again.

'Lively Epistle from a Gordon Highlander', *Manchester Evening News*,
12 April 1900, p. 5

115

Of all the reinforcements, though, the 1st Battalion, Devonshire Regiment
made the greatest impact. As Private W. Parminter informed his parents,

We have been in several fights, and we have been heroes, but I think
the worst was when the Boers tried to take Ladysmith on the 6th
January, and it was a very narrow escape that they did not have it. The
Boers attacked us about 3 a.m., and took our outposts by surprise, and
kept up the firing until 7 p.m. This was the fight that our Regiment
got their name up about, because they charged up the hill and drove
the Boers off it. Before our Regiment charged, the Gordons and
Rifles had a go at it, but failed in the attempt, losing many killed and
wounded. Then General White asked if our Regiment, Colonel Park
of the Devons would try and take it, and Colonel Park[9] told him he
did not have many men, but would try. General White told Colonel
Park if he would take the hill, he would do anything for him. He
charged up the hill and took it, losing several killed and wounded,
among them being 3 officers and Lieut. Masterton wounded in five
places, this officer has got all right again.[10]

'A Barnstaple Soldier on the Boer Repulse', *North Devon Herald*,
12 April 1900, p. 2

116

Another Devonian, Private W. Lyons wrote retrospectively that

---

8   Initially this was true. The British had about 1,000 men defending these positions.
Kruger, *Good-Bye Dolly Gray*, p. 171.
9   Cecil William Park became an ADC to King Edward VII and rose to the rank
of major general before his death in 1913. The attack of the Devons was dubbed the
'crowning episode of the day'. Donald Macdonald, *How We Kept the Flag Flying: The
Story of the Siege of Ladysmith* (London: Ward, Lock & Co., 1900), p. 175.
10   Lieutenant James E. I. Masterton (1862–1935) received a Victoria Cross for
managing to deliver a message to the I.L.H. despite being severely wounded in this
action.

We had all our time to keep the Boers from coming in; they tried five times but without success. At Wagon Hill, their last attempt, the gallant Devons showed how we could fight with fixed bayonets ... The Boer is a brave man, he 'sticks' fire pretty fair, but cold steel he cannot quite understand. They call the Indian contingent the 'Devils of Ladysmith' ...

'Letters from the Front', *Western Times*,
11 April 1900, p. 4

117

Devonian bravery, as exemplified in a close-order frontal charge with the bayonet, proved very costly.[11] Private Frederick J. Mulligan, 1st Battalion, Devonshire Regiment, recalled:

At the charge of Wagon Hill 50 men fell in 50 seconds: my dear old pal fell in the charge.

'A Brave Regiment', *Manchester Evening Chronicle*,
4 April 1900, p. 3

118

In Chieveley, the relief force followed the battle, as confirmed by a colour-sergeant of the 2nd Battalion, Devonshire Regiment:

We could hear it very plainly. The enemy occupied our position three times, and was repulsed each time. The last time they stopped in the trenches the whole of the day until dusk, when our 1st Battalion, led by Major Park, drove them out at the point of a bayonet. We received a helio message yesterday stating that the 1st Battalion behaved splendidly. They did not state our casualties, but the Boer loss was very heavy ...

The Gordons are not in it now. It is all the Devons here, but I suppose in England it is the 'Gordons did this and the Gordons did that', but don't you believe it. The Devons have won first honours in the defence of Ladysmith.

'Letters from the Front', *Western Morning News*,
6 February 1900, p. 8

---

11 Of the five officers and 184 NCOs and men engaged, three officers and 14 men were killed, one officer and 34 men were wounded. W. J. P. Aggett, *The Bloody Eleventh: History of The Devonshire Regiment* (Exeter: Devonshire and Dorset Regiment, 1994), vol. 2, pp. 336–7.

119

A member of the Rifle Association, Leonard Allsop, recorded that

> during the assault on the town on Jan. 6 we were out but only held
> in reserve in one of the numerous earthworks. The assault was a very
> warm affair indeed, lasting about 17 hours, and kept going the whole
> of the time.

Like Lieutenant Merriman and others he minimised the British casualties
and grossly exaggerated the Boers':

> Our loss was about 300, the enemy's loss from 800 to 1,200.
>
> 'The Siege and Relief of Ladysmith', *Derbyshire Advertiser*,
> 30 March 1900, p. 8

120

Yet the Gordons suffered an acute loss, too, as Sergeant Forbes
observed:

> our dear gallant Colonel.[12] Poor man he was shot in the morning by
> a stray bullet, which entered his stomach and he died the next day.
> Six officers and six sergeants of whom I was one buried him on the
> Sunday night at 11.30. It was a very solemn ceremony. The minister
> had to read the service by the light of a candle, and then we had to
> fill in the grave ourselves. At first we could not get shovels, and had
> to use our hands until we got them. Before we left we all saluted
> him for the last time.
>
> 'Letters from the Front', *Carlisle Journal*,
> 30 March 1900, p. 7

Preparations for crossing the Tugela River

If the battle of Wagon Hill convinced the Boers that they should revert
to their strategy of attrition, it also ensured that White was unlikely to
break out of the investment or attempt to assist Buller by any diversionary
actions. Meanwhile Buller, who had delegated command to Warren,
sought to outflank the Boers by crossing the Upper Tugela River. First, he
had to move his army westwards, with the mounted units under Colonel

---

12   Lieutenant Colonel William Henry Dick-Cunyngham VC. See chapter 1, note 18.

Lord Dundonald[13] leading the way, with the remainder of the army, involving some 25,000 men, 650 wagons, eight field batteries and the Navy's big guns, taking six days to catch up.

121

'Such a march, I shall never forget it as long as I live', wrote Lance Corporal J.A. Chinnery, 1st Battalion, South Lancashire Regiment. Having taken 'fifteen and a half hours to march ten miles' from Estcourt to Frere, with the last mile taking nine hours to cross the Little Bush River, which 'owing to the excessive rains, had become so swollen that to ford it was an impossibility', the soldiers were allowed a day's rest to dry their clothes beginning their

first night march (I am speaking of the 5th Division – 10,000 men) . . . Nothing was known of our destination, at least by Mr Tommy Atkins. Rain in torrents again, a pitch-like darkness, and wretched roads covered with four inches of mud. It was simply frightful, slipping and stumbling all over the place. I hadn't a watch, so could only guess that we had been marching about six hours when the last halt was given, and, completely exhausted, I threw myself on the ground, not caring about slush or anything else . . . At 4.30 a.m. we resumed our march until 9 a.m., when halt was ordered, and we got our breakfasts ready, bully beef, biscuits, and tea . . . At twelve noon we were off again, this time in a broiling sun, temperature about 100 in the shade. After covering about ten miles [16.1 km] we halted and bivouacked for the day and night on the banks of the Upper Tugela River . . . The next day at 11 a.m. the march began again, and although my company had been on alert all night without a wink of sleep, we had to fall in with the remainder, and plod on. However, we only marched about seven miles [11.3 km], and halted at the place where I am now writing. Every movement has been kept religiously secret from us until last night (January 14th), when we were told that we were the relief column for Ladysmith . . . The greatest trial we have is an awful thirst, the constant cry being water.

'Hardships of Campaigning in Natal', *Northern Whig (Belfast)*,
19 February 1900, p. 6

---

13   Colonel (later Major General) D.M.B.H. Cochrane, the earl of Dundonald (1852–1935) was an officer of the Life Guards, who had served in the Nile Expedition of 1884–5, before commanding the Mounted Brigade in Natal. He took part in the relief of Ladysmith and the advance into the Transvaal.

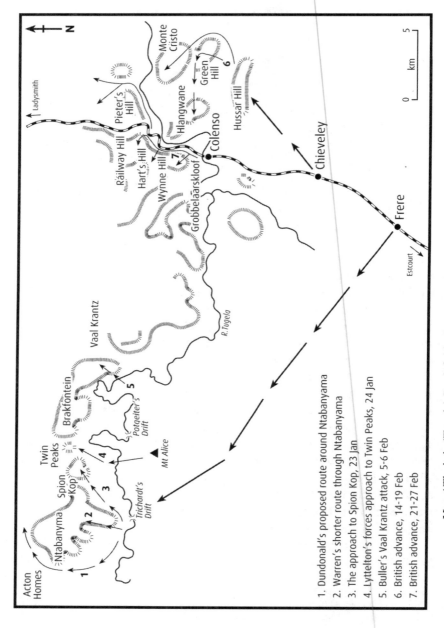

Map 4 Thukela (Tugela) Battlefields: January and February 1900

1. Dundonald's proposed route around Ntabanyama
2. Warren's shorter route through Ntabanyama
3. The approach to Spion Kop, 23 Jan
4. Lyttelton's forces approach to Twin Peaks, 24 Jan
5. Buller's Vaal Krantz attack, 5-6 Feb
6. British advance, 14-19 Feb
7. British advance, 21-27 Feb

122

'We are having a very hard time of it,' wrote Private E. Trout, 1st Battalion, York and Lancaster Regiment, to his sister in Doncaster:

The troops and waggons [*sic*] reach between six and seven miles on the road – when we are on the march. We have not had a good sleep this year, and the grub is very bad. One day I had nothing to eat, so I got a lot of green peaches that were not ripe and made me bad . . . We have crossed about a score of rivers, and only found one bridge – the others we had to march across . . . When we are marching the men are dropping all the way. We have too much to carry – topcoat, water bottle, haversack, with all our things in, rifle, bayonet, and shovel, and if we come to a slop-hole in the road we are glad to drink out of that.

'Letters from the War', *Sheffield Daily Telegraph*,
16 February 1900, p. 5

123

After reaching Spearman's Hill, a Cameronian, Corporal George Logan described how

On the 15th our brigade with two batteries (howitzer) received orders to occupy three kopjes in front, and make a demonstration against the enemy to assist Sir Charles Warren to get round the enemy's right flank. We executed the movement under General Lyttelton,[14] shelling the enemy's position and heavy rifle fire, but received no return from the Boers. We continued to occupy the three kopjes, doing outpost duty every second night, and living in the open, without tents, blankets, or sheets, in all sorts of weather. Then we had orders to make another demonstration, which had the effect of receiving the enemy's fire, 2 being killed and 16 injured of the Rifle Brigade. All this time, the naval guns and batteries of artillery had shelled the enemy's position with lyddite, but they masked their guns and remained silent.

'Letters from the Front', *Free Press (Aberdeen)*,
28 February 1900, p. 7

---

14 Major General Neville G. Lyttelton (1845–1931), having joined the Rifle Brigade in 1865, gained extensive service in India and Egypt, and commanded one of the two infantry brigades under Kitchener in the Sudan. He was one of the few British commanders to enhance his reputation during the South African War and later became the first chief of the general staff.

124

'On the 17th January', recalled Sergeant Catherwood of the 63rd Battery,

> we came into action on a high rocky hill overlooking the Tugela, and commanding the low-lying hills to the front and left flanks, but not within range of Speying Kop [*sic*] (or Look-out Hill), and covering Venter's Spruit, over which the sappers were to build pontoon and trestle bridges for the convenient crossing of the division, the passage of the river being most dangerous. We shelled every probable cover ... As soon as our infantry crossed the river, they advanced towards the hills to the front and left flank covered by artillery fire, but not many Boers showed themselves – none within range. We remained in action all day, and at night bivouacked by the south bank of the Tugela.
>
> 'Letter from the Front', *Bristol Observer*,
> 10 March 1900, p. 2

125

Writing from Spearman's Hill Camp on 18 January, Private Lionel Graham, 2nd Battalion, Somerset Light Infantry, indicated that he was part of

> the reserve brigade. Our artillery is firing at the Boers a couple of miles from here. We can hear the guns firing all day long. We are expecting orders to shift every minute. Everything is all ready to march away . . . We get no bread here; plenty of bully beef and biscuits. There are fourteen of us in our tent, so there is not much room to stretch ourselves.
>
> 'Interesting Letters from a Somerset in South Africa', *Somerset County Gazette*,
> 10 March 1900, p. 2

126

A sapper of 17th Company, Royal Engineers, affirmed that

> Our Company and the pontoon troop put the bridges across the Tugela to take our army across to the district of Acton Homes. The engagement started the day after we got across, and it lasted about six days, finishing up with the attack on Spion Kop. The right half of my Company, to which I belong, was engaged.
>
> 'The Battle of Spion Kop', *Devon and Somerset Weekly News*,
> 1 March 1900, p. 6

The Battle of Spion Kop, (23–24 January 1900)

Although Dundonald found a possible way to outflank the Boers round the north-western end of the hills, known as Ntabamnyama, Warren considered this option as too distant and dangerous. He preferred to advance by a shorter route from Trichardt's Drift with 15,000 men and 36 guns, while Lyttelton, with 9,000 men, sought to distract the attention of the Boers by firing at Potgieter's Drift. Having encountered Boers hastily dug-in on the crest of the height, where as Reitz recalled, they resisted 'any further encroachments',[15] the British sought to exploit the diversionary feint by assaulting the bastion of Spion Kop. The first phase of this action involved the crossing of the Tugela.

127

Sergeant Catherwood continued his narrative **124**:

Next morning we crossed the river, and in the early morning of the 19th we came into action below the crest of a hill and shelled Speying [*sic*] Kop and hills to the left, over the heads of our infantry, afterwards changing our position to the left, and engaging the enemy on the left flank, and covering the advance of Generals Hart's and Hildyard's brigades. It was in this position that we remained in action for seven days continuously, the detachments sleeping at their guns … The first day my guns (No. 4 in action) fired seventy-nine rounds, some of the others firing many more.

'Letter from the Front', *Bristol Observer*,
10 March 1900, p. 2

128

On 20th and 21st Warren's troops fought a series of indecisive actions along the Ntabamnyama Hills. 'We crossed the river and advanced up the hill without opposition', wrote Private W. Aspden of the Border Regiment,

but there was a hill behind on which they had taken position. However, we did not attack them then, but moved in the night to a position further on at a place called Ventur's Spruit. We then attacked them and drove them from their first position and held it for a week under heavy fire. They fired some of our own shells at us. We lost heavily on the first day, but on the remaining six days we fought them

---

15 Reitz, *Commando*, p. 71.

in their own way, firing at them from behind rocks. In these positions we lost very few . . .

'The Men in Natal Not Starved', Blackburn Times,
17 March 1900, p. 3

129

The lack of progress on this front prompted the decision to seize Spion Kop, a prominent hill (1,470 feet (448 m) in height) that overlooked the theatre of operations. 'We had been fighting five days up to the 23rd of January', recalled Private O. Turner, Royal Lancaster Regiment,

> and we lost between 30 and 40 men of my regiment. My mate was gathering a few stones for our bed when an order came that we were going to have a night attack . . . So we began our marching, and we were on our feet all night. We landed about 3 or 4 in the morning at a place called Spion Kop. It is the highest hill in Natal. We got to the top however, and the Boers fired on us in the dark and wounded about sixteen of our fellows. We were given two hours to make some trenches, then they got the ball rolling. There were three regiments on the top – the Lancashire Fusiliers, the South Lancashire and ourselves, the Royal Lancaster.

' "They Mowed Us Down Like Rabbits", The Story of Spion Kop Again',
Blackburn Times, 17 March 1900, p. 3

130

A sapper of the 17th Company, Royal Engineers, continuing his letter **126,** described how

> the right half of my Company climbed up that terrible hill at night with slung rifles and a pick and shovel, so as to make some hasty defence works. When we reached the top there were only four companies of the Lancashire Fusiliers in front of us, but a lot of troops were coming up behind . . . Just then a terrible fire commenced. The Boers were all round us, and bullets came from every direction. However, our troops charged, and drove them back amongst the rocks. It was an uncomfortable time, and I thought my last hour had come. We then commenced to make some kind of defence works, and the ground being so rocky we had to make them of stones. We

only had an hour to make a covering for some thousand men. It was impossible to do it to perfection.[16] A heavy fog was on the hill all the time, and for an hour after daylight, but the Boers kept firing through the fog, and killed and wounded a lot of our men whilst they were working. When daylight came the bullets came like hail, and hundreds of men were killed and wounded. Out of my Company we lost the Major commanding and three sappers killed, a lieutenant and four sappers wounded. I should have been killed myself . . . [but] kept under cover as much as possible.

'The Battle of Spion Kop', *Devon and Somerset Weekly News*,
1 March 1900, p. 6

131

The night assault and capture of Spion Kop had surprised the Boers: Reitz realised that 'This was most serious, for if the hill went the entire Tugela line would go with it, and we could hardly believe the news.'[17] Like the other Pretoria volunteers, he rushed to join the reinforcements mounting a counter-attack on the northern slope. Meanwhile Lancastrian units[18] and Thorneycroft's Mounted Infantry[19] bore the initial brunt of the Boer counter-attack. At the top, recalled Private W. Taylor, 2nd Battalion, Royal Lancaster Regiment,

we were met by a volley from the Boers, but we charged them with fixed bayonets and drove them off the on to another hill, where they started firing at us all night and then when morning came and they found out we had no big guns, they came nearer and started firing their big guns on us, and they kept it up all the blessed day and part of the next night, bullets and shells flying around and among us all the time . . . We came down the night after, or else I think we should all have been killed and wounded. We had over 200 killed and wounded,

---

16   Quite apart from the makeshift nature of the defences, particularly the lack of cover against shell fire, their location, chosen in the dark, was short of the crest and allowed the enemy dead ground that they could employ in mounting assaults on the British position.

17   Reitz, *Commando*, p. 72.

18   Lieutenant Colonel John Downham, *Red Roses on the Veldt: Lancashire Regiments in the Boer War, 1899–1902* (Lancaster: Carnegie Publishing, 2000), pp. 105–17.

19   Irregular Horse raised by Major General Alexander ('Alec') W. Thorneycroft (1859–1931), who had served in the Anglo-Zulu and the Anglo-Transvaal Wars. After Major General Sir Edward Woodgate was fatally wounded on Spion Kop, he assumed command on the summit.

and the Lancashire Fusiliers lost about 450 killed and wounded.[20]

His regimental comrade, Private Turner, continuing his letter **129**, described how

> They mowed us down like rabbits. Fancy having dead and wounded men on either side of you, and the moans of the wounded would break the heart of a stone. Hundreds died from loss of blood.
>
> 'A Blackburn Man Killed. Another Narrow Escape' and ' "They Mowed Us Down Like Rabbits", The Story of Spion Kop Again', *Blackburn Times*,
> 17 March 1900, p. 3

132

Surviving Lancashire Fusiliers were particularly graphic in the their reflections. 'We cleared the hill before the other regiments had time to come up' wrote Sergeant Hartley, a veteran of Omdurman:

> Then we gave three cheers, and the R.E. came up to make trenches. The Boers kept firing on us from an adjoining hill during the time we were making the trenches, and someone fell almost every shot because we were all in groups in the dark. Dawn came and the fun commenced. Well murder was not in it, as from dawn until dark the enemy kept up a fire like hailstones. Our regiment and Thorneycroft's Mounted Infantry were in the front line and we caught the brunt of it. Our fellows fought like lions. Time after time the Boers tried to rush our trenches, and every time we drove them back with heavy losses. Our general was shot down, our staff officers, our own officers – we had no one to command us, our ammunition very nearly gone. We sent a message for reinforcements, and the answer was 'Hold hill at all costs, reinforcements coming.'
>
> 'An Awful Day on Spion Kop', *Liverpool Courier*,
> 27 February 1900, p. 7

133

Of the same regiment, Private Halliwell recalled that

---

20 The casualties of the Royal Lancaster Regiment are correct (72 killed, 102 wounded of whom 18 died of their wounds and 31 missing) but the losses of the 2nd Battalion Lancashire Fusiliers, though the heaviest of all units engaged, were not quite so grim (88 killed, 182 wounded of whom 19 died of their wounds, and 138 missing). Maurice and Grant, *History of the War in South Africa*, vol. 2, p. 507.

It was five o'clock when the Boers commenced with their artillery at Spion Kop, but we despised them. Then the rifle fire came which we returned with all the heart of a British soldier. The Boers advanced to within fifty yards [45.7 m], and it was then that we fixed bayonets, and the cowardly wretches retired. Later some Boers rushed up with the white rag, and our men thinking they were surrendering, rushed out to take them prisoners when we received a heavy fire, which knocked a great many of our men over. Mad with rage the few men left rushed the enemy with the bayonet killing a few, but they fled.

'Soldiers' Letters. "The White Rag"', *Manchester Evening Chronicle*,
16 March 1900, p. 3

134

Herbert Unwin, a native of Sheffield, then serving in Thorneycroft's Mounted Infantry commented:

I was laid [*sic*] in one position nearly all day, cramped, and parched with thirst; the trenches piled with dead and dying men. One poor fellow in our trench had his arm blown off close to his shoulder. He picked it up with the other hand, saying 'My arm, my arm. Oh God, where's my arm!' Quite mad with pain, he jumped out of the trench, and was instantly shot again, and saved further pain.

'The Story of Spion Kop. Told By A Sheffield Soldier', *Sheffield Daily Telegraph*,
12 March 1900, p. 6 and repeated in the *Devon Weekly Times*,
16 March 1900, p. 7

135

Among the reinforcements were the 2nd Battalion, Scottish Rifles (Cameronians), who had already crossed the Tugela as part of Lyttelton's brigade in true Covenanting fashion, with 'our minister', as Private James Murray recalled, 'offering a few short prayers before we set off'. They now

got up the hill – Spion Kop – and every step we took up we could see men of the Lancashire brigade coming down, some of them horrible to behold.[21] We then got to the zone of fire, and if ever I was glad that I was a short man it was at that moment. Just as I was turning

---

21 Many of the reinforcements shared these feelings. As Private W. Rutland, 2nd Battalion Middlesex Regiment, remarked, the sights and comments of the wounded 'did not improve our feelings', NAM Acc. No. 1981-07-18, Rutland, diary, p. 14.

a corner to get into the firing line (and we had to go one at a time, in single file), three shells flew in rapid succession over my head, and if I had been only a few inches taller I should not have lived to write this letter. At last, however, we got into the trenches . . . [and] I then had time to look about me, and what did I see – dead, dying, and wounded scattered all over the field . . . Well as soon as the Boers slackened their fire, we poured volleys hot into them, and after seven hours hot firing and hard fighting, in as tight a hole as it was ever the lot of any of us to be in, we had to retire leaving our dead and wounded on the field, to be catered for by the Boers.

'Graphic Description of Spion Kop, Startling Experiences', *Blackburn Times*, 17 March 1900, p. 3

136

The Imperial Light Infantry (I.L.I.), as Tom Davis recounted, were also among the reinforcements:

When we reached the front line, which we had to do on the right of the hill, we found them behind the rocks peppering it into the enemy as hard as they could. This was the Middlesex and Lancasters, and soon the I.L.I. was in the thick of it. But how sadly handicapped our braves, both soldier and civilian were. The instant you put your head up to take aim properly you had a bullet unpleasantly near, and that is an awful feeling . . . Firing ceased by mutual consent about 7 p.m., and the regulars left and went to bed, the I.L.I. being in charge of the position, so there was not much sleep for us.

'Letter from Tom Davies [*sic*] now fighting in South Africa', *Stroud Journal*, 9 March 1900, p. 3

137

Another battalion, the 3rd Battalion, King's Royal Rifles attacked the Boer positions to east of Spion Kop, specifically the Twin Peaks from which the enemy had delivered a withering fire upon the summit. Sergeant G. Shirley recorded that this was a very costly operation:

we had our colonel and two more officers killed, besides others. Our total casualties were 98 – 19 killed, 78 wounded, and one missing.[22]

---

22 This data is almost correct. Lieutenant Colonel Robert George Buchanan-Riddell (1854–1900) had led the successful assault on Twin Peaks before he was killed, part of the 102 casualties (24 killed and 78 wounded) in this Battalion. Maurice and Grant, *History of the War in South Africa*, vol. 2, p. 597.

We fell in about two miles [3.2 km], halting this side of the river Tugela, being formed up in quarter column. The right half battalion crossed first and then the left. We had to cross the river, which is about forty yards [36.5 m] wide and a very strong stream, with everything on . . . After we were all over we were formed up and told that two regiments were in great trouble, and that we had to relieve them if possible. The position that we had to attack was across an open plain, a mile and a half wide, and then up Spider's Kop, about 900 feet [274.3 m] high, and almost like a precipice, with the best shots of the Boers strongly entrenched on the top. All the time we were crossing the plain we were under a murderous fire from the Boers . . . At all events I was lucky to get to the bottom of the hill with my section, which was part of the firing line of the left half of the battalion. The firing line was composed of two sections of 'E' Company, Nos. 3 and 4, and two sections of 'F' Company, Nos. 1 and 2. So you see in all there were only four sections, that is just a company, to attack a position which seemed almost impregnable. But at all events we were successful and reached the top, driving the Boers from their position.

'Letters from the Front', *Lichfield Mercury*,
2 March 1900, p. 8

138

By seizing Twin Peaks, and forcing the Boers to remove their Krupp gun and pom-pom, one of the few epic feats in this battle,[23] the Riflemen were hardly impressed by a subsequent order to abandon the hill: 'We were wild', wrote one of the King's Royal Rifles,

at getting the order to retire after getting right up to the top. We had to come down again in the dark, nearly breaking our necks, falling over rocks and down into deep holes.

'The Rifles at Spion Kop', *Hampshire Observer*,
17 March 1900), p. 2.

139

Ironically the Boers, having seen their own casualties and desertions mount, and unaware of 'the cruel losses that the English were suffering',[24]

23 The ordinary soldiers knew nothing about the confusion and disputes among the high command, still less the desire of Thorneycroft to abandon the summit of Spion Kop on the same night that the Boers had decided to fall back. Pakenham, *Boer War*, pp. 295–307; Pretorius, *Historical Dictionary*, p. 427.
24 Reitz, *Commando*, pp. 75-77.

had decided to abandon the hill on the same night as the British. If the
Boer victory was, in the opinion of Viljoen 'a fluke',[25] the battle had proved
a daunting experience for the British on the summit. An officer candidly
highlighted the tactical difficulties experienced, the appalling sights on the
summit, and the 'post-traumatic' effects on some of the survivors:

> The Boers held the far edge of the hill with a very few men – probably
> not more than fifty, certainly not a hundred, but hidden behind the crest,
> and protected by rocks. All efforts to dislodge them proved unavailing.
> Our men quailed before their rapid and accurate fire and, though called
> on over and over again by their officers, they were driven back again and
> again. Meanwhile the Boer artillery had begun to play upon them with
> a cross-fire . . . The most horrible sights met the eye everywhere. Men
> with half their heads blown off, and others without legs or arms, and
> many disemboweled [*sic*] were seen on all sides. And in the narrow and
> crowded space one not only saw them, but was thrown in contact with
> them, and was even forced to walk amongst the heap of mangled bodies
> . . . Just before dark the Rifles from Potgeiter's Hill captured another
> point, after some loss, on the east side of Spion Kop, and established
> themselves pretty securely. If this had been done earlier in the day it
> would have had some effect, but it was now too late. The other troops
> were thoroughly disorganized, and had become practically useless . . .
> The general did not intend to retire, but the officer in command made
> up his mind that the position was untenable, and possibly he was right
> when the morale of the troops was taken into account . . . The effect of a
> terrible fire such as was experienced on Spion Kop on the minds of men
> is very curious. Soldiers who had gone through the day without a scratch
> were so overwrought that when, overcome with fatigue, they lay down
> to sleep, they sprang up again and ran off in the dark without knowing
> what they were doing or where they were going. At other times they ran
> round and round in circles, and threw themselves down again, crying
> out for the companions they had lost.
>
> 'The Massacre of Spion Kop', *North Down Herald and County Down Independent*,
>   30 March 1900, p. 3

140

Soldiers extracted what regimental pride they could from the debacle.
Private D. Beat, a Perthshire man in G Company, Imperial Light Infantry,
claimed that

---

25 Viljoen, *My Reminiscences*, p. 56.

Everyone admits that we saved the position that day. We got a biscuit the night before, and got nothing until the following morning (36 hours). Water was at a premium on the hill . . . The regulars speak very highly of us here, and they said – 'Thank God, boys, you got up, or else there would have been none of us left.'

> A Perth Man's Experiences at Spion Kop', *Strathearn Herald*,
> 3 March 1900, p. 2

Sergeant Hartley, 2nd Battalion, Lancashire Fusiliers, reflected ruefully,

We lost over 500 men in five days' fighting, and we lost nearly all our officers. Lancashire might well be proud of her pet regiment, although she has been hit very heavy. The men fought like lions and when the ammunition ran short we stood at fixed bayonets and challenged the Boers to come and take us.

> 'Enough To Turn A Man's Hair Grey', *Blackburn Times*,
> 17 March 1900, p. 3

Corporal Logan, 2nd Scottish Rifles, concluding his letter **123**, recorded that

General Buller said he was proud of us for the deed we had done, and would let Great Britain, Natal, and South Africa know of ours and the 60th's [King's Royal Rifles] deeds that day. We saved a complete defeat.

> 'Letters from the Front', *Free Press (Aberdeen)*,
> 28 February 1900, p. 7

141

Others found the experience quite galling. Private Louis Wilshaw, 2nd Battalion, Lancashire Fusiliers, wrote:

Omdurman was a picnic in comparison. Many instances of heroism were performed, but all paid for it with their life. The enemy's shell did deadly work, having free scope.

> 'Soldiers' Letters', *Manchester Evening Chronicle*,
> 3 March 1900, p. 3

Private J. E. Sharples, Royal Lancaster Regiment, remembered

lying down expecting every minute to be blown to pieces . . . Bullets and shells were now raining down on the hill, and our artillery could not touch the Boer guns. If we had had some guns on the hill it would have made a difference. All we could do was keep up a rifle fire.

'Bolton Soldiers' War Letters', *Bolton Evening News*,
28 February 1900, p. 2

'I probably fired 500 to 600 rounds,' reckoned Sergeant Raisbeck, 2nd Scottish Rifles,

although I must confess I aimed and fired in anything but a deliberate manner . . . For about six hours we lay packed in that trench – the well, the wounded, and the dead, and the two latter were greatly in the majority by nightfall. Our throats were parched with thirst, and the cries of the wounded for water were piteous . . . I am afraid that Spion Kop will count as another reverse, but the odds were too much for us altogether. . .

'On the Way To Ladysmith', *Leeds Mercury*,
17 March 1900, p. 8

142

The carnage[26] left a lasting impression on all who saw it. As Private G. Turner, Royal Lancaster Regiment, admitted:

I will never forget it as long as I live. They mowed us down like rabbits. Fancy having dead and wounded men on either side of you, and the moans of the wounded would break the heart of a stone. Hundreds died from loss of blood. . .

' "They Mowed Us Down Like Rabbits", The Story of Spion Kop Again',
Blackburn Times, 17 March 1900, p. 3

Private J. Hutchinson, York and Lancaster Regiment, agreed that

It was like being in hell, but there was no retiring. We had to stick it.

'Like Being in Hell But No Retiring', *Rotherham Advertiser*,
31 March 1900, p. 8

---

26 Memorably described as 'that acre of massacre', John B. Atkins, *The Relief of Ladysmith* (London: Methuen, 1900), p. 237. Over the period 17 to 24 January 1900, British forces suffered 1,733 casualties. Maurice and Grant, *History of the War in South Africa*, vol. 2, p. 597.

143

Writing from the Military Hospital at Pietermaritzburg, Corporal Lewis, Royal West Surrey Regiment, described his journey from the summit of Spion Kop, after he was shot in the arm:

> I first of all had my arm dressed, and then went back to the field hospital about two miles to the rear of where the fighting was taking place . . . I visited four hospitals on the road down here, sometimes staying two or three days at one place.
>
> 'A West Surrey Man's Battles', *Surrey Times and County Express*,
> 14 April 1900, p. 5

Private John Henderson, a Gordon Highlander attached to the relief column, reckoned that

> We had 700 Civilian and 200 Regimental Stretcher Bearers carrying away the wounded all that day and also the night following. Thirteen stretcher bearers were killed and 43 wounded.[27] It was a dreadful day, in fact a second Majuba. On the 25th the ambulance and doctors went to the top to bring in the remainder of the wounded, and when they reached the higher ground it was a sight never to be forgotten. British soldiers lay all over the field in sections of 20s and 30s. Some were unrecognizable, owing to the deadly shell fire blowing many a chap to pieces. On one small kopje I counted almost 200 killed alone . . .The South Lancashire Regiment lost very heavily and also the Lancashire Fusiliers and the Scottish Rifles, the Fusiliers having only about 400 of their regiment fit . . . It took us 24 hours to bury the dead alone. The Boers appeared to have laid a trap, from the accuracy of their guns upon the hill, and it was somewhat disheartening to have to return. We have gone back some miles to try and draw them but

---

27 The medical arrangements were more extensive than at Colenso. After field treatment, the wounded were carried by bearers, including M. K. Gandhi, one of the 1,100-man Indian ambulance corps, down a 2-mile descent from the top of Spion Kop and then by ambulance wagons and bearers to the base hospital near the Mount Alice. There the original 60 tents and 10 marquees had to be expanded by another 100 bell tents to cope with an additional 500 patients. If the men suffered less from the heat than at Colenso, they had incurred a much larger proportion of wounds from shell and shrapnel and were more exhausted by their hardships. After treatment at the base hospital, the more severely wounded were removed to hospitals in the rear. Frederick Treves and William Stokes, 'The War in South Africa', *British Medical Journal*, vol. 1, no. 2044 (3 March 1900), pp. 534–40; M. K. Gandhi, *An Autobiography* (London: Penguin Books, 2001), p. 204.

I am afraid it will not work. They will not risk much. We shall get to Ladysmith all the same, and every one has faith in Buller. You would need to see the country to understand the difficulty of moving nearer Ladysmith without danger of losing men.

'A Perth Man in the Ladysmith Relief Column', *Strathearn Herald*,
3 March 1900, p. 2

144

On the day after the battle Father Reginald F. Collins, chaplain to the forces, climbed Spion Kop and met with Boers, including General Botha, on the summit. He passed a message from the general on to Sir Charles Warren:

Tell him we want to fight out this quarrel in a Christian way; that it should be clearly understood between us what is to be done after a fight (*schlacht*) and during the war (*krieg*). But there must be reciprocity – there must be reciprocity. Ask him to send me a list of those of our people who are in his hands. Their relatives and friends want to know whether they are alive or dead. I myself will give at all times the fullest information of those we have belonging to you. That he may count upon. As I give up your wounded he should give up ours. You can now carry away the wounded and bury the dead. There are also six wounded who are prisoners in my hospital down there. They can also be taken away or I will give an order that one of my ambulances convey them to any place decided on by your medical authorities . . .' After shaking hands with the General and his secretary . . . I withdrew.

The officers of the R.A.M.C. then carried out the removal of the wounded, and the Rev. Mr Gedge, Church of England chaplain to the forces, and I, on Thursday, buried 138 dead. On Friday 20 were buried, and on Saturday 85.

I venture to think it a matter of considerable importance to draw attention to the attitude of the Boers whom we met during the carrying out of our duties on these three days. After collecting all the identification papers, letters, and personal property of the fallen, and whilst waiting for the graves to be dug, we chaplains were unoccupied, and therefore had plenty of time to talk to the Boers around us. For my part I confess that the deepest impression has been made on me by these conversations, and by the manly bearing and straightforward outspoken way in which we were met . . . there was a total absence of anything like exultation over what they must consider a military success. Not a word, not a look, not a gesture or sign, that could by the most sensitive of persons be construed as a display of their superiority.

Far from it, there was sadness, almost anguish, in the way in which they referred to our fallen soldiers. I can best convey the truth of this statement and show that there is no attempt at exaggeration in using the word 'Anguish' by repeating expressions used, not once, but again and again, by great numbers of them as they inspected the ghastly piles of dead. 'My God! What a sight', 'I wish politicians could see their handiwork.' 'What can God in Heaven think of this sight.' 'What a cursed war that brings these poor fellows to such an end.' 'We hate this war. This war is accursed. Everyday on our knees, we all pray that God will bring this war to an end' 'It is not our war: it is a war of the millionaires. What enmity have we with these poor fellows?' 'Would that Chamberlain, Rhodes, and the millionaires could see these trenches and graves. . .'

Apart from several foreigners, chiefly Swiss and Italians, the Boers seemed to me to belong to the farmer class, some dressed like English gentlemen farmers, and others, who formed the majority, less well dressed but with no signs of raggedness about them, and with scarcely any evidence of the wear and tear of the campaign. . .

Again and again, I will add, they expressed their admiration for the bravery of our men.

'Boers and British on Spion Kop', *North British Daily Mail*, 2 March 1900, p. 2

145

The whole mission now seemed quite daunting: 'The sight of the hills is enough to make your heart drop, never mind having to climb them', claimed a private of the West Yorkshire Regiment:

They seem to reach up to the very heavens. It is nothing to be up in the skies; we can get that height before breakfast. The Scotch lads can talk about the famous Dargai,[28] but my colonel was in that, and he said it was child's play to the hills here. The Scotch lads don't seem any better here than anyone else; not the same as they have been in every other action.

'A Liverpool Man on the Spion Kop Battle', *Liverpool Daily Post*, 1 March 1900, p. 8.

---

28 The storming of Dargai Heights by the 1st Battalion, Gordon Highlanders on 20 October 1897 was an imperial epic. The success of the Scots after various English and Gurkha units had failed was celebrated across the empire. So euphoric was the public response that it fuelled some feelings of enmity towards the Gordons. Edward M. Spiers, *Scottish Soldier and Empire, 1854–1902* (Edinburgh: Edinburgh University Press, 2006), ch. 6.

146

Buller sought to boost morale as Sergeant A.W. Kean, 2nd Battalion, Somerset Light Infantry, recalled:

> To-day (Monday, January 29th) General Buller had us all formed up on parade, and he gave us such good praise for the work we had done for him. He said he was more than pleased with the way the troops fought and bore the fighting which lasted, more or less, ten whole days, and you may guess that is no small joke.
>
> 'A Taunton Cyclist with General Buller', *Somerset County Gazette*,
> 10 March 1900, p. 7

147

There was grumbling about Buller after this defeat, with jibes about Sir 'Reverse' Buller and 'The Ferryman of the Tugela',[29] and Captain F.M. Peacock, 2nd Battalion, Somerset Light Infantry, testified to a growing scepticism within the ranks:

> One afternoon General Sir R. Buller held a parade of our brigade, and made us a speech. The troops had been, he said, through a most trying week, and the highest praise was due to them. They must not imagine that, because Spion Kop had been abandoned, their work had been thrown away, because he was now in hopes that he had found the 'key to the road to Ladysmith.' He then read a copy of a telegram from the Queen in which her Gracious Majesty expressed her sympathy with the troops for the arduous week they had experienced. Sir Redver's remark about the 'key' became the subject of rather sarcastic mirth amongst the soldiery. Weeks have elapsed since then, and we are still outside Ladysmith. The infantry will call out to the artillery as the battery passes them on the road, 'I say, found that key yet?' and the gunners call out above the rattle of their wheels, 'Yes, but it don't fit the lock.'
>
> 'The 2nd Battalion P.A.S.L.I. in South Africa', *Somerset County Gazette*,
> 7 July 1900, p. 3

148

Nevertheless, Buller's words of praise were appreciated as Private E. Pole of the King's Royal Rifles affirmed:

---

29 Pakenham, *The Boer War*, p. 307.

General Buller gave us a speech after the battle, and said better bravery he had never seen in all his career as ours when climbing the hill. He told us he had never seen better climbing nor better discipline in his life . . . We have been two months trying to get into Ladysmith, but have not succeeded yet, and cannot say when we shall. We are fifteen miles [24.1 km] away yet, with plenty of Boers in front of us, but we have great faith in General Buller.

'Three Battles, But Not A Scratch', *Leicester Chronicle*, 3 March 1900, p. 2

Battle of Vaal Krantz (5–7 February 1900)

Faith in Buller would soon be tested again. Having resumed direct command over all troops along the Tugela, Buller renewed his attempt to break Botha's lines by attacking three miles [4.8 km] east of Twin Peaks. With artillery on the high ground south of the river (on Mount Alice and nearby Swartkop), he sought to seize Vaal Krantz, move artillery forward onto these captured positions, enfilade the Boer defences and force his way through with his cavalry. Some 850 burghers, including Viljoen and his Johannesburgers, held Vaal Krantz. Although they would have to vacate the summit under heavy fire on the second day of the battle, they received reinforcements from another 800 Boers and the deployment of a Long Tom on Doornkop (Doringkop) southeast of Vaal Krantz.[30] On 5 February at 6 a.m. the battle began with a feint attack, and British field batteries opened fire, while a pontoon bridge was constructed. At 2 p.m. General Lyttelton commenced his attack, albeit without the supporting battalions he had been promised.

149

Sapper F. C. Poole, writing on 6 February, observed the opening exchanges:

Yesterday our troops started an attack on the Boer position, which consisted of a long range of hills. Our artillery and naval guns did some grand work. I saw a big party of Boers retiring from the hills, and the guns put at least ten shells amongst them, doing great execution. I was in charge of General Warren's headquarters telegraph office, just in the rear of the troops, so I saw what was going on. By nightfall we took part of the Boer position, and at daybreak our guns

30   Viljoen, *My Reminiscences*, p. 57; Pretorius, *Historical Dictionary*, p. 468.

advanced and simply showered the hills and trenches with lyddite. The battle is going on now continuously, and we are determined to get through to Ladysmith this time.

'Interesting Letter from a Bristol Sapper', *Bristol Observer*,
7 April 1900, p. 2

150

'Vaal Krantz,' as Sergeant Lambley of the 78th Field Battery informed his aunt was

about five or six miles [8 or 9.7 km] east of Spion Kop. We marched to the river, and came into action, and shelled all the trenches on the other side. Then the engineers built another bridge across, and we got over all right. Our naval siege guns shelled the Boer position from some high hills this side of the river. On Sunday night we crossed the river, and bivouacked under cover of a hill until daylight. Then about 4.30 we advanced across the open plain at a gallop about 200 yards [182.9 m], and came into action, the 63rd, 28th, and 78th batteries. Our orders were to shell every place we could for two hours, while our main body were to advance and attack the right flank. They had five more batteries with them. We got on all right, and shelled every place within range where we thought they were likely to be, without getting fired at in return, until the order came for us to retire, a battery at a time, from the left . . . The 63rd were the first to go, and as soon as their horses came up they opened fire on us from some big Creusot guns that throw a 100 lb shell 10,000 yards [9.1 km],[31] and, to make it worse, our guns would not reach them. It was just like some little dogs barking at big ones. Of course, we blazed away for all we were worth, but though we elevated our guns as high as we could, our shells fell a long way short. They had it all their own way. Our captain had his right foot blown off, four gunners were wounded, two of them at my gun, and any amount had their clothes torn by bullets or pieces of shell. We also had two ammunition wagons smashed, and one shell dropped in my team, killed the two centre horses, but did not hurt any of us . . . Anyhow we got the guns away safe at the finish, and Generals Buller and Warren, who were watching us the whole time, rode up and praised us greatly for the way we stuck to our guns, and got them out of range.

---

31 In fact, there was only one Long Tom engaged but its superior range and positioning to the east of Vaalkrans would prove crucial in the artillery duel that dominated the battle. Changuion, *Silence of the Guns,* pp. 60–1.

'On The Way To Ladysmith. A Loughborough Sergeant's Letter',
Leicester Daily Mercury, 31 March 1900, p. 6

151

When A Company of the 2nd Battalion, Somerset Light Infantry, served
as escort to the naval guns in the rear, Captain Peacock, continuing his
letter **147**, had an excellent view of the battle:

> The second day I watched from our hill the enemy shelling a battery
> of our artillery below us. It seemed to me that it must have been
> an awful time for the gunners, the enemy had got the range with a
> most unpleasant accuracy. Every now and then a shell would appear
> to land right on a gun and envelop it in a cloud of red dust, and the
> brave little guns would bang back at their distant adversary. I believe
> Colonel Montgomery, R.A., was wounded, and that the captain of the
> battery had to have his foot amputated.
>
> 'The 2nd Battalion P.A.S.L.I. in South Africa', *Somerset County Gazette*,
> 7 July 1900, p. 3

152

In the infantry advance, recalled a lance corporal of the 3rd King's Royal
Rifles,

> our Brigade [Lyttelton's] attacked and succeeded in taking two
> kopjes, one known as Vaal Krannz [*sic*], which we held in spite of a
> determined attempt by the Boers to regain their position. We were
> also subjected to a terrible shell fire from their big guns. In the attack
> the D.L.I. [Durham Light Infantry] and the R.B. were in the front
> rank, supported by the King's Royal Rifles and the Scottish Rifles.
>
> 'Letter from the Front', *Lichfield Mercury*, 23 March 1900, p. 5

153

These front-line units, as described by Sergeant Shirley of the 3rd King's
Royal Rifles,

> had to cross the Tugela, where they came under a very heavy fire from
> a gun, which our boys call the 'pom-pom,' with a 1lb shot. They lose
> pretty heavily, but British pluck and determination leads them on and
> eventually they get to the bottom of Val Krantz Kop, and fix swords
> ready for the charge. They work their way up the Kop, and when near
> the top give a ringing British cheer which throws panic into the Boer

lines and the Kop is ours. We get the position about 4.25 and keep up a very hot and heavy fire, and we are able to keep them away. At 6.10 p.m. our regiment gets the order to advance and take up a position overlooking the Boer lines, only having three shells fired into us without doing us any harm, and we make a breastwork during the night.

'The Capture of Vaal Krantz Kop Described from the Ranks', *Lichfield Mercury*, 23 March 1900, p. 5

154

Private R. Newton, 1st Battalion, Durham Light Infantry, informed his mother how

We had fourteen killed and eighty odd wounded altogether,[32] but we took the hill after a grand charge. We held it for forty hours without anything to eat at all. The Boers were in a strong force on some big hills further over, and they were firing at us all the time. You should have seen the gallant Durham Light Infantry take hill. It was a fine piece of work, taking it at the point of the bayonet . . . The English Brigade relieved us off the hill, after we had been under fire for 40 hours. They fired into us from the two flanks and in the centre.[33] They had some longer ranged guns[34] than ours.

'Letter from an Eldon Lane Man', *Auckland Times and Herald*, 16 March 1900, p. 5

32   The losses of the Durhams were heavy: two officers and 18 NCOs and other ranks were killed or mortally wounded; six officers and 70 NCOs and men wounded. This was a large proportion of the 333 casualties suffered by the British in the battle (27 killed, 300 wounded and six missing). S. G. P. Ward, *Faithful. The Story of the Durham Light Infantry* (Edinburgh: Thomas Nelson, n.d.), p. 296; Maurice and Grant, *History of the War in South Africa*, vol. 2, p. 598. Boer casualties amounted to 38 killed, and 45 wounded and four missing, Pretorius, *Historical Dictionary*, p. 469.

33   The British had only seized the southern kop, which was separated by a saddle from a higher northern kop, entrenched by the Johannesburg Commando. Despite suffering severely from the British shelling (of the 95 burghers with Viljoen, 29 were killed and 24 wounded) these Boers were able to sustain their musketry fire from there and from the nearby heights occupied by the Soutpansberg and Standerton Commandos. Only through a balloon launched on 6 February did Buller learn of the 'almost impregnable position further on', so contributing to his decision to 'give up once more and not waste any more lives in a useless attacks'. NAM, Acc. 1983-07-121, W. Greening, diary, 6 February 1900; see also Viljoen, *My Reminiscences*, pp. 58–9.

34   The artillery duel of the battle of Vaalkrans was the heaviest of the entire war. While Buller had assembled 72 guns to deliver 9,599 shells over the three-day period, the longer range and positioning of the 10 Boer guns ultimately prevailed. Changuion, *Silence of the Guns*, p. 61.

155

Another front-line unit was the 1st Battalion, Rifle Brigade, of whom Private T. Martin recollected that

Getting over the pontoon bridge was a shaky business, but advancing over the plain towards the hill was very rough indeed. I got over the ground very quickly. When I got near the Boer trenches with the Durhams, I fixed my bayonet and gathered speed. About 40 yards [36.6 m] from the trench we got a fierce fire from them. One chap there, quite a lad, rose up deliberately to his knees, and taking deadly aim (I was straight in line) fired at me. 'Whiz' the thing cut me close to the temple, clearing away some of my long hair. I felt mad, and I could not stop, but made at him. He threw down his rifle, and put up his hands, but he was too late, I bayoneted him. His wrist strap adorns my left wrist.

'Letter from a Nairn Soldier at the Tugela', *Daily Free Press (Aberdeen)*, 22 March 1900, p. 6

156

As the artillery duel dominated the battle, Sergeant Shirley, in continuing his letter **153**, recounted how

At 4.25 the next morning our artillery fire a shot and the Boers reply with rifle fire. We got under cover, returning the fire with energy and British pluck . . . They continued their fire all the morning, and my section, No. 3 of E Company was told to get up to the breastwork, and we get the ranges and give them a few shots. About 2.20 p.m., I notice one of the Boer ambulances coming over the veldt and report the same to our officer, who tells us not to fire on it; but one or two of our men seem to suspect that they bring guns in their ambulance wagons, and, on this occasion I am sure they were correct, for the wagon got into a donga for a short time and then went back again. Directly afterwards we were under a very heavy fire from the 'pom-pom' which wounded three of our men. Again the ambulance makes its appearance and we do not fire on it, for our soldiers always show respect for hospital conveyances. In about half an hour we were under fire from shrapnel shell, three of them dropping within a yard of me without doing me any injury, and I am firmly convinced that both guns were brought up in the ambulance wagon. We were to suffer for it, for they were to start shelling us as hard as they possibly could. The Boer riflemen were creeping up under the fire of the 'pom-pom' and shrapnel. While we were watching them in the front, the Durhams were driven from their breastwork, having one man killed, and they almost caused a panic among our own men, but with an English cheer, which would have frightened 10,000 Boers, we get at them again and drove them off. They tried this game on twice, but it failed, and night was drawing on, for which we were thankful. Having had nothing to eat for almost 36 hours and nothing to drink for 24. The sun was awful, almost scorching the skin off us, but we took no notice of this being thankful that our casualties were so light and our lives spared . . . We were relieved by the West Surrey Regiment.

'The Capture of Vaal Krantz Kop Described from the Ranks', *Lichfield Mercury*, 23 March 1900, p. 5

157

Among the relieving units were the 2nd Battalion, Devonshire Regiment, of whom Private John Ebur wrote that

I dare not write and tell you the horror of that fearful battle [Val Krantz], which lasted three days and two nights, only to find after losing so many valuable lives that Buller deemed it prudent to give up the position we had so gallantly earned, and once more for the second time recross the Tugela and retire back to Chieveley.

'With General Buller's Relief Force', *Devon Weekly Times*, 11 May 1900, p. 7

158

The order to withdraw caused surprise on both sides: the retreat for Viljoen, after such a heavy bombardment, 'was as much of a mystery to me as that at Spion Kop',[35] while on the British side the order produced a widespread sense of despair. 'Our fellows,' wrote the lance corporal of the King's Royal Rifles in his letter **152**,

were heart-broken at giving up the positions they had so hardly won, and saying 'Why did you not let us have our heads? We would have shown the Boers whether we could reach Ladysmith or not' . . . General Buller evidently has some good reason that we do not know of, or he would not have ordered us back here.

'Letter from the Front', *Lichfield Mercury*, 23 March 1900, p. 5

---

35 Viljoen, *My Reminiscences*, p. 60.

159

Captain Peacock's company of Somerset Light Infantry, having been sent forward to occupy supporting positions across the Tugela, had endured the effects of heavy shelling but in letter **147** and **151**, he added that the

> idea of a retirement was not exactly rosy. We should have to cross three quarters of a mile [1,200 m] of perfectly open plain, to say nothing of filing over sixty yards [54.9 m] of a pontoon bridge. However, the wise order was given that we should retire by sections, commencing from the right of our line, the sections following each other at 400 or 500 yards' [365.7 or 457.2 m] distance. The pontoon was well within range, we knew, having seen several shells pitched well beyond it that day. But as often happens in war, the 'unaccountable' occurred: not a shot was fired at the retiring regiment, though when we had all got well over the bridge one or two shells dropped some way to our rear.
>
> 'The 2nd Battalion P.A.S.L.I. in South Africa', *Somerset County Gazette*,
> 7 July 1900, p. 3

160

Finally, as Sergeant Lambley observed in his letter **150**:

> After three days' fighting General Buller ordered us to retire across the river again, which went very much against us against us again, but I suppose he knew best. Anyhow we retired to Chieveley, and stayed till the 13th. . .
>
> 'On The Way To Ladysmith. A Loughborough Sergeant's Letter',
> *Leicester Daily Mercury*, 31 March 1900, p. 6

161

On returning to Chieveley the men, wrote Driver G. Harrison, 19th Battery, Royal Field Artillery,

> are all like natives – such a dirty looking colour; and you would never think we were English to see us here, as our beards are a foot long, and during the time we were in action we got fair crummy [*sic*] with lice . . . But I soon got rid of them . . . A lot of the infantry are like it and being so hot they are black as the devil.
>
> 'Soldiers' Beards a Foot Long', *Stroud Journal*,
> 23 March 1900, p. 3

Chapter 4

Enduring a Siege and
Securing the Breakthrough

Siege Conditions Worsen

After the losses incurred at Wagon Hill, and the losses from the mounting toll of sick, the defenders of Ladysmith adopted a passive posture, enduring the shellfire of the Boers and waiting upon the relief forces to break through and scatter the enemy.

162

Writing on 20 January, and continuing the letter **39**, Lieutenant Guy Reynolds of the 5th Dragoon Guards, claimed that

> the only good fighting troops are the Indian Contingent, who have almost all been on service before, and who are all locked up here, and are in such a weak state that it will take a long time before they recover, if they ever do. All the regiments here (with a very few exceptions) have shown conspicuous gallantry whenever they have met the enemy, and it is a great pity that such a splendid division should have had to be sacrificed, though it has undoubtedly saved Natal. We have had baddish weather lately, and get wet through pretty well every night, and it is very miserable and cold and bad news on top of it all makes one rather low spirited. Buller seems to be so dreadfully slow, and our men are dying in numbers every day. The horses, who get only about 4 lb [1.8 kg] of grain a day, are fading away. I hear they are going to destroy 500 of the worst, so as to give more food to the others. This war will cost the country a nice little sum before it is all over, and afterwards they will have to reorganize the army, especially the artillery, in some way or other, either compulsory volunteering or compulsory militia, I expect. Our artillery

– except the siege train – has been absolutely unable to cope with the enemy's guns. It seems very humiliating to us during any of these battles, that the Boers, who are not much better than savages, should be able to hold us easily at arm's length. They have also a better rifle than ours . . .

6th February – Another week gone and no nearer relief. For the last three nights we have all been waiting for an attack from the Boers. The Intelligence Department have, or think they have good information that the enemy will make one more desperate attempt to take Ladysmith, and if they attack in great numbers, we shall have all our work cut out to beat them off, but I think we shall do it all right. At all events we are ready for them and they'll have a warm reception if they do come. If they are decisively beaten in their attack, I fancy they'll raise the siege and retire north to some strong position and probably Lang's Nek or Majuba Hill, in which case we shall be relieved without Buller's help. He was fighting the day before yesterday, but we haven't heard the result yet, I trust he wasn't beaten again. We have to live almost entirely on horseflesh and 2½ biscuits a day. I don't care much for horseflesh. It is rather sweet, and generally very tough, though ox is not much better in that respect. . .

10th February – We have heard Buller's guns going hard for the last four days, but he apparently is no nearer day by day. I expect the Boers have taken up some very strong positions. He is only about ten or twelve miles [16.1 or 19.3 km] from here, so we can hear him very plainly, and shall be able to see the Boers retreat if he can only manage to beat them. We complete the 100th day of the siege to-day.

'Letters from the War', *Warrington Guardian*,
31 March 1900, p. 2

163

A major in Ladysmith wrote:

Another attempt to get letters through our closely guarded investment is to be made to-night. We have got a Kaffir messenger who will make the attempt for £15, undeterred by the fate of previous messengers, who have nearly all fallen into the hands of the enemy. There are several of us engaging the boy, but in any case the postage of this letter will cost several pounds for the first eight or ten miles [12.9 or 16.1 km], and only a penny for the remaining 6,000 odd [965.6 km].

Those attempting to send letters have been warned to use utmost caution to mention nothing which will compromise or play into the hands of the enemy, who is exceedingly clever at using all available information. I think that we can make good our defences for another three months if typhoid does not attack us badly.

'Battle Stories', *Evening News (London)*,
22 January 1900, p. 1

164

Another letter got through to a resident in Durban, who passed it on to his brother in London. It had arrived

on Monday morning from Ladysmith. A Kaffir runner got through with two hundred and fifty letters, nearly all from volunteers. E— wrote brightly in a way, but somehow there was a sad note about it. He said the camp was well, but the whole tone was low. They had plenty of sports, and the military were very jolly with them.

'Life in Ladysmith', *Kent Standard*,
10 February 1900, p. 7

165

By 2 February, Corporal Eli Symonds, Royal Engineers, admitted that

We are very badly off here now. Half the troops are ill, and there is very little to eat, not half enough in fact. They vary our diet. One day we get 1 lb of white bread with ¾ lb of fresh meat, which it is almost impossible to chew, another day we have brown bread, with 1 lb. of horseflesh, which is far better than the beef, and another day we get ½ lb of corned beef. I am a bit better off now, for I went out to one of the Boer farms outside Ladysmith, and brought a sack of Indian corn, which when ground up makes very good porridge. There is a raffle here to-day for a case of whiskey [*sic*] (four bottles). A hundred are going in, and pay £1 a head. Just fancy £100 for four bottles of whiskey! Boxes of matches are 1 s [5 p] each, and are very difficult to get even at that price. A dozen potatoes cost 22 s 6 d [112.5 p]. It's impossible to get anything in the eating line. The fruit was all picked and eaten before it was half ripe.

'A Crewkernian in Besieged Ladysmith. Whiskey at £25 a Bottle',
Somerset County Gazette, 7 April 1900, p. 2

166

Another civilian, Leonard Allsopp, in his diary **119**, which he managed to send to his father, Reverend J. Allsopp of Castle Donington:

Jan. 22, 1960 – We are all right so far, although we have had a rough time of it . . . The Carabineers [*sic*] were quartered in our yard, in sight of a 6-inch gun on the Umbalwana [*sic*], so you can imagine the shells that have been fired near us, and yet strange to say the house has not been struck . . . The children all had a sort of low fever owing to bad food, etc. We had a deep hole dug near the house, and covered with sand bags, where we spent a good deal of our time. Four Carabineers were killed by one shell quite close to the house, and several wounded. A bugler of the Carabineers was put on the watch every day by our underground shelters . . . A good many horses were killed, at different times, but considering that about 10,000 shells have been thrown into the town I think very little harm has been done. They could not have hit blank spaces better if they had tried. As a member of the Rifle Association, I have done my share at guard both day and night. During the assault on the town on Jan. 6 we were out, but only held in reserve in one of the numerous earthworks . . .

Jan. 27 – The enemy began to shell the railway station, which I take as a sign that they have given up all hope of taking the town. We hear all sorts of rumours of what is happening, but the military authorities will not give us any information. If it had not been for the Indian Regiments, the Boers would most likely have been in Durban before the troops from England arrived. Britain was too slow altogether . . .

Jan. 30 – We started on biscuits and beef to-day, and from to-morrow we have rations of biscuits and horseflesh. It is rumoured [*sic*] we must hold out for another six weeks, so evidently the hard times are coming. The Boers will have grown tired of this before six weeks are over, or we shall be on our way to Pretoria.

Feb. 3 – The price of things has gone up. Fancy eggs at 40 s [£2]. a dozen, tin of milk 7 s 6 d [37.5 p], a marrow 8 s [40 p], whiskey £5 per bottle, and other things in proportion!

'The Siege and Relief of Ladysmith', *Derbyshire Advertiser*,
30 March 1900, p. 8

Seizing the South Bank of the Tugela

By switching his point of attack, and being willing to launch a flank assault away from the railway, Buller was finally able to stretch the Boer defences and take advantage of his numerical superiority in men and guns. Although the Boers had occupied key positions on the southern bank of the Lower Tugela from Hlangwane to Hussar Hill, they could spare only 1,500 men for these deployments leaving twice that number entrenched on the northern bank. Moreover, these were fairly isolated positions with little prospect of reinforcement or the provision of supporting artillery fire.

167

As Buller's forces switched their axis of attack, Sapper Charles Field wrote on 10 February 1900:

> We are now on the march in a direction towards Colenso, and I believe our intention is to attack them from the other side again. I am sure our good and clever Sir Redvers is doing everything for the best, although we have had several repulses. But we shall get our own back again before long. I'll bet you see some sights; they don't like the steel, neither do they like night attacks. The prisoners that we have captured are awful-looking creatures, and many of them are wearing our dead soldiers' uniforms . . . I must say our troops have done some splendid work out here, the Infantry especially, and I do not think they can ever be too much appreciated for their own work and the hardships the poor fellows have gone through. We are not allowed any luggage up to the front, and therefore we only have the clothes we stand up in . . . The water here that we have to drink is sometimes filthy and the colour of mud, and the best water we have got up to the present was from the Tugela river. Sometimes we are unable to wash for days, owing to the scarcity of water. I have just about trained my teeth to the bully beef and hard biscuits.
>
> 'A Colchester Man with the Ladysmith Relief Column', *Essex County Standard, West Suffolk Gazette, and Eastern Counties Advertiser*, 24 March 1900, p. 5

168

Trooper H. Clifton, South African Light Horse, participated in the first action on Hussar Hill. Writing on 17 February, he stated that

> We took up this position three days ago, after an hour's fighting. We had a hot time while it lasted, shot and shell pouring in upon us like

hail . . . We get quite a lively time when out scouting for it is risky work as we have to advance until we are fired upon and then retreat and report. This work is very hard on horseflesh for sometimes the poor brutes have not their saddles taken off for three days together . . . I have already killed six of mine with hard riding,[1] for although of the Light Horse I am too heavy to be carried for a week without a change of mounts . . . At Hussar Hill we had 7 horses killed and 8 men wounded. We are a rowdy lot in our regiment for in it we have Yankees, Australians, Canadians, Africanders [*sic*], and almost every other white faced nation. Yet we get on well together for we are agreed upon one thing, and that is British supremacy in South Africa.

'News from the Front', *Auckland Times and Herald*,
23 March 1900, p. 5

169

The mounted forces enjoyed the initial stages of the flanking movement as another trooper, an Irishman, serving in the South African Light Horse recalled:

Our regiment did a lot in turning the flank, and we quite surprised the Boers by appearing suddenly beside them. The prettiest ride I ever had was the morning we started from Hussar Hill. Of course we left before dawn, but when the day broke we were among the mountains, and it was just like riding through Kilarney, only much more extensive. It took us six hours to get to the foot of the hill,[2] where we met the Boers, and then we had to dismount and lead the horses up. They opened fire first, but retreated when we advanced . . . We had with us the mounted infantry of the King's Royal Rifles, some Natal Carabineers [*sic*], and Imperial Light Horse.

'Letter from an Irish Trooper', *Northern Whig (Belfast)*,
25 April 1900, p. 6

---

1   British and imperial forces 'expended' 400,346 horses, mules and donkeys during the war. Among the causes were the inadequate standards of horse mastership, as reflected in this letter, compounded by the availability of vast numbers of remounts, and the enfeebled condition of many horses after long sea voyages, inadequate periods of rest and horse mastership, and the ravages of African horse sickness at lower altitudes in the wetter months. *Minutes of Evidence before the Royal Commission on the War in South Africa*, Cd. 1792 (1904), XLI, q. 19299, p. 258; Anglesey, *History of the British Cavalry*, vol. IV, pp. 363–4.

2   After Hussar Hill, the British advanced in an anti-clockwise direction, seizing Green Hill and Cingolo before they took Monte Christo.

170

Artillery and infantry followed. Lance Corporal Charles Langston, 2nd Battalion, Dorsetshire Regiment, informed his sister that

> On 14 Feb. we attacked and carried by assault Hussar Hill. Some hard fighting followed for the next two days, till, by the 19th, we were in possession of Monte Christo and the Hlangwane valley. On the 20th we seized Hlangwane Hill and drove the remaining Boers across the Tugela.
>
> 'Incidents of the War', *Morning Leader*,
> 4 April 1900, p. 2

171

Gunnery was now being applied in a more systematic manner, not least in the assault on Monte Christo. 'We opened fire', commented Bombardier W. C. S. Motton, 7th Battery, Royal Field Artillery,

> on the right flank of Monte Christo and kept this up for three days, ceasing at sunset and commencing at daybreak. At last the infantry pushed well forward and we were ordered to advance and open fire on the left of Monte Christo. We had to cross a level plateau of two and a half miles [4 km] and the bullets fell like hail. It is a wonder we did not lose more men than we did, but we lost a lot of horses. Once more coming into action we fired on the Boer laager. It was there the murderous fire was issuing from. The distance from our guns was 1,075 yards [983 m] and rifles carry 3,000 [2.7 km], so you can guess how we were getting it. After a quarter of an hour's fire their Maxim Nordenfelt, better known as 'Buck-up'[3], opened fire on our infantry and we had to turn a section or two guns on that – it was in a wagon at 3,000 yards on our left. After we got the range and put in a few shrapnel and lyddite we heard no more of that for a day. Then our attention was turned to the laager. After about twenty rounds had been sent up they were retiring fast, so we quickened our fire and took the laager and Monte Christo with two guns and all the spoil.
>
> 'An Artillery Man's Experiences', *Middlesex County Times*,
> 14 April 1900, p. 2

---

3   Also known as the 'pom-pom' because of the noise of its steady rate of fire from these hand-cranked guns. This 1-pounder (1.457-inch/3.7-cm) gun was a mobile and versatile weapon that laid down a heavy rate of fire over a range of 3,000 yards (2,740 m). Once the British had learned to take cover, the Maxim-Nordenfelt was used less to inflict damage than to restrict movement and prevent the return of fire. Marix Evans, *Encyclopedia of the Boer War*, pp. 176–8.

172

For 'the first few days', recalled Private W. Law, 1st Battalion, Royal Welch Fusiliers,

> we gained a few little hills, and on the fourth day we got Monte Christo after a hard fight by General Barton[4] and his Union Brigade. It was all over then, for we could see that we had command of the chief part of Colenso. Next day we bombarded till we set on fire their chief position, and eventually we got on top of Hlangwane.
>
> That was quite enough for the Boers, although they were still in a good position on the Ladysmith side of the river. They fled in all directions, and we got Colenso quite simple, the enemy only molesting us with a few shells from Long Tom[5] to try and upset the pontoon bridge, which we had across in a few hours.

'Letters from the Front', Midland Counties Express,
14 April 1900, p. 6

173

Capturing Monte Christo was one of the two pivotal objectives on the southern bank. The 'great battle,' stated Corporal A. Hawkins, 2nd Battalion, Devonshire Regiment,

> took place on the Sunday when we took Monte Christo. We turned the Boers' flank, and got the key to Ladysmith. It was a terrible charge, but we took the position about half-past one. I thought of home and all of you sitting down to your dinner, and I would have given all the world, if I had it, for a drink of water.

'More Letters from the Front', Mid-Devon and Newton Times,
5 May 1900, p. 3

174

'After a hard fight' at Monte Christo, wrote Sergeant Lambley, Royal

---

4   Major General Geoffrey Barton (1844–1922) entered the army in 1862 and saw active service in the Asante War (1873–4), the Anglo-Zulu War (1879), Egypt (1882) and the Sudan (1885). Having displayed little initiative in the battle of Colenso, he led his men with more verve in battle of Tugela Heights. He took part in the counter-guerrilla operations and later commanded the Pretoria garrison.

5   As there is a dispute in South African historiography over whether the Long Tom, brought to support the Boers, actually took part in the battle of Tugela heights, this letter like several others in this volume is further confirmation that some British soldiers thought that they had come under fire from a Long Tom. Changuion, *Silence of the Guns*, pp. 85–6.

Artillery, continuing his letter **150** and **160**,

we drove them out, and captured their laager, where they had been for four months, so the fellows we took prisoner told us. They went off in a deuce of a hurry when they did leave, for we captured tons and tons of ammunition, dozens of saddles were lying about, dozens of horses killed by our shells, there were suits of clothes and things of every description thrown about everywhere. The stench was awful, but they must have took [*sic*] most of their dead and wounded with them, as we only found a few lying about and a few graves. We stayed in their camp one night, and then advanced again, and since then we have taken Hlangwana, [*sic*] and driven across the river, and captured Colenso.

'On The Way To Ladysmith', *Leicester Daily Mercury*,
31 March 1900, p. 6

175

The capture of Hlangwane was, as Private J. A. Duncan, a Mancunian Reservist attached to the 7th Royal Fusiliers, remarked:

the key to the position at Colenso, and we occupied it for 23 hours amid a perfect hurricane of shot and shell, but we stuck on until the artillery came up; we were drenched to the skin all the time . . . We then took the River Tugela with a rush, completely surprising the enemy . . . There is one thing a man could not help but admire in the troops, and that was the earnestness of their determination to relieve Ladysmith at any cost. Under all the hardships there was not a growl to be heard, officers and men had but one intention, and that was to beat the Boers.

'A Manchester Fireman's Story', *Manchester Evening Chronicle*,
3 April 1900, p. 3

176

After the capture of Hlangwane, the British were in a position to affect a crossing. As Private Paul Curtis, 2nd Battalion, Devonshire Regiment, wrote:

We have taken Colenso, one of the Boers' strongest positions and the place that has cost so many lives. We are now between Colenso and Ladysmith, and occupying a hill with the enemy about 800 yds [731 m] from us, so we are playing their game behind big boulders. I

am in a sangar built with big stones, so as to be bullet proof . . . When
we took a hill that the Boers were on (Hlangwana [*sic*]) we looted
over 10,000 rounds of their ammunition and my chum and myself
went into some of their stores, and found a lot of nice sponge cakes.
I picked up a nice pair of boots, just the thing as the others were
nearly off my feet. I slipped them on and a few new shirts and caps we
captured as well. The Boers are well off for food, as this lot around
here left a lot of bread and fancy stuff behind. Yesterday we had an
awful day on this hill, shells and bullets whizzing around us from all
directions.

'Letter From Bovey Men', *Totnes Times*,
14 April 1900, p. 3

Morale in Ladysmith

The breakthroughs on the southern side of the Tugela undoubtedly
boosted morale in Ladysmith. They heard the constant pounding of
Buller's heavy guns, reportedly saw guns being dragged to the crest of
Monte Christo, and received his heliograph, claiming possession of the
'main ridge and spurs'.[6]

177

Promising news, though, did little to alleviate the worsening conditions in
the town. Private G. Sharpe, 1st Battalion, Leicestershire Regiment, felt
that

From the time we were first besieged it has been a life of torture, what
with sickness, through the men being out all night during the rainy
season, and the bad food; they have caused the downfall of so many of
us. Probably you may doubt our having to live on horseflesh and one
biscuit for a day's ration, but it's the solid truth. I have been down
with dysentery, but am all right now.

'The Relief of Ladysmith', *Leicester Daily Mercury*,
10 April 1900, p. 2

178

Bombardier C. Syms, 13th Battery, Royal Field Artillery, also dwelt upon
the misery of the final days of the siege:

---

6   'Ladysmith Again Watching and Waiting', *Yorkshire Post*, 23 February 1900, p. 5.

during the siege sometimes they would get four ounces of biscuit, with eight ounces of meat, and four ounces of that horseflesh Three ounces of maize was also served out which they boiled with a little salt and eat like oatmeal. He had been to bed hungry on many a night during the 118 days siege. By bed . . . he means lying down with a big coat, one blanket and a waterproof sheet kit for a pillow on the ground, under a railway tarpaulin, propped up with a few posts and a small dry stone wall built around.

'A Totnesian on the Siege of Ladysmith', *Totnes Times*, 7 April 1900, p. 5

179

Writing home to Manchester, from Ladysmith on 1 March 1900, Private J. Scanlon, 1st Battalion, Manchester Regiment, confirmed that

I am in the best of health, and thank God for it. I only got a very slight wound on the hand on the 6th January. I was hit about three o'clock in the morning, but I still kept fighting till seven o'clock at night. We had the Boers all round us for 119 [*sic*, 118] days. As for shot and shell we got used to it. We all got our share of starvation. For the past three months, we had to [live] on 4 ozs of biscuits and a ¼ lb horse beef, but we kept the Boers out, and we got great praise for it. I could fill the newspaper with the siege, but I will send you a paper with the price of things that were left in Ladysmith, but poor Tommy could not buy them, and he had to go home with a hungry stomach. As for smoking we were smoking leaves off the trees.

'Smoking Leaves off Trees', *Manchester Evening Chronicle*, 10 April 1900, p. 3

180

The diminishing rations had a deleterious effect upon heavily pressed soldiers. As a sergeant of the Gordon Highlanders explained:

You must bear in mind that during all this time we had harder work to do than would have been necessary under ordinary circumstances to keep up a bold front, to keep the whole surroundings in a perfect state of defence, and especially at the weak points, which every now and then showed themselves when the enemy attacked time after time. It was hard, indeed, to work for several days from four to six hours a day, and then most part of the night amongst rocks and cactus trees of a horrible kind tearing your hands and legs, breaking off nails, etc.

and coming home tired and sore, bleeding all over, and full of thorns that in two days' time turned into large swellings, leaving holes in the arm and leg into which one could insert a finger. No medical comforts being to hand, these sores had no help, and the coloured water left for blood lent to the festering, and that with the fearful heat and sweat and flies made it miserable. Scarcely a man escaped from diarrhoea and dysentery, and some pitiable sights were to be seen. Like others, I had my share of this, and the pain and suffering I am not ready to forget in a hurry. To see poor objects – shadows – death staring at his comrade, who also looked death, men wasted away with this terrible scourge till the skin and bone were alone left; to see these men drawing themselves, or crawling outside their crude places of abode to make for the w.c.s but never getting the length, the blood and slime running and leaving traces here and there and everywhere all the time. These were the men who had to fight for Ladysmith . . . All this was going on while day by day the enemy who surrounded us kept up shot and shell whirring and whizzing amongst us, causing us so much trouble in making new places of abode for shelter from shots coming from different directions.

To be dressed in the kilt for months and wearing 150 rounds of ammunition round one's stomach, and with belts, etc. about us, to lie down in the hope of getting sleep, and to up at 3 a.m. daily, and 'standing by', ready for the usual daybreak attack. If we worked till 1.30 a.m. or 2 a.m. in a drenching rain and black darkness, and had then to get turned out at 3 a.m., you may guess what comfort, what rest, the hour in between afforded, with diarrhoea, dysentery, fever, etc. on you, and pained with torn and bleeding arms and legs, with the poisoned pricks and thorns from the trees still smarting . . . All this sort of thing, added to by the want of water and food, made it a miserable existence in the extreme, for it was *nothing* more than existing, nothing more than drawing life out as far as possible as one would do an elastic, making it thinner and thinner the longer you pull it without actually breaking it, which would make the fatal deal.

'Letters From A Ladysmith Defender to Friends in Crieff', *Strathearn Herald*, 21 April 1900, p. 3

181

The wounded hardly fared much better. Writing home to Openshaw, Private E. Dance, 1st Battalion Manchester Regiment, admitted that

They had a good try to kill me, but just missed it. I was hit on the

18th December by a piece of shell on the top of the head, just missing the brain. Everybody are [*sic*] surprised that I am living. Even the doctors thought it was serious, but I have pulled through. I have been in hospital eight weeks with it, I will soon be right. We have been living on horse-beef, mule flesh, and horses' corn ground and made into a porridge, a pint of water a day which you could cut with a knife, and a wash once a month. Some of the men have no socks and no boots and their clothing is in threads. And fancy having to lie down on your stomach for four months under shot and shell without cover. I would tell you more only it would make you cry. Even the papers don't publish it from what I have seen.

'More Ladysmith Experiences', *Manchester Evening Chronicle*,
23 April 1900, p. 3

182

The hospital at Intombi, which originally had a capacity for 300 patients, was now vastly overcrowded. As a Highland officer of the Royal Army Medical Corps wrote on 23 February 1900:

There is a large hospital there, which at present has about 1600 patients.

As long as we got full rations no one minded staying here very much, but latterly our rations have been cut down to very little. The 60th have eaten all their stores, so our food is not of the best, mostly horse-flesh with not much bread or biscuit, although latterly the biscuit ration has been increased. For breakfast we have mealie porridge, and either mince meat or slices of tough horse grilled. Lunch – more meat and either mealie porridge or boiled starch (the kind you stiffen collars and shirts with). Dinner – more tough horse or mule, sometimes beef, soup, and mealie pudding. Our only vegetable is wild spinach.

On 26 February, he added:

Buller has been fighting hard for the past week, but we have had no authentic news as to what has happened. If all goes well, he ought to be in by the end of this week. We hear his artillery every day. There are very few Boers around us now. Only one big gun and about five small ones have been left behind. All the others are with the force opposing Buller. I shall be glad to get out of this place; it is dreadfully slow! I hope we are not left behind if the whole force advances, as

I want to see some more fighting, and to see the Boers get a good beating. They have fought very well, and will give us some trouble yet. This force will not be much good without six weeks rest and good food. It is pitiable to see the cavalry horses going about camp. They have no forage and are driven out every day just outside our outposts to get what grazing they can. There is not much grass for them now. The enemy fire at them daily, and generally kill a few, but not many.

Letters from Ladysmith', *Inverness Courier*,
6 April 1900, p. 5

183

Deaths from enteric fever continued to mount and demoralisation[7] ensued. 'One of our very best comrades', wrote the Devonian Private Will. Satterford to his parents in Newton Abbot was

poor Fred Leonard, who died at our hospital here on February 13th from enteric fever. I expect the sad news will be sent home to you all before this reaches you, as it is sent by cablegram. Still, I suppose it was ordained for him. Poor fellow! He was not very ill before going into hospital. It came on worse after his admission. It grieves me to think about him, and I deeply sympathise with his people, to whom I shall write soon.

'Torquinian's Letter from Ladysmith', *Devon Weekly Times*,
12 April 1900, p. 6

184

In these circumstances trying to communicate with the outside world helped to sustain morale. W. A. Weir of the Ladysmith Intelligence Department sent home to Ealing a description of

the working of the pigeon post. The messages which had to be sent were, of course, in cypher, and were reduced by photography to a small size. Sometimes they were maps drawn by a man, who used to go up in the balloon, of all the Dutch camps round the town. At other times they handed us a tiny bit of tissue paper with a few words written on it. These were tied to the upper part of the leg of the bird, and let him go about sunrise. He would fly straight to Durban, and from there the message would be sent back to General Buller,

---

7   'It was the dangerous stage', wrote Macdonald, 'No one had the vitality to fight the disease.' Macdonald, *How We Kept the Flag Flying*, p. 135.

who was only about twenty miles [32.8 km] away from us. To send them out, I had to go out on to the hills outside the town, and as near the Dutch lines as possible, the idea being to let the birds have a good start from high ground. Of course I could never get far out, as the enemy were well on the watch for people trying to escape with despatches.

'The Ladysmith Pigeon Post', *Middlesex County Times*,
14 April 1900, p. 2

Battle of Tugela Heights (21–27 February 1900)

Even with reinforcements Botha's forces, possibly numbering about 5,000 men with seven guns and three pom-poms, found themselves hopelessly outnumbered. Buller commanded some 28,000 men and over 70 guns, with several guns occupying dominating positions on the southern bank of the Tugela River. On 21 February, the British began their final advance by throwing a pontoon bridge across the river and enabling Major General J. Talbot Coke's Brigade, with the 2nd Battalion, Somerset Light Infantry in front, followed by the 2nd Battalion, Dorsetshire Regiment, to attack the Colenso kopjes (koppies) and capture Fort Wylie.

185

Writing on the following day, Private Lawrence, 2nd Battalion, Somerset Light Infantry, described how

We advanced on Colenso, and had to wait until the pontoon bridge was put down to cross the river. As soon as it was ready we extended out for attack, and were soon under terrific fire from the Boers. We being the only regiment to attack the position, we soon found it a pretty warm shop, bullets flying around us like a hail storm, such a thing as I have never witnessed before. As soon as they opened fire on us we lost about five men, who got knocked over before we had time to realize where we were. The idea of our being sent out there was to draw the enemy's fire, so as to allow the remainder of the troops to work around their flanks. We did not know they were so strong a force, but we got into position and could not retire, so we had to stick it, which we did, as, of course, Britons only could. As soon as it was dark we retired for the night behind a hill. Next morning we were relieved by three brigades (twelve regiments)[8], who took up the same

---

8   The Somerset Light Infantry were part of Major General J. Talbot Coke's

position as we had the day before, and soon drove the enemy back a little. Of course, it could not be expected that our regiment could do as much as twelve, but we got great praise for what we did do . . .

'A Tauntonian's Description of the Fighting', *Somerset County Gazette*, 31 March 1900, p. 2

186
Private H. Downs, 2nd Battalion, Somerset Light Infantry, recalled how

We started attacking the enemy early in the morning and about twelve o'clock we crossed the Tugela, and we split up in companies, some of us going to the left and some to the right. We were being shelled all the time while we were advancing by one of their 'Long Toms', a big gun which carries five or six miles [8 or 9.7 km]. It was nearly too warm for us and we had orders to lay [*sic*] down, so as to prevent them (the shells) doing much damage. Our front at length was reported 'all clear' and we again advanced. We had only a shot now and again and – nothing to speak of until we came within 800 yards [731.5 m] of the enemy. The bullets then fell all around us like hailstones. We stuck to it, however, and when I saw my right hand man shot down I thought my turn would come next. The bullets, however, passed over me alright [*sic*], and now I am at Colenso ready for another fight.

'A Bridgwater Man At Colenso', *Somerset County Gazette*, 7 April 1900, p. 9

187
As Lance Corporal Charles Langston observed in his letter **170**, the 2nd Dorsets had crossed the river in support, whereupon

An order came to reinforce a company of Somersets, who had crept round the base of the hill to a ridge further on. The roll of musketry had become almost deafening. The sergeant in charge of my section got in a funk and hesitated about taking his men through the awful hail of lead. The men seeing him hesitate shouted to me: 'For God's sake, Langston take us across.' As soon as I heard them I dashed to the front and raced across the open ground, the men following. We

---

Brigade. The other brigades were those of Major Generals Hildyard, Lyttelton and A. S. Wynne, who was wounded in the subsequent action and his command passed to Kitchener's brother, Lieutenant Colonel F. W. Kitchener. Major General A. F. Hart's Irish Brigade followed on 23 April.

got to the shelter of the ridge, but not without losing a couple of men. We stayed there till dark.

'Incidents of War', *Morning Leader*,
4 April 1900, p. 2

188

Private G. W. Davis, B Company, 2nd Battalion, Somerset Light Infantry, reckoned that he would

never forget the 21st February, when our regiment was facing that severe fire at Grobler's Kloof [9] for six hours, and I don't believe one of our men caught sight of a blessed Boer; and yet our men were knocked over to the tune of 100 killed and wounded. We were firing where we thought the Boers were concealed, but as for seeing Johnny Boer, not a sight of one. So there we were lying down and being fired at, while we could not even get a glimpse to aim at in return. But the fun of the thing was the pontoon bridge which the Engineers were laying across the Tugela. The Boers were shelling all the time. We were in a donga just behind, and every time we heard a shell whizzing over we held up our heads to see where it would strike, thinking that every shell would strike the bridge, but, thanks to the Boers' bad shooting, they all went without doing any damage into the river.

'A Stroud Soldier on Army Biscuits', *Stroud Journal*,
17 August 1900, p. 3

189

Less amused by these events was Sapper Key Hobbs, who saw

four wounded in putting up the first bridge; one died from wounds. If the Dutch were good shots they would have killed every one of us. We were one and forty minutes, under a shower of shot, and could not see where they came from. There were nine altogether out of two companies wounded.

'Letter from a St. Columb Engineer', *West Briton and Cornwall Advertiser*,
3 May 1900, p. 3

190

Private John Davis of the Somerset Light Infantry,

---

9   A kloof is a mountainous valley, and this valley (Grobbelaarskloof) was to the west of the railway line.

was shot through the right buttock on the 21st February about
four hours into the afternoon, but dare not move, there was such a
murderous hail of shell and rifle fire, so I had to lie until about ten in
a pool of blood until the stretcher bearers came out. In our regiment
alone we lost 121 killed and wounded.[10] To look at the place you
would never believe it could be taken. Our regiment was the first to
cross the river at Colenso.

'With General Buller', *Somerset County Gazette*,
14 April 1900, p. 11

191

On the following day, 22 February, Major General Wynne's 11th
(Lancashire) Brigade seized the next hill above the railway line, one that
became known as Wynne's Hill, 3 miles (4.8 km) north of Colenso. The
1st Battalion, South Lancashires took the crest, followed by the Royal
Lancasters, with the 2nd (Hildyard's) and 4th (Lyttleton's) brigades providing support. The 11th Brigade along with the 4th Brigade comprised
the 5th Division under Sir Charles Warren. Private William Barnes of the
1st Battalion, South Lancashire Regiment, recalled that

Our artillery had been shelling a strong Boer position for three days
and nights. About one o'clock in the afternoon General Buller and Sir
Charles Warren, who is in command of our brigade, gave the order
to advance and attack the Boer forces. There were thousands of them
strongly entrenched all around. My regiment was in the fighting line.
As soon as the Boers saw us coming they commenced to fire on us
with their big guns and rifles. You talk about thunder and lightning! It
was something horrible . . . Before we reached the bottom of that hill
hundreds were shot dead or wounded. A bullet went clean through my
haversack. As soon as we commenced to climb the hill it was awful. I
could hear men shouting for stretcherbearers and doctors and saw men
lying wounded all over the place. During the afternoon I came across a
poor fellow who had got both his legs blown off just below the knees by
a Boer shell, and his moans were heartrending. There was not a doctor
to be seen. I gave him a drink out of my water bottle, but all I got from
him was that he belonged to Lancashire and was a married man.

'Letters from the Front', *Carlisle Journal*,
20 April 1900, p. 7

---

10   The 'principal' casualties for the Somerset Light Infantry were five officers and 87
other ranks. Maurice and Grant, *History of the War in South Africa*, vol. 2, p. 600.

1   The observation balloon at Ladysmith
(Navy and Army Illustrated *for 1899)*

2   Sir George White
(Illustrated London News, *21 October 1899, p. 568)*

3 Devons advancing at Elandslaagte
(Illustrated London News, 25 November 1899, p. 779)

4   *Naval Brigade at Ladysmith*
(Illustrated London News, 9 December 1899, p. 831)

5   *Dublins boarding an armoured train*
(Illustrated London News, 16 December 1899, p. 866)

6 Dead on Spion Kop
(A. T. Mahan, The War in South Africa, *New York: Collier, 1902, p. 162)*

7 *Night signalling*
(Illustrated London News, 27 January 1900, p. 170)

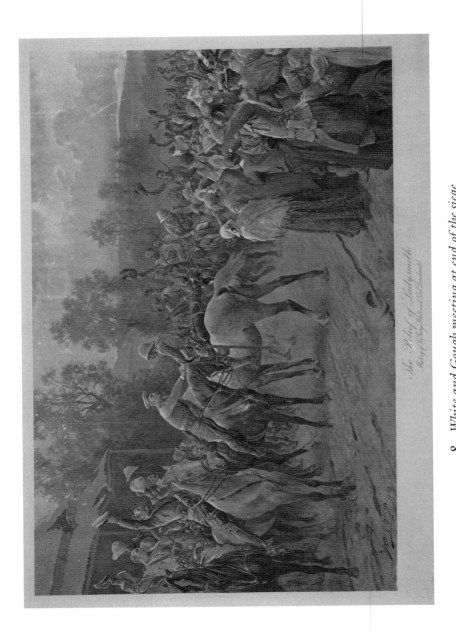

The Relief of Ladysmith
Meeting between White and Dundonald

8   *White and Gough meeting at end of the siege*
(*Photogravure after John H. F. Bacon, London: C. W. Faulkner & Co. 1900*)

192

Underscoring the stresses of this battle were the reflections of Private G. T. Jerram, King's Royal Rifles, in a letter to his wife:

> We were on our way to take possession of a hill. We were at it all that day and night, and part of the next day. The Boers sent some shell trying to put our guns out of action . . . Several of our men were wounded on the same day, and our Major had a narrow escape, a shell dropping behind the little wall he was sitting in front of just to his right.
>
> 'Soldiers' Letters', *Cheltenham Chronicle*, 19 May 1900, p. 6

Another Rifleman, Private Walter Rhodes confirmed that it had been

> uphill work, as the Boers are entrenched on all the hills between us and Ladysmith, and we have to drive them out under heavy fire. They are like little natural forts, but our naval guns and howitzers have been giving them snuff this last week. I am completely lost in time.
>
> 'Losing Count of Time', *Manchester Evening Chronicle*, 1 May 1900, p. 3

193

Far worse was the fate to befall the Irish Brigade on 23 February, as Major General Arthur Fitzroy Hart drove the Inniskillings, Connaught Rangers, Imperial Light Infantry, and the Dublin Fusiliers up the next hill to the east. It would become known as Hart's Hill or Inniskilling Hill. Having advanced along the railway line, and crossed a railway bridge under fire, the Irish were sent in piecemeal fashion up the rocky hillside out of sight of the Boers above and protected by artillery from south of the Tugela. At the crest, the artillery fire had to cease lest it killed their own men but the Irish found themselves facing Boer trenches some 150 yards (137 m) ahead across open ground. Twice the Irish charged and failed each time, resulting in some 500 casualties, the majority in the Inniskillings – 72 per cent of their officers and 27 per cent of their men.[11] One of the surviving Inniskillings, Private David Mulligan recalled ruefully:

> We had a heavy battle here on the 23rd and 24th February, in which

---

11   Ibid. See also the extracts from Captain H. F. N. Jourdain's diary quoted in Field Marshal Lord Carver, *The National Army Museum Book of the Boer War*, pp. 118–22.

I got a slight wound, but thank God, I am all right now and out of hospital again . . . Our regiment lost heavily . . . we went out with over eight hundred men, and between that and Saturday we lost almost five hundred between killed, wounded, and missing. The killed, I understand, numbered about one hundred. We lost all our officers, but three or four.[12] There was one officer got twenty-seven bullet wounds but strange to say, he is still alive.

'Interesting Letter from One of the Inniskillings at the Front', *Northern Whig (Belfast)*, 21 April 1900, p. 6

194

Another Inniskilling, Private Hugh Coffie confirmed that he had survived:

battle on the 23rd February and got out of it alright [*sic*]. It was terrible to hear the moans of the dying that night on the hill. We took the hill. We fixed bayonets and cheered and charged. Our fellows were falling as thick as mist. It was terrible. We lost all our officers but four. They were all crying for water. Some of our fellows were riddled with bullets. There was some blood spilled that day.

'Letters from the Front', *Fermanagh Times*, 26 April 1900, p. 4

195

Private E. J. Hart, Imperial Light Infantry, explained that

The Boers were strongly entrenched, and they held other hills on both flanks, enabling them to get a cross fire into us. Great gaps were mown through the Inniskillings, and they fell in all directions. However, the forty or fifty survivors managed to occupy a trench, but they were not strong enough to hold it, and they had to leave it. The Boers the following day turned our flank. This was largely the fault of the officers, who ought to have shifted us to a more effective position at daybreak. With the Durhams and a number of Maxims[13] we put in

---

12   This muddles the casualties of the Royal Inniskillings, who suffered 13 casualties out of 18 officers and 238 casualties out of 877 men, and of Hart's Irish Brigade that suffered 27 casualties among the officers and 500 among the men. Maurice and Grant, *History of the War in South Africa*, vol. 2, p. 600.

13   The Maxim-Vickers machine gun was a .45 calibre weapon that fired the 'small' .303 bullet with smokeless powder. It had a notional rate of fire of 500 rounds per minute but as the belts held only 250 rounds and firing had to be in bursts to avoid overheating, the normal rate of fire was somewhat less. Marix Evans, *Encyclopedia of the*

some very effective work. This undoubtedly saved us from a severe reverse, as the Boers had a deadly cross fire on us, as well as that infernal pom pom.

'The March to Ladysmith', *Northern Whig (Belfast)*,
1 May 1900, p. 6

196

The 1st Battalions, Durham Light Infantry and Rifle Brigade reinforced the position on the following day where Rifleman T. Plowman recalled the

terrible work. How I got through day after day, exposed to bullets and shells, I can't think but I was one of the lucky ones. Several times I thought my last moment had come as I lay on the ground with no shelter . . . It was a horribly dark night and stormy, and I can tell you it was no joke lying down until next morning exposed to bullets.

'Another Letter from the Front', *Dorset County Chronicle and Somersetshire Gazette*, 19 April 1900, p. 12

197

An armistice on the morning of Sunday 25 February enabled the British to remove the wounded and bury the dead from Hart's Hill. 'Today (Sunday)', wrote Sergeant Lambley, continuing his letter **150**, **160** and **174**,

there is an armistice, to bury the dead and bring in the wounded, as there were a lot they could not get at while the firing was going on. It seems so strange to be quiet after the continuous roar of guns and the rattle of rifle . . . They found 87 of our men dead on a hill that our fellows took, but the Boers retook it again as the supporting line did not get up in time. There is a lot more along the line.

'On the Way to Ladysmith', *Leicester Daily Mercury*,
31 March 1900, p. 6

198

Lance Corporal J. Tonkin, 2nd Battalion, Devonshire Regiment, described how

We had an armistice for about eight hours; that is peace to bury the dead and pick up the wounded, and there was a lot I can tell you

Boer War, pp. 179–80.

. . . We were able to walk about the battlefield and see everything. Between our position and the Boers they came halfway and we the same, talking to one another.[14] It was quite safe, for no one was allowed to fire while peace was proclaimed. I wish it was for good.

'Letter from the Front', *Western Times*,
29 March 1900, p. 4

199

A Sunderland soldier recorded that

They buried several Boers at the foot of the hill close to where 87 of our brave Irish brigade lie. Poor lads. They were killed charging a hill in the dark, upon which a footing could not be obtained owing to the large rocks lying about: didn't have a chance. Enemy lying down in trenches at the top of the hill taking shots at them struggling up If the Irish lads could only have got amongst them a different tale would have been told.

'The Relief of Ladysmith', *Sunderland Herald and Daily Post*,
11 April 1900, p. 3

200

In another letter written during the armistice, Lance Corporal William Burgin, 1st Battalion, Border Regiment, affirmed that, unlike General Roberts in the Free State,

General Buller has the hardest job on hand. It is all big hills here, and the Boers swarm like bees on the top, and will take some shifting. We have 72 guns and 21,000 infantry firing at them, and can't shift them, but are gaining ground slowly. We have got over the Tugela River, and that is one great thing. The river is 80 yards [73.1 m] wide and 14 feet [4.3 m] deep, with a very strong current . . . We believe Sir George White can only hold out 13 days longer, so Buller says there is to be no returning this time – no matter what lives we lose, we must push the fight on. The poor women and children in Ladysmith, we believe, are living on horseflesh, and all their houses are knocked down by the Boer shells.

'A Sheffield Man in the Ladysmith Advance', *Sheffield Daily Telegraph*,
30 March 1900, p. 5

---

14 Although MacBride's Irish Brigade had fought in this action, they did not take part in the armistice, McCracken, *MacBride's Brigade*, p. 66.

201

Following the armistice, Buller decided to pivot the point of attack. He withdrew the bulk of his force to the south bank and deployed them across the river via the pontoon bridge repositioned below the Tugela falls. He concentrated his guns to cover the final stage of the attack against an exhausted enemy that would be demoralised further by the reports of General Piet Cronjé's predicament at Paardeberg.[15] 'The next move for our battery', wrote Gunner H. Lambert, 61st Howitzer Battery, Royal Field Artillery, to his father,

> was again to cross the Tugela . . . and we had a time of it getting across. Just imagine, we had to bring our horses and guns down a place exactly like the Cliff Rocks, and then as it were to cross the Avon. You will, no doubt, see the picture and be able to judge for yourselves what a job we had. We had to use drag ropes, and it took us nearly the whole day.
>
> 'Interesting Letter from a Bristolian', *Bristol Observer*,
> 7 April 1900, p. 4

202

'But the great day of all', claimed Corporal A. Hawkins, 2nd Battalion, Devonshire Regiment, continuing his letter **173**,

> was Majuba day – the 27th Feb. They even signaled [*sic*] to Buller to tell him it was Majuba day. We gave them Majuba day! The artillery started fighting six o'clock in the morning and we advanced under their fire right up to the Boer trenches, when the order was given to charge. We charged and drove them in all directions – that's when we came across the Germans and French. I never saw such a cowardly lot in all my life; they even laid down to surrender, but we showed no mercy, but served them all alike, and we had won a great battle. . .
>
> 'More Letters from the Front', *Mid-Devon and Newton Times*,
> 5 May 1900, p. 3

---

15 Although the Boers knew about the surrounding of Cronjé's 4,000 forces, Viljoen telescopes his recollections by claiming that news of the surrender demoralised his men, *Reminiscences*, p.67. So does Blake, *West Pointer*, pp. 127–8. The Boer authorities held back this news until 5 March lest it dishearten other men on commando. Fransjohan Pretorius, 'Boer Propaganda During the South African War of 1899–1902', *The Journal of Imperial and Commonwealth History*, vol. 37, no. 3 (2009), pp. 399–417, at pp. 406–7.

203

An East Surrey private soldier asserted that

On the 27th of February, Majuba Day, we rushed their many positions[16] with the bayonet; the slaughter was awful. My regiment lost 292 killed and wounded, including nine officers.[17] We had troops all along their positions for over 12 miles [19.3 km]. Altogether we have been fighting 16 days, and never took our boots off, or coats, sleeping with all our straps, with nothing to cover us only our khaki suits we stand up in, and that is the same suit we left England with ... The bullets few around like hailstones, but they could not drive us back this time. No one could see fear; we jumped right into their trenches on top of them. They wanted to surrender, but we were not having any, but stuck them all except the 200 that General Hart told us to take prisoners. Our men were mad, for no officer could control them, firing until long after all the Boers were gone.

'How They Relieved Ladysmith', *Dover Express*,
20 April 1900, p. 7

204

Private Frank Thompson, 2nd Battalion, South Lancashire Regiment, confirmed that little mercy was shown:

The 27th was the anniversary of Majuba, so the general formed us all up, and told us we were going to avenge it, and that we would have to charge the Boer trenches. We advanced about 1,000 yards [914.4 m] from the enemy, and then we were ordered to charge. It was something awful to see the Boers asking for mercy. We gave them the bayonets. If you had seen me you would not have known me, as I was covered with blood from head to foot. I was one of the first in the trenches of our regiment. Our men said I should get the Victoria Cross for carrying a wounded man out of the firing line. No officer

---

16 Buller launched three brigades against the Boer positions on Railway Hill to the north-east of Hart's Hill, Pieter's Hill to the east of the railway, and Hart's Hill. Once Railway Hill was seized at 17.00, concerted pressure broke the Boer resistance on Hart's Hill and, after a renewed assault launched at 18.00, the Boers were compelled to vacate Pieter's Hill. All three hills were in British hands by midnight. Pretorius, *Historical Dictionary*, p. 328.
17 This is an exaggeration. The East Surreys lost 7 officers and 141 casualties, Maurice and Grant, *History of the War in South Africa*, vol. 2, p. 600.

saw me, or else I might have got it. I don't want medals, I want to get home out of it.

'Five Engagements without a Scratch', Sheffield Daily Telegraph,
3 April 1900, p. 7

205

Reitz recalled that the bombardment of the crest of Pieter's Hill was so intense that 'it was almost invisible under the clouds of flying earth and fumes, while the volume of sound was beyond anything that I have ever heard'. When the burghers broke, they streamed down the hill 'in disorderly flight. The soldiers fired into them, bringing many down as they made their way blindly past us, not looking to right or left.'[18] From the perspective of Private George Bird, a Reservist of the 2nd Devons,

> On the day we made the enemy retire it was a grand sight, I can assure you, to see them retiring in all directions, and our artillery pouring shell after shell at them, mowing them down like grass. Especially our Maxim gun did some excellent work that day, and the next morning when we advanced a few miles further ahead we found trenches full of dead Boers, and blood, brains, and men's fingers and thumbs all over the place, but the worst of it was that the Boers had women and children along with them, and they were killed and buried with the men, because we could not help it.

'The Relief of Ladysmith. Letter from a Tauntonian. The Horrors of War',
Somerset County Gazette, 7 April 1900, p. 2

206

Rifleman T. Plowman recalled in letter **196** that

> After firing was over we bivouacked on the ground, kept a sharp lookout. Next morning we heard the news that the Boers had cleared off and that the cavalry had got into Ladysmith. We lost more men in this last fight than we did in the whole of the 15 or 16 days. I helped to bury seven of our men the next morning – a sad duty to perform. We then marched towards Ladysmith and bivouacked within three miles [4.82 km].

'Another Letter from the Front', Southern Times,
21 April 1900, p. 3

---

18 Reitz, *Commando*, pp. 87–8.

Reflections on the Battle of Tugela Heights

207

The experience had been appalling. As Private Dolan, a South Lancashire Reservist, observed:

> It rained almost every night, and we were wet through, and had to sleep in our clothes when we could get a chance, and then in the day it was burning hot. We have had to let our clothes dry on us the best way they could. We lost ever such a lot of our regiment and of all the other regiments that were with us.

'Letters from the Front', *Liverpool Echo*,
28 March 1900, p. 4

208

An East Surrey private observed that

> The fighting, and the sights to be seen afterwards were most horrid, but, thank God, I have come safely through it, although expecting every moment to be my last. I may say that at one time I was lying in a trench, which was shelled by the Boers for 36 hours and we had not a drop of water or food till we managed under cover of darkness to creep out and get away.

'Our Soldiers' Hardships', *Surrey Times and County Express*,
14 April 1900, p. 5

209

Sapper Field reflected that

> If you only saw the positions that the Boers held you would think that they could be held for ever and so they would have been if we had held them instead of the Boers. Our men have done splendid work out here, I can tell you. The Engineers have had a lot of work to do, what with telegraph, railways, bridgings, roads for the troops and naval guns, and getting guns up the hills. They have had to work day and night preparing roads for the troops to march on. We have lost a lot of R.E.s out here and I can tell you we have never had more than four hours sleep at a time. Marching is very rough in this country, and we have had a great deal of trouble to get water, and then it is filthy. My boots are very bad and my toes are projecting from one, but that is not half our luck on active service . . . A lot of people thought this affair

was going to be a picnic, but they were mistaken.

'The Relief of Ladysmith', *Essex County Standard, West Suffolk Gazette, and Eastern Counties' Advertiser*, 7 April 1900, p. 7

210

Gunner Lambert, continuing his letter **201**, was mightily impressed by the Boer trenches:

In places their trenches were seven feet [2.1 m] deep, and as thick, with boulders of rocks, and to look at them they seemed impregnable. This was the first time I saw the effect of lyddite, and it was horrible. I went over to look around, and saw our infantry burying their dead, and the Boers at the same time. They left tons of ammunition behind, as well as bags of flour, clothes and all kinds of kit. Dead horses had been lying about in the sun, which made it horrid.

'Interesting Letter from a Bristolian', *Bristol Observer*, 7 April 1900, p. 4

211

In his letter **203**, an East Surrey private claimed that

I did not do as most did, rob the dead and wounded Boers. I think if he is dead let him rest, although I think it is a sin to bury all the money and watches they seem to have on them. It is said that the Boers lost about 5,000 killed and wounded and prisoners [*sic*]. I quite believe it, for dead Boers are lying everywhere you look.'

'How They Relieved Ladysmith', *Dover Express*, 20 April 1900, p. 7

212

On the fighting qualities of the Boers, opinions were mixed. 'I see by the papers', observed Private James Hart, 1st Battalion, South Lancashire,

that they say Boer is a brave, plucky fellow. If he is I know where there are plenty. They cannot fight when you get them on equal terms, and they have their wives with them loading their rifles.

'Soldiers' Letters', *Liverpool Daily Post*, 5 April 1900, p. 7

After learning from a wounded Boer girl, who had wanted to go home, that her father 'kept her in the trenches fighting with them, because she was a very good shot', Private George Bird of the 2nd Devons reckoned in his letter **205** that 'you can guess what sort of people we have had to fight against, more like savages than human beings'.

'The Relief of Ladysmith', *Somerset County Gazette*,
7 April 1900, p. 2

'The enemy are a cowardly lot', wrote Private Charles Lines, 1st Battalion, Border Regiment,

and they are not such good shots as they are supposed to be. They are all right if they are lying down with something to rest their rifles on, but as soon as you go towards them they fire very wild.

'What a Bilton Youth Thinks of the Boers', *Rugby Advertiser*,
7 April 1900, p. 3

213

An experienced Devonian officer in Natal was much more appreciative:

I am very much struck with the Boers I have caught myself or spoken to. They are so brave and so modest that all my preconceived ideas of the truculent Dutchmen have evaporated. It is a great pleasure to fight these men. They are brave and intelligent, and it is some credit being able to get the best of them. To beat an ignorant savage, such as I have had the pleasure of doing on very many occasions, is no criterion of an army. Certainly at Abu Klea[19] we had a warm corner, but the Arabs proved they were not an enemy at all against disciplined troops when 14,000 could not beat 800. But to defeat the Boer, to 'best' him at his own game, to catch him asleep, is a real lively pleasure, and for my own part, I think it is a task to which any man might be proud to devote himself. What a lot they are teaching us, these farmers! When we have settled them we shall be the most magnificent army in the world . . . But one must confess war against the Boers is a hazardous business. Fighting begins at 3,000 yards. [2.7 km] You never see your enemy, even at 900 or 500 [823 or 457 m]; and the Boer is a busy fellow if he feels so inclined. He will stay and fire 300 shots at you before you can clap your hands. If

19   In the battle of Abu Klea (17 January 1885) a small British desert column of 1,100 officers and men held off attacks by approximately 12,000 Mahdists.

he wants to go to a better place he will go, but you can't see him move. Taking one consideration with another, the Dutchman is a fine enemy, and if he did not misuse the white flag, he would be universally respected. . .

We are stronger as an army than we were six weeks ago. We have health, and the Army has confidence in itself, and supreme confidence in Sir Redvers Buller.

'The Boer As A Fighting Man', *North Devon Herald*,
15 March 1900, p. 8

214

Sergeant A. W. Keen, 2nd Battalion, Somerset Light Infantry, amplified this praise of Buller and placed it in the context of the conditions encountered in the relief of Ladysmith:

There is no doubt General Buller deserves the greatest praise for the way in which he has manouevred the troops about from one place to the other. I assure you we used to do a good grunt when we had to retire, especially as we have had it impressed upon us so much never to retire, but to keep going forward. But there is no doubt that General Buller foresaw things and knew that his losses would be very severe had he continued the advance, and especially at Spion Kop. Our losses were pretty heavy as it was, but had the advance been continued our losses would have been beyond estimation. I think it is General Buller's great motto to manoeuvre and take positions with as few casualties as possible and not to rush a position which means sure death, especially against such positions and fortifications as the enemy possessed.

'The Doings of the Somersets in South Africa', *Somerset County Gazette*,
7 April 1900, p. 2

215

Soldiers appreciated the praise of Sir Redvers. As Private T. Connor, 2nd Battalion, 7th Royal Fusiliers, recorded:

Our regiment and the Welsh Fusiliers received special mention from Sir Redvers Buller. We held a hill[20] . . . for four days and five nights under a murderous cross fire from the Boers. We lost 150 men on the

---

20 Wynne's Hill

hill.[21] On the fifth morning to our surprise that the Boers were gone, and I can assure you we were not sorry, as we couldn't lift up our heads for bullets. We had to crawl like worms for our food.

'A Very Tough Job', *Middlesex County Times*,
7 April 1900, p. 3

216

Again Devonians lauded their general, commending 'General Buller's bull-dog tenacity', as characterised by a soldier wounded at Pieter's Hill, inasmuch as

checked three times, he yet went for them a fourth, and, if ever there was an example of putting one's hand to the plough and not turning back, we have it in General Buller.

'Another Good Word For Buller', *Devon Weekly Times*,
20 April 1900, p. 6.

Sergeant W. C. Mitchell, F Company, 2nd Battalion, Devonshire Regiment, added:

About General Buller (God bless him). I hear they are making severe remarks about him at home. But I for one would go with him anywhere, and there is not a soldier in South Africa but has full confidence in him.

'Unbounded Confidence in Buller', *Mid-Devon and Newton Times*,
10 March 1900, p. 3

217

Soldiers from other units echoed this praise: 'It was not,' asserted Private W. H. Green, 2nd Battalion, 7th Royal Fusiliers,

a very easy job for General Buller, and it is a great pity the people have nothing else to do but to run him down. Some of them should make a trip to South Africa.

'Buller's Difficulties', *Surrey Times and County Express*,
20 April 1900, p. 5

---

21 The casualties of the Royal Fusiliers were 4 officers and 80 men, and of the Royal Welch Fusiliers 4 officers and 63 men, so 150 represented a combined total. Maurice and Grant, *History of the War in South Africa*, vol. 2, p. 600.

Private C. A. Pettifer, 2nd Battalion, Middlesex Regiment, agreed that

> only those who have been in this country can tell what a job he [Buller]
> has had. Talk about kopjes: I have been on top of some hundreds of
> them since I have been here, and we have had to drive the Boers off the
> lot of them one by one. However, we have done it after fourteen days'
> fight, during which time we were under fire night and day.
>
> 'Letters from Natal', *Middlesex County Times*,
> 7 April 1900, p. 3

Corporal George Logan, 2nd Battalion, Cameronians, agreed that

> Buller is just what he was represented to be, a great general.
>
> 'The Relief of Ladysmith. Interesting Letter from an Aberdonian Soldier',
> *Aberdeen Journal*, 4 April 1900, p. 6

'Music' of the Guns and the 'Dash' to Ladysmith

218

Within Ladysmith, where civil–military tensions had mounted over the
billeting arrangements, rationing and the destruction of property,[22]
hopes had risen during the last few days of the siege. In his diary (**39,
162**) for 20 February, Lieutenant Reynolds noted that

> 5,000 Free State Boers left here when they heard of the relief of
> Kimberley. Altogether the news to-night is good, and I hope we shall
> get something to eat before long. I am ravenous . . .

> [*23 February*] A great number of Boers have left, and Buller thinks
> there are only 5,000 or so against him now. His guns sound very
> close, and their music is very pleasant to us after more than 16 weeks
> siege . . . What a terrible thing it would have been for the army if the
> Boers had captured the 10,000 odd men that are here. I think we are
> spared even the anxiety of that now, as Buller is keeping them rather
> too busy for them to think of attacking us.
>
> 'Letters from the War', *Warrington Guardian*,
> 31 March 1900, p. 2

---

22 Watson, *The Siege Diary of William Watson Oct. 1899–Feb. 1900*, pp. 37–8.

219

In his letter from Ladysmith **182**, the Highland medical officer recorded:

On February 28th, we first knew that the Boer army was retiring. I
was out at one of the outposts during the afternoon, from where we
could see long lines – thousands of horsemen and waggons moving
over the plains from south to north. They were quite close, only about
four miles [6.4 km] away, and it made one very angry to think that
we had no cavalry nor artillery in a fit state to go after them – most of
our cavalry horses having been eaten and the artillery horses too weak
from want of food to pull a gun. Our naval guns were all on the other
side of the camp, so they were out of range.

The Boers commenced taking away the big gun on Bulwana [*sic*]
Hill, and managed to do so although they were heavily bombarded
by us. How we longed for Buller's cavalry to appear! It was most
tantalizing to see the Boers getting away so easily.

'Letters from Ladysmith', *Inverness Courier*,
6 April 1900, p. 5

For their part, the Boers were all too conscious of their own vulnerability
in spite of beginning the withdrawal at night. By daybreak, as Reitz
described: 'In all directions the plain was covered with a multitude of
men, wagons, and guns ploughing across the sodden veld in the greatest
disorder . . . Had the British fired a single gun at this surging mob
everything on wheels would have fallen into their hands. . .'[23] It was a 'sad
sight', recalled Viljoen, 'to see the commandos retreating in utter chaos
and disorder in all directions'.[24]

220

On 15 March 1900 Edgar Palmer, Natal Carbineers, wrote to his mother
that

You've all heard that we, and the Imperial Light Horse, were the first
in. On Wednesday morning, very early, we recrossed the Tugela to
a position from which we had been withdrawn some days earlier to
get out of the Boer shell fire, and pushed right forward, passing our
gallant infantry, who'd been so successful the previous day (the 27th,
Amajuba's Day). We scouted right out in open ground scattering

---

23   Reitz, *Commando*, p. 90.
24   Viljoen, *My Reminiscences*, p. 70.

small parties of Boers, capturing a few here and there, and three encampments . . . They must have been in a terrible hurry as everything to private letters and photos, were left behind. We captured a great quantity of small arm and big gun ammunition, and then pushed on to a line of kopjes, which we occupied, about one and a half miles [2.4 km] in front of our fighting line, and about four and a half miles [7.2 km] from Ladysmith, from which we were separated by a very long hill on our front. We worried scattered parties of the enemy from these kopjes, and got them well on the run . . . In the afternoon we went forward to thoroughly clear the country before a general advance was ordered. It was tricky work, but we had very little opposition, and went steadily on till we reached the top of the hill in our front.

When we were on a level with the top of Mount Bulwan,[25] and running parallel with it, and momentarily expected a visitor from the Boer 'Long Tom' thereon. We knew we were getting near Ladysmith, and all necks were crammed for first view. I was only about 100 yards [91.4 m] in front of our advance, scouting and cautiously creeping on to a ridge, expecting to find foes there. Right down in the hollow, about three miles [4.8 km] away, was our much looked for goal, looking most peaceful and calm – the last place in the world one would think to be the scene of a bloody four months siege. I'm rather proud of the fact of being the first of the relieving force to see Ladysmith and I couldn't help being selfish and enjoying the feeling alone for some minutes before calling our crowd up. The excitement then was intense, and we stood on the skyline regardless of Boers or anything else, and let off cheer after cheer. An order then came to retire to our intense disgust, and as it was nearly sundown we gave up the idea of getting to Ladysmith that night.

Just then up came our Major Mackenzie and Major Gough[26] (later on Lord Dundonald's staff, and as big a dare devil as our major), and in full hearing of all us chaps we heard the following. I must say that previous to this we heard that Dundonald had expressly ordered us not to go further forward than the top of the hill on which we were,

---

25 Umbulwana Hill.

26 Major (later General Sir) Hubert de la Poer Gough (1870–1963) had a father, uncle and brother who all won the Victoria Cross, the only family ever to win the Victoria Cross three times. His meeting with Sir George White in Ladysmith was depicted in a famous painting by John Henry Frederick Bacon. Gough later commanded the 3rd Cavalry Brigade at the Curragh in 1914 when he opposed the use of force against the Ulster Volunteers. He subsequently commanded the British Fifth Army (1916–18).

as the other part of the cavalry division had been driven back from
Mount Bulwan, so what ensued shows what dare devils our officers
were:

Major Gough – Are we going through to-night Mackenzie?
Major M. – Can we go through?
Major G. – Can we go through?
Major M. – By G— we can
Major G. – Then let us go.

That was enough. We waited for no orders, but giving one yell,
down the hill we went pell-mell. There was no path down, and the
whole hillside was a mass of big boulders, but we managed to get
to the bottom without breaking anybody's neck. I managed to get
a front seat, and off we went at a racing pace across broken country
and over Boer trenches . . . We expected a volley every minute, but
I don't think anything could have stopped us then. We were simply
mad for the time being. Our majors splendidly mounted as they were,
had all their work cut out to keep in front, and were swearing at us
for all they were worth to keep us in hand. Hats and blankets off,
saddles were discarded; and men down were left to get up unaided.
As we got near Waggon [*sic*] Hill, held by our Naval Brigade, we
began to be anxious lest in the half light we should be mistaken for
the enemy, so we shouted and cheered the louder to warn them,
and then just as we swept round the base all doubt was ended by a
rousing cheer from the top, and the guns burst out in triumphant
fashion over our heads at Mount Bulwan, where the Boers were
trying to shift their big guns.

Then we dashed through our outposts, Carabineers [*sic*] that day,
as it happened, and we knew our object was attained.

'The Dash on Ladysmith', *Liverpool Daily Post*,
20 April 1900, p. 8

221

Corporal Eli Symonds, Royal Engineers, continuing his diary **165**, noted
for 28 February,

Still in good health, but, how hungry! It is real starvation now, and no
mistake, the rations having been greatly reduced The porridge we get
is not at all good, it is very old and nasty, and makes some of the men
ill, but I manage to eat it. February 28th (later) – We were relieved

to-day, thank God! Two troops of cavalry came in about five o'clock in the afternoon. It was a fearful afternoon and night. It rained in torrents, and the thunder and lightning were something awful.

'A Crewkernian in Besieged Ladysmith. Whiskey at £25 a Bottle', *Somerset County Gazette*, 7 April 1900, p. 2

222

The Highland medical officer, continuing his letter **182** and **219**, added that

In the evening we heard cheering in the town, so after dinner I walked down with one of the 60th Rifles to the hospital to try to pick up some news, and there we heard that a body of Colonial Horse had just ridden in. There was great excitement, and every one was delighted to think that our troubles were now over.

'Letters from Ladysmith', *Inverness Courier*, 6 April 1900, p. 5

Chapter 5

Relief, Rejoicings and Reflections

Relief of Ladysmith

However welcome for both the besieged and the relieving forces, the relief of Ladysmith surprised both parties in many respects. Contrary to the assumption (**200**) that all the houses would have been demolished by three-months of shelling, the basic structures were still recognisable.

223

'Anyone,' wrote Middlesex soldier Private C. A. Pettifer in his letter **217**,

> who comes out here expecting to see something wonderful will be very disappointed, for they will see nothing but a few tin-roofed houses and some low hills round it, with a few stone walls and trenches along the top.
>
> 'Letters from Natal', *Middlesex County Times*,
> 5 May 1900, p. 3

Sergeant William Browne, 1st Battalion, Royal Inniskilling Fusiliers, agreed:

> Ladysmith is not much of a place. It is very small and all shattered. I think the people in it were on their last hopes

and Private T. Orr, of the same regiment, writing to his sister, stated

> You would drop tears if you saw the way they destroyed the lovely convent in Ladysmith, and those are the brutes that Irish have pity on.
>
> Letters from Ladysmith', *Fermanagh Times*,
> 19 April 1900, p. 4

224

'The Boers,' observed Lieutenant Robert Hannay Fuhr, Royal Army Medical Corps,

> had big guns on Umbulwana Hill, and how they failed to capture the place long ago is a profound mystery to me, for it lies half on a flat plain, and half on a gentle slop at a distance of only three miles [4.8 km] from the batteries on Umbulwana, with the river winding in between. Any other enemy would have captured Ladysmith on very short notice, but the Boers, great in defensive tactics, as we have found them to our cost, seem to lack fitness for attack except in the way of laying ambushes.

'Letter from a Medical Officer', *Northern Whig (Belfast)*,
7 May 1900, p. 6

225

There was extensive damage as the intelligence officer W. A. Weir conceded in his letter **184**:

> The town was in a dreadful state when General Buller's troops came in. The fever has been terrible, and the semi-starvation as well. My rations were half-pound horse flesh, one biscuit, one teaspoon full of tea, and one desert spoon full of sugar. We did not do badly, as we sometimes boiled up the pigeon's food and made a sort of porridge, but the men in the trenches had it pretty rough. You can have no idea of the terrible state the country is in. There is not a family which has not suffered in one way or another; but there is not the slightest sign or hint of giving in, and won't be until the law in South Africa is that all white men are to be on an equal footing. Then all the white races, English, Dutch, Hollanders and Germans will find their true level by their merit and ability.

'The Ladysmith Pigeon Post', *Middlesex County Times*,
14 April 1900, p. 2

226

Following his entry into Ladysmith, Mr Frederick Treves,[1] the distinguished surgeon, visited the various trenches:

---

1   He wrote an important account of his medical experiences in Natal: F. Treves, *The Tale of a Field Hospital* (London: Cassell, 1900)

The first of the camps we reached was that of the gallant King's Royal Rifles. They had made some sort of a home for themselves on the side of a barren and stony hill. They had, of course, no tents, but had fashioned all sorts of fantastic shelters out of stone and wood and wire. They had even burrowed into the ground, and had returned to the type of habitation common to primeval man. Among the huts and burrows were many paths worn smooth by the restless tread of weary feet. The path most worn of all was that which led to the water tanks. The men themselves were piteous to see. They were thin and hollow-eyed, and had about them an air of utter lassitude and weariness. Some were greatly emaciated; nearly all were pale; nearly all were silent. They had exhausted every topic of conversation, it would seem, and were too feeble to discuss even their relief. I reached Ladysmith at 2.30 p.m., and the food convoy did not arrive until late the same evening, so we had the sad opportunity of seeing Ladysmith still unrelieved – unrelieved, so far as the misery of hunger was concerned. I had no food at my disposal, but I had fortunately, a good quantity of tobacco, which I doled out in pipefuls so long as the supply lasted. It would have taken many pounds, however, to satisfy the eager, wasted, trembling hands which were thrust forward on the chance of getting a fragment of the weed. We out-panned on the outskirts of the town, and the first person to come up to me was a skeleton of a Kaffir, who offered me a shilling while he pointed repeatedly to his mouth. He was really starving, and devoured the biscuits I gave him like a wolf. There is no doubt the coloured people left in Ladysmith have suffered very severely. The main street of the town has no pretension to beauty, and is merely a broad road with corrugated iron shops on either side. On walking into 'starvation city' one's first impression was that of the utter emptiness of the place. Most of the villas were unoccupied, were closed up, and indeed, barricaded; the gardens were neglected, and everything had run wild. The impression of desolation was accentuated by an occasional house with a hole in its roof or its wall due to a Boer shell. All the people we met were pallid and hollow-eyed, and many were wasted; all were silent, listless, and depressed. There was no evidence of rejoicing, no signs of interest or animation, and indeed, as I have said, Ladysmith was unrelieved. Nearly every shop was closed or barricaded.

'Impressions on Entering Ladysmith', *North Devon Herald*,
12 April 1900, p. 2

227

Private Alexander Campbell, 2nd Volunteer Battalion, Manchester Regiment, agreed that

> Anyone can see that Ladysmith was once a beautiful place, but it is
> now up to the eyes in dirt and wreckage, and the stench is horrible.
> I don't think there is one sound building in the town. The Town
> Hall has been knocked about terribly. We went up to Caesar's Camp
> at sundown to join the Manchester Regiment, and found them a
> regiment of living skeletons – and no wonder. They were living on
> one and a half biscuits per day and mule flesh. All the graves of the
> men that have fallen are on the hill. There are as many graves here as
> there are in Stretford Cemetery. The Manchester men say the relief
> came just in time. They could not have stood up another fortnight
> ... All the men are in a bad way, but the Manchesters are the worst.
> Nearly all of them are suffering from dysentery, and many of the
> Volunteer Company too. I suppose it is through drinking the bad
> water. It is worse than the Mersey water . . . The Boers are in the hills
> 15 miles [24.1km] away from here, but I am afraid we shall not see
> any of the fun on account of the poor condition of our brigade ...
>
> 'The Manchesters. A Regiment of Skeletons', *The (Stockport) Advertiser*,
> 27 April 1900, p. 8

228

Where meetings occurred, the besieged were quick to comment on their near escapes as Private C. West, Army Service Corps, mentioned:

> Four weary months have we been besieged, during which time I have
> narrowly escaped death some dozens of times. It has been shocking
> to see our comrades being blown to pieces by monster shells, and
> then wondering whose turn it will be next to meet with such a fearful
> death. Hundreds have died of fever and dysentery, but at present there
> is a large camp filled with the sick and dying.
>
> 'Letters from the Front', *Poole, Parkstone and East Dorset Herald*,
> 29 March 1900, p. 5

'General Buller', wrote Corporal J. F. Crompton, 1st Battalion, Manchester Regiment,

> was just in time, for we were all dying almost for want of food, for we
> have been living on horse beef and one biscuit per day, and lying out

in the rain all night and dried again by the sun . . . We might have lost many men, but we have fought hard and proved what we are, true British soldiers and the pride of Ladysmith, which all the civilians say . . .
'Another Stockport Man among the Gallant Manchesters',
The (Stockport) Advertiser, 20 April 1900, p. 6

Sergeant E. Grant, 1st Battalion, Manchester Regiment, agreed:

I am a very lucky man . . . The Boers managed to hold us up here for 18 weeks, and we had an awful time of it . . . We were walking about half dead, and all the time we had to keep on fighting. Our clothes are falling off us, and there isn't a man in the regiment with a decent pair of boots, so we have to wait here to be equipped . . . The regiment is not really fit for marching after the hardships we have gone through . . .
'Better Times at Ladysmith', *Manchester Evening Chronicle*,
11 April 1900, p. 3

229

Some of the relieving force appeared apprehensive about entering Ladysmith. Writing on 3 March 1900, Lance Corporal J. Tonkin, 2nd Battalion, Devonshire Regiment, reported that after the battles:

We marched off expecting to get some more hard fighting, but we marched about five miles [8 km] and halted . . . I don't know if we shall go right into Ladysmith owing to the disease there. It cannot be very nice there after the time they have stopped there.
'Letter from the Front', *Western Times*,
29 March 1900, p. 4

230

In fact, a ceremonial entry was organised. Continuing his letter of **201** and **210**, Gunner Lambert recalled that

On the 3rd we had orders that the whole force would pack up and march to Ladysmith, where Generals White and Buller would see us, and when we arrived there we saw something that would make anyone's heart quail. The beleaguered garrison formed a guard of honour along each side of the streets as we marched along. The poor fellows were too weak to stand up and so they sat down, looking thin and haggard, not a smile to be seen except when they happened to see a face they knew . . . Well we gave them our biscuits, tobacco, and bully beef as we marched in, and they scrambled for them. There was not much damage done to the town except the town hall, which had the top clean blown off by a shell. The shops were empty and closed.

'Interesting Letter from a Bristolian', *Bristol Observer*,
7 April 1900, p. 4

231

The perceptions about the state of the inhabitants were widely shared. Gunner J. Taylor of the 19th Battery described how

the streets were lined with troops and we were cheered all the way through the town. It was heart-aching to see them; they were so weak they could hardly carry their rifle [*sic*].

'A Chagford Artilleryman at Spion Kop', *Totnes Times*,
14 April 1900, p. 5

An East Surrey soldier, continuing his letter of **203** and **211**, added that

It was a sight to see the poor women and children come out of Ladysmith to meet us half-starved. I had three fowls on my saddle which I looted from a Dutch farm. Although I had thought of having a good feed for myself and messmates, I saw them look at them with hungry eyes, so I gave them to the women, and was contented with my biscuit.

'How They Relieved Ladysmith', *Dover Express*,
20 April 1900, p. 7

232

'We had a triumphal march through Ladysmith, whose troops lined the streets', observed Corporal J. Austin, 2nd Battalion, Royal Scots Fusiliers,

it was a most impressive sight. The Gordons were just in front of Sir G. White, and when our regiment passed them they nearly went mad with delight. We are the only Scotch Regiment on this column, except the Scottish Rifles, but we had pipers with us. Though the Ladysmith troops were a little thinner and paler than us, they were much better clothed, and looked smarter, for we were all in rags. Some had no coats, some had boots with soles off – I had but one good boot myself – those who had good clothes were those who were wearing Boer clothes we took in the Boer camps.

'At Ladysmith', *Coventry Herald*,
6 April 1900, p. 6

233

Private Voce, of the 3rd Battalion, King's Royal Rifles, writing to his mother at Leicester, observed that

> The scene on the day when we marched into Ladysmith was one never to be forgotten. Every man that could stand turned out to meet us, and many a poor fellow in the hospitals that was hanging between life and death rolled out of bed to see us march past. It was pitiful, indeed, to see them stricken with fever and reduced to living skeletons, trying to stand up and cheer us. I think a sight like that would touch a heart of stone. It put new life into the fellows to see us, though I heard of two poor fellows that were in such a weak state that the excitement was too much for them, and they died. They told us they could not have held out two weeks more, and it is a well known fact that some of them were praying to get shot. Great credit is due to Sir George White and his little garrison for the way in which they held out against such terrible odds. They dug places underground and stayed there while the Boers were shelling the town; they were like so many rats creeping in and out. To them poor fellows, being hemmed in as they have been all this time, the relief is like awakening from a living death . . . Men were nearly hugging one another, officers shaking hands with privates, ranks made no difference.

> 'The Relief of Ladysmith', *Leicester Daily Mercury*, 10 April 1900, p. 2

234

The survivors of the siege were, of course, delighted to see the relief force and the supplies of food. Writing to his parents, Trooper W. C. Ryder, 5th Royal Irish Lancers, noted how the early visitors to Ladysmith

> were skinned of every bit of tobacco and eatables they had got. On the 3rd of March we had full rations of everything. I can tell you we were pleased enough to get it. Well I must tell you I have had pretty good health. Poor Boxer French died from enteric; Joe was in hospital about three months; also Hooker about the same time. Newbury has had diarrhoea very badly this last month, but stuck it pretty well. Our troop was fifty-four strong when we left Pietermaritzburg, and I am the only one that has not been in hospital and yet have been in every action. I have had one horse killed under me and another wounded in the back, and had some very narrow escapes from shells.

> 'Life in Ladysmith', *Middlesex County Times*, 7 April 1900, p. 3

235

Conversely Sapper H. Nadin, 37th Company, Royal Engineers, admitted that

Our Company have been very fortunate indeed, for we have only had five wounded up to the present, one of them dying three days after. We have been under the enemy's fire for three days at a time, in front of the firing line, making breastworks and cover for the Infantry, and it is marvelous [*sic*] we were not all killed or taken prisoners. So you see we have had a very warm time. We are now having a rest, which we require, as we have had to work night and day for several days with only about two hours' sleep, and then we have had to make cover for ourselves before we could do so, and then a shower of bullets would come whistling over your head and all around you. We have only about forty of our Company here, the others having gone to Elandslaagte and Dundee.

'Work of the Engineers', *Manchester Evening Chronicle*,
26 April 1900, p. 3

236

Continuing his letter of **182, 219** and **222,** the Highland medical officer reflected upon the

day most of Buller's army marched in, and are at present encamped around Ladysmith. What magnificent troops they are! – mostly reserve men,[2] looking fit and strong for anything. I have seen our troops under fire pretty often now, and do not think there are better fighting men in the world.

We have moved our hospital from the old drain in which we lived up to barracks, and are now comfortably quartered in the huts. At one bound we have jumped from famine to abundance, and all sorts of good things are flowing in. The difficulty is to restrain one's appetite and not to eat too much.

'Letters from Ladysmith. A Highland Officer's Experiences', *Inverness Courier*,
6 April 1900, p. 5

237

Exercising restraint, however, was a demanding expectation. A corporal of

---

2   In a short-service army, where infantry spent seven years with the colours before entering the reserve for five years, the more mature soldiers were the reservists.

the King's Royal Rifles, who had been eating mule-flesh 'in some tallow, which was served out to us for greasing boots and straps' prior to relief, was

> now on full rations and enjoying the fat of the land. The plum-duff arrived in splendid condition, and was much appreciated by 'yours truly' and his chum. As the latter was able to contribute to the above half a cake and three mince pies, as well as a tin of condensed milk, a tin of treacle, some fresh bread, and about three quarts of tea, we had a 'buster', and felt so happy and contented that I think I would have invited Oom Paul[3] himself to have tucked in had he been in the neighbourhood.

> 'Faring Sumptuously in Ladysmith', *Hampshire Observer*,
> 28 April 1900, p. 2

238

The medical fraternity had to deal with the consequences of the siege long after 28 February. Lieutenant Robert Hannay Fuhr, Royal Army Medical Corps, who had served with the relief force now joined the medical authorities in the 5th Brigade, Field Hospital. On 12 March, continuing his letter **224**, he wrote that since

> *December 1st* we have had 876 wounded through our hospital, and upwards of 600 cases of illness. The more trivial cases are cured by ourselves, while the severer cases are as a rule as promptly passed on to the base hospital. At present we have as many as 140 men in accommodation intended for only 100, and, notwithstanding such overcrowding, which cannot in an emergency be avoided, no one lacks any attention or comfort we can give. There are about thirty cases of enteric fever and several very bad ones of dysentery.

> *March 31st* – Since my last short scrawl upwards of 240 new cases have come in, so that we had to take possession of a farmhouse and turn it into a deputy hospital. My own share there was 37 – 24 enteric, 7 dysentery, and the rest light attacks of inflammation, etc. – besides which I have had to attend 66 men lying under canvas, so my hands have been very full. At present we have only 123 cases left altogether . . .

> 'Letter from a Medical Officer', *Northern Whig (Belfast)*,
> 7 May 1900, p. 6

---

3   This was a popular British nickname for President Paul Kruger.

239

The demands were equally pressing at the Stationary Hospital, Chieveley.
Writing on 14 March, Private W. J. Brown, Royal Army Medical Corps,
affirmed that

> We are still very busy here as there are so many sick and wounded, and
> all the big hospitals down the country are full up . . . it was something
> awful to see the wounded coming in. One man had his thigh shot
> away, his arm shot and broken, and was shot in the back and neck in
> several places. We are at work day and night, and the nursing sisters
> the same. The medical officers are operating all day as fast as they
> can. We are still getting very hot weather . . . We get very heavy
> thunderstorms, and they make it a bit miserable being under canvas.
> We are all hoping to get to Pretoria shortly to see old Kruger, and
> then I hope it will be an end to the war.
>
> 'Letters from the Front', *Somerset Standard*,
> 27 April 1900, p. 7

Rejoicings

The feelings of elation in Ladysmith paled by comparison with the
rejoicings throughout the United Kingdom and much of the empire.
Richard Price has likened these scenes of jubilation to the 'celebratory'
crowds that gathered on 'Armistice Night and VE Night'. He distinguished between the 'jingo mobs', reportedly containing prominent
groups of middle-class youth, including students, who tried to break up
anti-war rallies, and these crowds that were simply 'rejoicing: England
had regained her honour. And that is what these crowds were about.'[4]
As an attempt to absolve the working class from any taint of imperialism,
this thesis has been challenged both for the United Kingdom generally,
and for Scotland in particular.[5] There were certainly elements of relief in
the wave of spontaneous enthusiasm that swept across the country from
mid-morning on 1 March 1900. As *The Times* intoned, 'ever since the
'unhappy entanglement of Ladysmith', with the confinement of 10,000
soldiers,

4   Richard Price, *An Imperial War and the British Working Class: Working-class
attitudes and reactions to the Boer War 1899–1902* (London: Routledge & Kegan Paul,
1972), ch. 4 and pp. 131, 241.
5   M. D. Blanch, 'British Society and the War', in P. Warwick (ed.), *The South
African War: The Anglo-Boer War 1899–1902* (London: Longman, 1980), pp. 210–
38; Spiers, *Scottish Soldier and Empire*, pp. 171–5, 183, 196–7.

a great fear has hung over us . . . Week by week the chance grew ever stronger that, for the first time for a hundred years, a great British army might be forced by famine, by disease, and by exhaustion of their ammunition to lay down their arms.[6] The military effects of such a calamity would have been serious, but it was not the military effects the nation feared. They feared for the prestige of the flag, and to-day they are rejoicing with an exuberant gaiety they rarely display because Sir Redvers Buller and his gallant troops have removed that fear from their hearts.[7]

In its account of the siege, the *Yorkshire Post* also compared the siege of Ladysmith with other epic imperial investments – Lucknow during the Indian Mutiny (1857) and the Yorktown surrender (19 October 1781) – and reckoned that the 'pluck of the Ladysmith garrison has been beyond all praise. Their inactivity has probably been their hardest trial . . .' It also reported on the scenes of enthusiasm in Montreal, Calcutta, St John's Newfoundland and Kingston, Jamaica.[8] Even the leading anti-war organ, the *Manchester Guardian* recognised that the 'dark shadow that has lain over the country since December last has been at length removed . . . We rejoiced over the relief of Kimberley and the victory at Paardeberg', it added,

but the public joy over General Cronje's defeat[9] was as nothing compared with the joy over Ladysmith relieved. And the popular instinct was right yesterday . . . There is no pleasure so keen as that of rescue, and the pleasure is doubly keen when the rescue has been hard, and seemed at times almost impossible . . . But the spirit of the soldiers seemed to rise with each succeeding failure, and success is always valued in proportion to the effort it has cost.

Ironically the *Manchester Guardian* then proceeded to claim that the truth about the sufferings of Ladysmith would come neither from 'accounts' of the siege nor 'the letters' but from the death toll caused by disease.[10] This

---

6   At Yorktown on 19 October 1781, General Lord Cornwallis surrendered an army of over 8,000 soldiers, practically ending the American War of Independence.
7   *The Times*, 2 March 1900, p. 9.
8   'The Story of the Siege of Ladysmith' and 'Enthusiasm in the Colonies', *Yorkshire Post*, 2 March 1900, p. 6.
9   The nine-day battle of Paardeberg (18–27 February 1900) resulted in the defeat of the veteran Boer commander Piet Cronjé and the surrender of 4,019 men and 50 women.
10   *Manchester Guardian*, 2 March 1900, p. 5.

was emphatically not the view of the Mancunians, who had gathered in vast crowds in Albert Square at noon on the previous day. The square was

> filled with men and women, some of them relatives or friends of soldiers in the Lancashire and, perhaps, other regiments who are with General Buller . . . One of the most remarkable things of the day was to be seen at the head Post-office. For more than two hours after the receipt of the news the office was filled by people anxious to wire off at the earliest possible moment the news to their relatives and friends . . . The detail in the account of the day is newsworthy. It helps to illustrate the fact that interest in the doings of the troops was very real, and that the Lancashire men at the front have always been in the nearest memories of their friends.[11]

In cities, towns, market towns and villages, crowds paraded through streets bedecked with flags and bunting, gathered to sing patriotic songs, and celebrated into the night, burning effigies of Kruger and Cronjé. After all the disappointments of the campaign, this was not just an outburst of relief but, above all, an imperial triumph that celebrated the confounding of the queen's enemies. Students from the Yorkshire College in Leeds led a vast crowd to the Town Hall, where they 'sang with characteristic vigour the National Anthem, and cheered for Buller and White and the Queen'. There were similar celebrations all over Yorkshire, with Sheffield described as 'Buller daft' and scenes that had 'not been seen in Sheffield since Waterloo'.[12] Some 30,000 were thought to have paraded through the streets of Liverpool, singing patriotic songs and executing effigies of Kruger, Cronjé and Joubert. Among the many speeches delivered, Mr Sandbach, the chairman of the Exchange Newsroom reminded his audience that 'The people of Liverpool and of Lancashire had a special reason for pride in the gallantry shown by the Lancashire brigade, and especially by the men of the South Lancashire Regiment mentioned in a recent dispatch.' In this 'magnificent hall', a former Inniskilling, Trooper A. Forbes, now of the 31st Imperial Yeomanry and dressed in khaki uniform, was brought to the front and compelled to make a speech. He reminded his audience of 'the gallant fight and the fearful loss by his old regiment. He called for cheers for the Queen, which were heartily given.'[13]

---

11 'Manchester', *Manchester Guardian*, 2 March 1900, p. 3.
12 'The Relief of Ladysmith', *Leeds Mercury*, 2 March 1900, p. 6.
13 'National Jubilation over the Relief of Ladysmith', *Liverpool Courier*, 2 March 1900, p. 8. On the recognition of the praise for the South Lancashire Regiment, see also the editorial in the *Liverpool Daily Post*, 1 March 1900, p. 4.

While the student-led processions provoked Nationalist hostility in Dublin, Nationalist as well as Loyalist bands and processions appeared in Enniskillen (albeit on separate nights), paying tribute to local Inniskillings, many of whom were Roman Catholic.[14] In Scotland, the emotional outburst convulsed communities from Kirkcudbright to Kirkwall, Stornoway to St Andrews, Glasgow to Edinburgh. There were celebrations throughout Lanarkshire, a county from which the Cameronians had traditionally recruited, and at the evening bonfire in Stonehouse, the *Hamilton Advertiser* recorded that a local magistrate, Mr John Borland

> eulogised the victories of British arms in South Africa, and the noble and determined manner in which General Buller has successfully accomplished his task. When we say that there are eleven men out of Stonehouse at the front, it is in no way surprising that there should be such loyal hearts ready to celebrate the success of such great events as are now taking place in South Africa.[15]

After all the letters that had cemented ties between the soldiers at the front and their friends and relatives at home, and then the fitful communications from Ladysmith over four months, concern about the survivors of the siege was understandable. Unprecedented scenes of enthusiasm swept through Aberdeen and its neighbouring communities – the heart of the recruiting district of the Gordon Highlanders. Vast crowds, including Gordons from the regimental depot, gathered in the leading thoroughfares of Aberdeen, where Union Street was 'swathed in bunting'. Joiners on strike greeted the news with 'tremendous enthusiasm', students proved conspicuous in all the parades, and amid the cacophony of noise, the 'whistles of the steamships and steam trawlers united in a great chorus'. In nearby Stonehaven, 'the residents' had 'more than usual interest in the good news from the fact that a number of our young men are in the 2nd Gordons, confined in Ladysmith, as is also Lieutenant Walter Baird, of that regiment, the second son of the lord lieutenant'. Similarly in the twin villages of Garmouth and Kingston, where about 'two per cent of the natives' were 'fighting for the Queen and country, or are on their way to the seat', the 'good news was received with numerous manifestations of public rejoicing'.[16]

The heroes of the hour, White and Buller, were praised in the press,

---

14   'A Characteristic Celebration by Dublin Students', *Yorkshire Post*, 2 March 1900, p. 5; 'Relief of Ladysmith', *Fermanagh Times*, 8 March 1900, p. 3.
15   'The Relief of Ladysmith', *Hamilton Advertiser*, 3 March 1900, p. 5.
16   'The News in Aberdeen' and 'Rejoicings in the North', *Aberdeen Journal*, 2 March 1900, p. 6.

the meeting of White and Gough in Ladysmith was both chronicled and painted,[17] and, in some newspapers, the achievements of these generals juxtaposed with letters of praise from soldiers at the front.[18] There was also widespread coverage of White's speech after he had met Gough and knew that Ladysmith had been relieved:

> People of Ladysmith, I thank you one and all for the heroic and patient manner in which you have assisted me during the siege of Ladysmith. From the bottom of my heart I thank you. It hurt me terribly when I was compelled to cut down rations, but thank God we kept the flag flying.[19]

Reflections

In Natal the British soldiers faced an uncertain future despite the lack of any threat from the Boers, who had blown up their central supply dump at Elandslaagte and withdrawn to Glencoe, but as Reitz described were in 'such confusion that most of the army had continued straight on' (to the Boer republics).[20]

240

'We are encamped about a mile [1.6 km] from Ladysmith', explained Gunner Lambert, concluding his letter of **201**, **210** and **230**:

> They have been losing 16 men a day with enteric fever, and the fellows told us when once a man got that he was sure to die, as they had no medicine or milk to give them.
>   Well here we are, one good job completed, and wondering what the next move will be . . . I hope it won't be long, as I would rather be on the move than sitting here watching the horses graze. The Naval Brigade are joining their ships, leaving the guns with the artillery, but our horses are badly in want of rest – they are all bones; this country would pull the fat off of anything.
>
> 'Interesting Letter from a Bristolian', Bristol Observer,
7 April 1900, p. 4

---

17 A notable painting was *The Relief of Ladysmith* by John Henry Fredrick Bacon.
18 'Sir George White', *Sheffield Daily Telegraph*, 2 March 1900, p. 6; 'Honouring Sir George White' and Soldiers' Letters', *Liverpool Courier*, 2 March 1900, p. 8 and 'Relief of Ladysmith' and 'At the Front', *Fermanagh Times*, 8 March 1900, p. 3.
19 'The Relief of Ladysmith', *Coventry Herald*, 9 March 1900, p. 6.
20 Reitz, *Commando*, pp. 90–1.

241

Further north the York and Lancaster Regiment had moved its camp from Nicholson's Nek to Elandslaagte but, in a letter dated 6 April 1900, a Rotherham soldier reported that

> Water is very scarce in this place . . . There are a lot of troops here – infantry, cavalry, and artillery. I suppose we are waiting for other things arriving before we make an advance . . . I am sorry to say fever and dysentery are very prevalent here, very likely owing to our having to drink bad water.
>
> 'Soldiers and Sickness', *Rotherham Advertiser*,
> 12 May 1900, p. 6

Rifleman Plowman, continuing his letter **196**, also found himself at Elandslaagte, which

> is about 20 miles [32.2 km] from Ladysmith. We are here repairing the railway. We have plenty of hard work, but very poor living.
>
> 'Another Letter from the Front', *Dorset County Chronicle and*
> *Somersetshire Gazette*,
> 19 April 1900, p. 12

242

The war was over for the severely wounded. Private W. Knight, who had been shot in the shoulder and leg at Lombard's Kop, informed his parents that he was

> booked for Netley.[21] My leg was hit with an explosive bullet, and shattered. I don't know whether I shall keep it or lose it until I get to Netley. My shoulder is all right.
>
> 'A Wounded Cheltonian', *Cheltenham Chronicle*,
> 14 April 1900, p. 6

243

Many others expected that their war would soon be over, too. 'They are sending some of us down to Durban', wrote Private C. Brown of the 1st Battalion, Gloucestershire Regiment,

---

21 This was the Royal Victoria Military Hospital, on which construction began after the Crimean War in 1856.

that is about 200 miles [322 km] from Ladysmith, for our health. I expect to be down there soon . . . They have got the news that this battalion is coming home when we get our prisoners from Pretoria.

'A Nailsworth Men on the Siege of Ladysmith', *Stroud Journal*,
11 May 1900, p. 3

Others were still obsessed with their recent privations. Writing on 28 March, Trooper J. Chorlton, 19th Hussars, informed a friend in Manchester that

You do not know what it is to be hungry. We ate our horses like cannibals. We did not suffer much by casualties in the field, but have lost heavily by sickness.

'What a Man Can Survive', *Manchester Evening Chronicle*,
4 April 1900, p. 3

244

On returning home, there was still interest in their sufferings. Interviewed in Swindon on 18 June, Private Illsley, 19th Hussars, who had twice been hospitalised with enteric, claimed that

We had 480 horses in the regiment . . . at the commencement of the hostilities. We had 60 when we were relieved. Poor brutes, it was only humane to put them out of their misery, for we had nothing for them to eat; we wanted all ourselves. What are the symptoms of enteric? Oh, your tongue and lips get dry as possible, and you feel as though you could stick your head in a bucket of water. You can't perspire, and you seem to be burning inside.

'Home from Ladysmith', *Evening Swindon Advertiser*,
19 June 1900, p. 2

245

Soldiers had revelled, nonetheless, in the support from home, including the receipt of incoming mail. 'Part of the mail', claimed Private Satterford in his letter **183**,

was a 'bumper', there being over 11 tons of letters for the troops that been sieged [*sic*] in Ladysmith.

'Torquinian's Letter From Ladysmith', *Devon Weekly Times*,
12 April 1900, p. 6

Writing from Durban, Private H. Tibbles, 1st Battalion, Gloucester Regiment, maintained that

> The people can't do enough for us – we are called the Ladysmith heroes, and the 'toffs' give us much as we want to drink when we tell them about Ladysmith. We have had presents from England, including Gloucestershire, too. They think a lot of us as we kept the Boers back.
>
> 'Soldiers' Letters', *Cheltenham Chronicle*,
> 19 May 1900, p. 6

246

However weary of the fighting, many had a real sense of accomplishment: 'I can tell you we will all be glad when this is over', wrote Private W. Jeffrey, 1st Battalion, Devonshire Regiment:

> We have had enough of it, but our regiment has got a splendid name out here in Natal, and also in England. Of course we had all the hardest fighting to do in this place, and our regiment saved Ladysmith from being captured on January 6th, when the Boers made their attack on the town. Our regiment made a charge that day that will never be forgotten . . .
>
> 'Letter from an Ashburton Man', *Totnes Times*,
> 5 May 1900, p. 3

247

When soldiers left Ladysmith and saw some of the battlegrounds along the Tugela, they had a better appreciation of what the relief force had overcome. As Private S. Coles, 1st Battalion, Devonshire Regiment, admitted:

> We thought that Buller was never going to relieve us, and we used to call him all sorts, but we altered our tune when we went to Spion Kop for three days to have a look at the position the Boers held: it was something marvelous [*sic*] how they ever took it at all.
>
> 'Letter from the Front', *Devon Weekly Times*,
> 1 June 1900, p. 6

248

Sergeant George Thompson, 68th Battery, Royal Field Artillery, writing in reply to letters and the receipt of newspapers from home, maintained:

I am proud to be thought so much of, and also to belong to such an
army as ours. Such pluck and courage; I never saw any to equal it,
especially on the part of our infantry. The poor fellows have fought
hard. They have had trying marches, night and day, but they have
gone at it with good hearts and spirits.

'A Loughborough Artilleryman with Sir Charles Warren', *Leicester Chronicle and
Leicestershire Mercury*, 21 April 1900, p. 3

249

Optimism had grown after the victory at Paardeberg, and the relief of
Kimberley and Ladysmith, that the war would be over soon. Some had
anticipated that the relief would be the beginning of the end: 'as soon as
we are relieved', wrote Private Albert Preece, 5th Dragoon Guards, in a
letter smuggled out of Ladysmith on 19 January, 'it won't be long before
it is over'.[22] After the relief Private John Mullen, 1st Battalion, Royal
Inniskilling Fusiliers, reckoned that 'the Boers are sick of the war from
what the prisoners tell us'.[23] and Corporal E. Pugh, 1st Battalion, Royal
Welch Fusiliers, agreed: 'I don't think the war will last much longer,
because the Boers are about fed up with it. Dear old England will show
them what she is made of.'[24]

250

Writing from Natal on 27 March, Staff-Sergeant Wallace H. Wood, Army
Medical Staff Corps, was

proud to-day to say I am a soldier, and have been side by side with
such heroes, for heroes they are every one of them, facing death
without a tremor[25] . . . I hope the people of England will not forget
them, and the gallant way they saved the Empire, or rather, I should
say made it, for in my opinion . . . this is the beginning of an empire
which will be the means of preventing in future such wars as this; as
no country in the world, knowing the Empire is one in deed as well as
in name, will ever dare to throw down the gauntlet to us.

---

22 'Letter from a Bridgwater Man at Ladysmith', *Somerset County Gazette*, 17
February 1900, p. 2.
23 'The Inniskillings at the Relief of Ladysmith', *Fermanagh Times*, 12 April 1900,
p. 3.
24 'Soldiers' Letters', *North Wales Guardian*, 6 April 1900, p. 2.
25 Somewhat bombastic in light of the well-publicised surrenders (see Afterword)
but it is noticeable that this was the phrase that the *Stroud Journal* chose to highlight
in its headline.

'Facing Death Without A Tremor', *Stroud Journal*,
18 May 1900, p. 3

251

Some desires were simpler; 'I hope it will soon be over', stated Private S.
Coles, 1st Battalion, Devonshire Regiment, in his letter **247**:

I have had quite enough – not seen a bed for eight months

'Letter from the Front', *Devon Weekly Times*,
1 June 1900, p. 6

252

How the war would end was still a matter of concern: as an Ulster doctor
observed in a letter dated 14 March 1900:

The only anxiety we have now is lest anything should occur to prevent
Great Britain settling the South African question once for all. The
Boers have been playing for a big stake, and they must take all the
consequences. The time for half-measures is gone, and they must
be taught that there can only be one Power in South Africa. The
Uitlanders and colonials have fought well and have done their share,
and it is only fair to them that the Boers should never have another
opportunity of ruining their property and homes.

'Letter from an Ulster Doctor', *Northern Whig (Belfast)*,
9 April 1900, p. 8

253

Writing from Estcourt on 22 March, Private C. F. Berry, Durban
Volunteer Light Infantry, echoed these anxieties:

To treat the Boers as the Englishmen have been doing is only making
things very similar to the 1881 affair, as the Boers have proved
themselves thoroughly untrustworthy and incapable of governing.
Some people are in favour of giving them their independence back
again.[26] If they get this where are the Uitlanders and the loyalists to
come in . . . The idea of England, or rather of some people there,
thinking of calmly giving these rebels back the country is absolutely
absurd and cruel.

---

26 Stephen E. Koss, *The Pro-Boers: The anatomy of an anti-war movement* (Chicago:
University of Chicago Press, 1973); Bernard Porter, 'The Pro-Boers in Britain' in
Warwick (ed.), *The South African War: The Anglo-Boer War 1899–1902*, pp. 239–57.

'A Tauntonian in the Durban Light Infantry', *Devon and Somerset Weekly News*,
3 May 1900, p. 6

254

Continuing his letter, **173** and **202**, Corporal A. Hawkins, 2nd Battalion,
Devonshire Regiment, evinced confidence that Buller's army could prevail:

I am in good health and spirits, thank the Lord, and will fight to the
last for the honour of my country, and help to rub off the disgrace of
what Gladstone did when he had the place in 1881.

'More Letters from the Front', *Mid-Devon and Newton Times*,
5 May 1900, p. 3

255

The intelligence officer, W. A. Weir, in his letter **184** and **225**, was rather
more perceptive:

A lot of fellows here are all for confiscating the Boer's property and
putting him out of the country (as far as rights are concerned and as
far as getting temporary satisfaction, I quite agree with them); but
then they would suffer the same way as we have been doing, so that
the friction would still be going on. The leaders at home have a tricky
problem to decide. However, it is a bit previous talking of what is to
be done after we have conquered. The Boers are the most suspicious,
smartest, craftiest people on the face of the earth; and, if the people at
home stick up for them at all, it must be out of sympathy for them, as
being 'a brave and simple people'. That was Gladstone's idea of them,
but without doubt they are every bit as cute as we are, if not more so.

'The Ladysmith Pigeon Post', *Middlesex County Times*,
14 April 1900, p. 2

Despite the capture of their capitals, Bloemfontein on 13 March 1900 and
Pretoria on 5 June 1900, the Boers resorted to guerrilla warfare, which
they waged until signing the peace of Vereeniging on 31 May 1902.
Winning this war required the services of 448,435 British and imperial
soldiers, the adoption of ruthless methods of counter-insurgency warfare,
and cost the British taxpayer some £201 million.

Afterword

The Letters and Their Legacy

The siege of Ladysmith proved an unexpected and exacting test of the late Victorian army, one that examined its powers of endurance, resilience and resourcefulness. The investment of some 12,000 soldiers for 118 days was both a national and a military humiliation, one that aroused intense concern among contemporaries and considerable debate between subsequent historians. Although Sibbald argues that the press commentary on Ladysmith represented a contrived 'siege epic' intended to mask the pervasive boredom of the event, and that the focus upon the gallantry of the besieged deflected attention from the limited developments elsewhere in the war,[1] there is plenty of evidence that moods oscillated within Ladysmith and that anxieties increased during the siege.[2] Many diaries kept by civilians and soldiers have survived and were published, notably the accounts of various war correspondents, some twenty of whom remained in Ladysmith.[3] Some accounts appeared as regimental histories,[4] or were published subsequently and used in the standard histories of the siege.[5] The Ladysmith Historical Society published several works privately,[6] and

1   Raymond Sibbald, *The War Correspondents: The Boer War* (Stroud: Alan Sutton, 1993), p. 84.
2   Angela V. John, *War, Journalism and the Shaping of the Twentieth Century: The Life and Times of Henry W. Nevinson* (London: I. B. Tauris, 2006), pp. 31, 34.
3   Ibid. p. 30; for example, George Warrington Steevens, *From Capetown to Ladysmith: An Unfinished Record of the South African War* (Edinburgh: Blackwood, 1900); McHugh, *The Siege of Ladysmith*; Macdonald, *How We Kept the Flag Flying*; and Henry W. Nevinson, *Ladysmith: The Diary of the Siege* (London: Methuen & Co., 1900) among others.
4   Lieutenant Colonel St John Gore, *The Green Horse in Ladysmith* (London: Sampson Low, Marston & Co., 1901).
5   Griffith, *Thank God We Kept the Flag Flying*; Sharp, *The Siege of Ladysmith*.
6   *A Diary of the Siege of Ladysmith Written by Miss Bella Craw* (Ladysmith:

numerous diaries and collections of letters have been used to illustrate the major histories of the war, including the Ladysmith campaign.[7] So the siege is hardly a neglected topic of historical inquiry.

This account of the siege is different: it does not rely upon the diaries of a few individuals, but seeks a broader range of insights from the writers of some 250 letters, diaries and interviews reproduced in 78 metropolitan and provincial newspapers. Such a collection has never been brought together before. Many of these correspondents were ordinary soldiers, a testimony to the improvements in elementary and army education in the later decades of the nineteenth century,[8] and despite their limited perspectives, sometimes blinkered by regimental rivalry, and their propensity to exaggerate the numbers of the enemy, especially after a reverse, they proffered eyewitness commentary of considerable significance. Unlike the reports of the war correspondents, none of their letters, other than those of the prisoners of war, were subjected to censorship. Their writings were all personalised accounts, whose value as a source of public interest was perceived by the recipients, whether friends or family at home, who passed them on to the editors of local newspapers. Their reproduction in so many provincial newspapers reflected the enduring interest in the actions and accounts of local soldiers in an era when infantry regiments had county affiliations or regional identities, and found at least a core of their recruits from within their regimental districts.[9] Moreover, the readiness of these newspapers to supplement their reportage from British soldiers with letters from their colonial counterparts underlined the continuing bonds between the latter, often first-generation emigrants [**136, 253**], and their former communities in Britain.

Despite the vast expansion of popular journalism in the 1890s, and particularly war correspondence with about 70 journalists covering the war at its outset, and possibly 200 to 300 individuals involved in

Ladysmith Historical Society, 1970); Lieutenant Colonel C.W. Park, *Letters from Ladysmith* (Ladysmith: Ladysmith Historical Society, 1972); Watson, *The Siege Diary of William Watson*; Driver, *Experience of a Siege*.

7   Pakenham, *The Boer War;* Lord Carver, *The National Army Museum Book of The Boer War.*

8   Alan R. Skelley, *The Victorian Army at Home* (London: Croom Helm, 1977), ch. 2; see also Tabitha Jackson, *The Boer War* (London and Basingstoke: Channel 4 Books, 1999), pp. 80–1 and on the press generally, Lucy Brown, *Victorian News and Newspapers* (Oxford: Oxford University Press, 1985).

9   The localisation of linked-battalion regiments within specific recruiting districts never worked as smoothly as the reforming secretaries of state – Edward Cardwell and Hugh Childers – envisaged. Edward M. Spiers, *The Late Victorian Army, 1868–1902* (Manchester: Manchester University Press, 1992), ch. 5.

the newsgathering process over the course of the war,[10] there were still many provincial and evening newspapers that could not afford their own correspondents. While they often used material from the central news agencies to cover the war, editors appreciated 'letters from the front' as personalised, often highly graphic, accounts of the military action.[11] As the letters took several weeks to reach their recipients in the United Kingdom, and then be passed on to local editors, they continued to provide fresh information about the earlier battles that preceded the investment of Ladysmith long after the siege had begun, and most communications, including reports from the beleaguered war correspondents, had been severed. By continuing to provide accounts of the battles, the treatment of the wounded, and the heart-rending scenes along the railway as Uitlanders fled from the Transvaal, and Natalians abandoned their homes, the soldiers' letters sustained popular interest in the siege and conveyed images that the official despatches could never capture.

That newspapers were willing to publish this flow of correspondence, partly from those besieged before the investment, then largely from soldiers serving in the relief force, and finally from both groups of letter-writers, underscores how the level of anxiety about the siege mushroomed. There was pride at home in the stoicism, resolve, and determination of the besieged to persevere in a form of warfare that few had anticipated and against a foe that had been vastly underestimated. There was an understanding, too, that the stakes were particularly high in Ladysmith, and that the potential loss of some 12,000 soldiers within a British colony would have been a devastating blow [**218**]. Ladysmith may not have been vital, in the way that contemporaries regarded the advance of the army of Lord Roberts into the Orange Free State, heading towards the Boer capitals, but, as *The Times* emphasised, the relief of Ladysmith had a great 'moral value' for Britain and the empire.[12] As feelings about the siege built up among a people that followed the trials and tribulations of the abortive attempts to break through the Tugela defences, they led to the unprecedented eruption of emotion after the relief of Ladysmith. The widespread rejoicing expressed relief, too, that the queen's enemies

---

10   Stephen Badsey, 'War Correspondents in the Boer War' in John Gooch (ed.), *The Boer War: Direction, experience and image* (London: Frank Cass, 2000), pp. 187–202, at pp. 190–1.

11   For a fuller study of the value of these letters for the provincial press and of the methodology by which they can be found, see Edward M. Spiers, 'Military correspondence in the late nineteenth-century press', *Archives*, vol. 32, no. 116 (April 2007), pp. 28–40.

12   *The Times*, 2 March 1900, p. 9.

had been confounded, however belatedly. In many communities, where the letters had sustained contacts with local soldiers at the front, friends and relatives wanted to learn of the fate of the British forces, both those in Ladysmith and their comrades who had breeched the Boer defences. Once again the readiness of the press to keep publishing letters from Natal for months after the relief testified to an acknowledgement of the sacrifices involved, the sense of a major accomplishment in the successful relief operation, and an assumption (erroneous though it proved) that a turning point had occurred in the war. Many of the correspondents had contributed to this growing sense of optimism [**249**].

The wide array of letters from which extracts are published in this volume, many of which have not been read since their publication over a hundred years ago,[13] provides a focus upon the Ladysmith campaign. This was only one of several concerns at the outset of the war when Mafeking and Kimberley were also invested, and newspapers published letters from across the various fronts in South Africa. Extensive coverage occurred in provincial papers such as the *Somerset County Gazette,* with its series 'Our County's Share in the War', and the regular columns of letters in newspapers such as the *Blackburn Times, Leicester Chronicle* and *Rotherham Advertiser.* The Natal campaign, though, was a particular test of the British military system, engaging the services of colonial forces; the 'Indian contingent' fresh – in some cases – from laurels won on the north-west frontier; and subsequently home-based units, some of whom had seen colonial service, including veterans of Omdurman, but many of whom, whether serving on short-service enlistments with the colours or Reservists, were to experience their baptism of fire [**24**].

Brimming with self-confidence [**1**], soldiers soon encountered the devastating effects of modern firepower from smokeless, flat-trajectory, magazine rifles supported by long-range artillery. The sights [**17, 142**], sounds [**6, 142**] and stench [**174**] of a modern battlefield, particularly in the hot daytime conditions of Natal, where water was often scarce [**30, 84**], ensured a flow of anguished commentary, first from northern Natal and later from the relief force. Neither in the official despatches, nor the regimental histories nor the major accounts of the war is the writing so graphic as in the post-battle accounts of the soldiers involved. Soldiers were only too willing to recount their sights of men and horses wounded, killed, or blown apart by modern weaponry, the sounds of shellfire (and then conspicuous by its absence during the eight-hour armistice on 25

---

13   There are odd exceptions, notably V. Peach, *By Jingo! Letters from the Veldt* (Totnes: Totnes Community Archive, 1987).

February), the cries of the wounded and dying, and the smell of shells, dead bodies and enemy entrenchments [**210**]. The pre-war confidence derived from underestimating the enemy, despite the previous experience of the First Boer War (or Anglo-Transvaal War as it is now known),[14] and from recent epic victories (the storming of the heights of Dargai and the routing of the khalifa's army at Omdurman), soon dissolved. Veterans of the Tirah and Sudanese campaigns admitted that their previous experiences paled by comparison with fighting an enemy skilled in the use of modern weaponry [**85, 141**]. Similarly, reputations forged in these former triumphs now seemed eclipsed, at least in the opinion of some soldiers after the bayonet charge on Wagon Hill [**118**] or after enduring the carnage on Spion Kop [**144**].

Yet the battlefields of Natal had much deeper effects upon the psychology and values of the British soldier. The modern battlefield was a profound shock, particularly the task of crossing a fire zone swept by smokeless magazine rifles. Many of the surprises reflected reliance upon outmoded tactics and an abject lack of field intelligence,[15] compounded by Botha's tactics of withholding fire until the advancing British were well within range. Yet it was the inability to see an enemy, often entrenched with excellent fields of fire and crossfire, which caused massive frustration. Soldiers emerged from battles, complaining bitterly that they had never seen a Boer throughout the exchange of fire [**14, 65, 82, 83, 188**]. Even worse the gunners, apart from their naval compatriots, found themselves out-ranged by the Boer artillerists [**100, 101**] and although the shelling was found to have limited effects in causing casualties [**42**], it certainly depressed morale in the early engagements. Fundamentally, the combination of magazine rifle fire and long-range artillery thwarted the British soldiery in their desire to close with the enemy. This was not only a dimension of battle in which they felt that they could prevail (as the Lancers did at Elandslaagte) but it was also an integral assumption in their heroic-warrior ideal. The repeated criticisms of the Boers for their lack of 'pluck' [**57, 95, 100, 224**] reflected as much the primacy that the British army accorded to mounting an offensive, and seeking a decisive outcome through battle in colonial warfare,[16] as it did to any measured appreciation

---

14 There were some veterans of the previous war fighting in the South African War, including Sir Ian Hamilton, Major General Hector Macdonald, later commander of the Highland Brigade, and Sir Percival Marling VC.

15 Edward M. Spiers, 'Intelligence and Command in Britain's Small Colonial Wars of the 1890s', *Journal of Intelligence and National Security*, vol. 22, no. 5 (2007), pp. 661–81.

16 Sir Charles E. Callwell, *Small Wars: A tactical textbook for imperial soldiers*

of the limited Boer resources and their tactical aims.

Intensifying this sense of frustration were the costs, both physical and psychological, of fighting against a resourceful foe, able to fight from prepared positions, well armed and highly mobile. The most obvious cost lay in the heavy casualties incurred whenever the British mounted their offensives. These casualties, particularly those incurred at Colenso and Spion Kop, were much higher than the British army had recently suffered (even if the proportion of fatalities was higher at Isandlwana and Maiwand). Certain formations, like those of Hart at Colenso, and reckless deployments, like Long's artillery at Colenso, compounded the likelihood of casualties, and these formations incurred the wrath of surviving soldiers [67, 68, 79, 80]. Even in the victories of Talana Hill and Elandslaagte, British forces took heavy casualties in crossing fire zones and when these were followed by a mass surrender at Nicholson's Nek, the embarrassment was acute [34]. The spectacle of some 900 British soldiers surrendering was bad enough; the surrender after only seven and a half hours' fighting some 300 Boers, albeit with little hope of escape or relief, [35] was nothing less than a humiliation.[17] Almost certainly the events on 'Mournful Monday' stiffened the resolve to hold Ladysmith, where again the prospect of enduring a protracted siege contravened all the assumptions of British military thinking. In *The Soldier's Pocket Book*, distributed to all soldiers, Lord Wolseley, the commander-in-chief, never even referred to being besieged only to the 'defence of posts'. He urged commanders to 'show' resistance 'as long as [it] can be offered', and maintained that 'even at the last moment, if he still commands a disciplined body of men who are in good heart, he may perhaps hope to cut his way out and join his armies in the field'.[18]

In recounting such events soldiers were not merely describing sequences of events, even if they often wrote in narrative form, but they were also selective in their writing, highlighting episodes that illustrated their recent experiences. While these sometimes involved near escapes, examples of gallantry, the thirst for vengeance, and the loss of friends, they were often intended to make a point whether about the need to overcome the effects of a demanding climatic and topographical conditions [4, 199], or the formidable physical barriers north of the Tugela [99, 217] or the difficulties encountered in the field [209]. Similarly soldiers sought to inform their readers about the privations of the siege [162–5], the shared sacrifices of officers and men [19, 20, 193] and the continued support

---

(London: HMSO, 1896; reprinted, London: Greenhill Books, 1990), pp. 44, 57–68.
17 Amery, *The Times History*, vol. 2, p. 253.
18 General Viscount Wolseley, *The Soldiers' Pocket Book for Field Service* (London: Macmillan, 1886), pp. 302, 406.

for Buller despite the criticisms of him by the press [92, 214–17]. In so doing, they conveyed their own values, diverse experiences and impressions of fighting in Natal, namely, the sensation of charging the enemy [204], the predicament of the wounded on the field of battle, being conveyed from it, and then being treated in hospital [20], the feelings of prisoners moving into captivity [33–5], the demands upon the medical profession that extended long after the siege was over [238–9], the contributions of the chaplains in burying the dead and in negotiating with the enemy [47, 144], and the invaluable roles of the engineers and the other support services [37, 44, 74, 126, 130, 235]. All these accounts are selective, emphasising aspects of recent activity, possibly serving as an apologia for soldiers after a reverse or by prisoners of war. These soldiers were writing to people who cared about their actions and whose approval they wished to cultivate. They also tended to telescope events (and so accounts of the siege at the end, dwelling on the privations, have to be balanced by accounts from the outset). Soldiers often exaggerated numbers of the enemy (perhaps through ignorance, possibly scepticism of Boer reports but often probably, after camp or hospital gossip, to excuse reverses or mitigate losses) and, in their commentary, indulged in regimental rivalry [140, 145, 228, 246]. Yet these letters retain a lasting value by illustrating the feelings, values and attitudes of officers and men. They reflect, too, the prominence of the support staff, who were always important on colonial campaigns but who had even more significant duties during a siege, not least in bolstering morale.

After extensive experience in small colonial warfare the British army understood the importance of securing their lines of communication. The inhabitants of Ladysmith recognised that the siege had started not when the shelling from the Long Tom on Pepworth Hill began [27] but when the railway and telegraph were cut [37, 39]. For the next two months the railway remained the focus operationally as the Boers pushed south and then Buller's relief forces pressed northwards across the Mooi River and thence along the railway to Colenso. Just as the railway proved critical in the ability of Buller to assemble a massive preponderance of men and guns in a relatively short period of time, it also enabled him to bring an abundance of supplies forward to sustain his force in the field [102]. The railway also served to remove the wounded and prisoners from the front, and the reference to the treatment of wounded from Talana Hill and Elandslaagte at Wynberg hospital [22] demonstrated an early example of the British efforts to expand their support capacity. This small hospital of fifty beds, though located 8 miles (12.9 km) outside Cape Town, but close to the railway at Simonstown, was ideally situated near a forest of pine and gum trees, and was promptly expanded by utilising the 500 beds of a nearby barracks.[19] Improvisation was equally to the fore in the arrangements for the treatment of the growing number of sick and wounded at Intombi [**46, 182**] and for the treatment and removal of the wounded after the battle of Spion Kop [**143** and note 26].

Quite apart from the essential need to provide soldiers with best available medical treatment, both logistic support and communication contributed powerfully to the maintenance of morale on active service. The fragility of morale was not evident at the outset of the siege as few anticipated either the length of the siege to come or the horrors that it would involve. The range of the naval gunnery, the capacity to keep flying the balloon despite the enemy's rifle fire, the relative ineffectiveness of enemy shelling, the ability to play sports and mount the occasional sortie all boosted confidence. Yet morale would slump fairly quickly with complaints about boredom, tedium and the demoralisation after Buller's defeat at Colenso (chapter 2). In these circumstances, the ability to communicate with the relief forces by searchlight and heliograph [**94, 103**], pigeons [**184**] and messages smuggled out by black runners [**163–4**] boosted morale – not in the sense of being able to co-ordinate action with the relief force, which was precluded by the enfeebled state of the horses in Ladysmith, but primarily as a means of reassurance and an ability to bypass the Boer efforts to keep Ladysmith isolated and to intercept its communications.

Nevertheless, any sense of satisfaction appears to have been momentary in its effects. As the siege dragged on, with a mounting toll of sick and the introduction of rationing, soldiers became less and less positive in their mode of expression. If they still passed the decisive test of Wagon Hill, survivors were all too aware that this had been an exhausting and costly victory, and one that the enemy had contested fiercely [**106–20**]. Thereafter the letter-writers became increasingly introspective, obsessed with derisory rations, improvised cigarettes and the exorbitant costs of foods sold at auction. Probably the most instructive of all these letters is the testament to the grim squalor of life in the trenches [**180**]. Few memoirs and certainly no despatches would describe how the increasingly enfeebled soldiers spent long periods of time on duty over a period of four months, wearing the same kit, encrusted with the effects of diarrhoea, dysentery and fever, and encumbered by 150 pounds of ammunition round the waist, and how they suffered from festering sores caused by

---

19 'The Wounded at Wynberg', *The British Medical Journal*, (11 November 1899), p. 1380.

thorn-inflicted cuts, sleep deprivation amidst drenching thunder storms at night, and the sight of emaciated comrades unable to reach the latrines – 'the blood and slime running and leaving traces here and there and everywhere all the time'. Writing in such an unheroic style does not make the letter of this Gordon Highlander representative of feelings on the front-line, and the misery of wearing a kilt for four months doubtless intensified his own feelings, as he indicated, but the letter has a real feel of authenticity in its account of conditions at the front.

All sieges involve the risk of deteriorating morale as the period of investment lengthens and the conditions worsen. Ladysmith was actually the shortest of the three sieges (the siege of Mafeking lasted for 217 days and Kimberley, 124 days) but it contained the largest concentration of troops and suffered by far the largest number of fatalities (some 600 of which 510 died from enteric or dysentery). Doubtless the reliance upon the polluted water of the Klip River, and the dwindling stocks of food, contributed to the growing sense of malaise. After the siege ended, many asserted that Buller's relief force had only arrived just in time [227–8] and even if these claims contained an element of exaggeration (both food, including horses [244], and ammunition had been husbanded carefully),[20] there was no disputing the mounting toll of hospital admissions. Throughout the siege, some 10,688 patients had been admitted and the overcrowded facilities contained 1,996 patients on 1 March (708 of whom were suffering from enteric fever and 341 from dysentery).[21] While soldiers regretted the deaths of all their comrades, they felt particularly distressed about fatalities from disease [183].

Frustration was just as evident among the forces engaged in mounting the relief operation. There was no concealing the evidence of three withdrawals, of outranged field artillery [100, 150], and of ten guns lost at Colenso. In their correspondence, soldiers repeatedly claimed that the Boers must have suffered prodigious losses, even in one bizarre case

---

20   At the end of the siege the 18th Hussars still had 71 of their 288 horses remaining, Burnett, *The 18th Hussars in South Africa*, p. 75. On 1 March the artillery also had 42 rounds for 4.7-inch naval guns, 252 rounds for naval 12-pounders, 102 rounds for howitzers and 7,200 rounds for field artillery, 'Siege Statistics From Ladysmith', *Highland News*, 24 March 1900, p. 5. Had Buller failed for a fourth time to break through, the commissariat authorities, namely Colonel Edward Ward and his second-in-command Colonel J. Stoneman, reckoned that they could extend the starvation rations for another two or three weeks. Melton Prior, *Campaigns of a War Correspondent* (London: Edward Arnold, 1912), p. 305. White had planned to hold out until 1 April, Maurice and Grant, *History of the War in South Africa*, vol. 2, p. 578.
21   Maurice and Grant, *History of the War in South Africa*, vol. 2, pp. 655–6; 'Siege Statistics From Ladysmith', p. 5.

claiming that the British had had 'the best of the scrimmage' at Colenso
[**90**], and assumed that the absence of Boer corpses merely meant that
the enemy was particularly adept at removing its dead [**174**]. After the
shocking experience of Colenso such claims, possibly the product of
camp gossip, were clearly intended to excuse an outcome that no one had
expected. In mitigation, any Boer losses at Colenso had to have been the
product of artillery bombardments, and none of the soldiers knew how
ineffective their own artillery was in general, and how ineffective lyddite
was in particular. The rate and concentrated impact of Boer rifle fire also
gave the impression that the unseen foe was much more numerous than
he actually was. Finally, much of this confusion derived from the lack of
field intelligence, and the ineffectual reconnaissance, at Buller's disposal.
If it was unfortunate that all the Natalian intelligence officers were trapped
in Ladysmith, and that the Boers proved so adept at firing warning shots
at mounted scouts [**169**], the failure of Buller to gather intelligence
by other methods before launching his forces in frontal assaults was an
oversight that few of his soldiers appeared to grasp.

In praising Buller repeatedly, soldiers commended his personal bravery
and 'bull-dog tenacity' [**92, 216**], personal qualities that reflected the
enduring appeal of the heroic warrior ideal. These qualities, though,
were hardly sufficient to overcome the concentrated firepower of modern
weapons, especially when employed from carefully prepared positions.
Fighting on the defensive by a resourceful enemy, as the more astute
soldiers recognised [**86, 213**], had acquired advantages over the offensive
(a foretaste of what would happen in the First World War). Tactics had
to alter (as the Devons found to their advantage at Elandslaagte [**18**]),
but soldiers still emphasised the daunting challenges that Buller faced in
breeching the Tugela defences [**99, 143, 200, 216–17**], and his readiness
to manoeuvre and not waste lives [**92, 214**]. He would eventually find a
way to exploit his overwhelming advantage in numbers of men and guns,
largely by attacking the Boers across a broad front and by co-ordinating
artillery in support of advancing infantry. Once again Buller's men, aware
of the criticisms of him in the press [**217**], rallied to his defence. This
adulation, stretching as it did beyond the Devonians and the Riflemen
with whom Buller was most connected, and overcoming moments of
grumbling after Vaal Krantz [**147**], derived in part from the bonding
experience of soldiers under sustained stress [**148**]. Buller's injury at
Colenso underscored the fact that officers shared the risks of modern
war, and often became the casualties themselves. Officer–man relations
probably varied across the many units engaged, and Hart's tactics
understandably incurred a degree of censure from below [**68, 195**],

but soldiers were concerned about the high-casualty rates among their officers, helped stricken officers on the field, and grieved over the loss of particular commanders [19–20, 120, 132, 193].

If the letters are revealing on such issues, they also confirmed that the modern battlefield, where combat or preparation for combat was waged by night and day [192], was a hugely stressful experience. Climatic factors compounded these stresses when soldiers found themselves pinned to the veldt over many hours in broad daylight. Soldiers undoubtedly suffered from the combination of extreme heat and lack of water at Colenso [84–5], and if they found the heat less oppressive on Spion Kop, soldiers and particularly the wounded bemoaned the lack of water here and at Vaal Krantz [140–1, 156]. The frustrations of fighting a largely unseen enemy, compounded by a succession of reverses and reports of the enemy's abuse of the white flag and firing on ambulance wagons, clearly affected many soldiers. Letter-writers admitted that they were virtually out of control when they eventually managed to engage the enemy hand-to-hand, bayoneting Boers in the act of surrender [155, 203–4]. Just as remarkable is the candid description of what would now be described as post-traumatic stress syndrome among some of the unscathed survivors of Spion Kop, who broke down in the aftermath of that horrendous battle [139]. What the correspondence confirms is that smokeless magazine rifles and long-range artillery, if employed effectively, could have psychological as well as physical effects.

Of all these effects, the most sensitive concerned what contemporaries described as unsteadiness or 'funk'. Given all the stresses of contemporary battle – an unseen enemy, fire zones swept by magazine rifles, friendly fire incidents [6], miscommunication [34] and thwarted assaults [115, 193] – a loss of nerve whether by individuals [187] or collectively could ensue. Sometimes they resulted in humiliating surrenders, notably at Nicholson's Nek and Spion Kop (where some 200 men, mainly Lancashire Fusiliers after the loss of a high proportion of their officers, were induced by Boer white flags to surrender). Apart from the prisoners[22] and certain diarists, including Donald Macdonald of the *Melbourne Argus*, who referred to the 'excellent opportunity in Ladysmith of studying the physiology of funk',[23] only very candid letter-writers alluded to such matters [139].

In fact, there was little time to reflect on such matters in an army that regarded reverses as temporary incidents in the drive towards Ladysmith.

---

22 'A Blackburn Man at Pretoria', *Blackburn Times*, 14 April 1900, p. 3.
23 Macdonald, *How We Kept the Flag Flying*, p. 129; see also NAM, Acc. 1956-03-10, Lieutenant H. F. N. Jourdain, dairy, 29 January 1900; Pakenham, *Boer War*, p. 298; Baring Pemberton, *Battles of the Boer War*, p. 175; Downham, *Red Roses*, p. 113.

Buller, having recovered from his vacillation after Colenso, sustained the momentum of his operation, so giving his soldiers every opportunity to avenge themselves and deliver on their 'determination . . . to beat the Boers' [175]. As soon as Buller's movements achieved tactical successes, and secured the high ground south of the river, discipline, motivation and an overwhelming superiority in numbers and guns became decisive factors in probing for, and then exploiting, breeches in the Tugela defences. Attitudes towards the enemy remained a crucial motivating factor. In early letters from the front, disdain and dislike of the enemy were all too prevalent. Soldiers criticised the mistreatment of the Uitlanders and the ransacking of homesteads in northern Natal [3] and were hugely indignant over the misuse of the white flag and the firing on ambulance wagons and hospitals, even when it was reportedly in error [10, 14, 41, 87, 133]. While some acknowledged the marksmanship of the Boers, their advantages in the range and weight of their artillery and the accuracy of their gunners, and their bravery in the assault on Wagon Hill [100, 113], many soldiers, particularly in the relief force remained fiercely critical of an enemy that rarely ventured out of their trenches [100, 212]. Lacking any understanding of the history and culture of Boers in their treks, they found it incomprehensible that Boers should bring women and children into their trenches, hence the claims that the enemy were cowards, even 'savages' in their approach to war [212].

In making such assertions, soldiers were probably giving vent to personal feelings and not seeking to influence the debate about the war at home. They were concerned about press coverage of the war, not least the criticisms of Buller, and were certainly interested in press reports about themselves: after the relief, Private C. West, Army Service Corps, asked his mother to 'look out for the *Graphic* in which will appear a photograph which includes myself'.[24] At this time, though, soldiers were probably not so concerned about the anti-war, or as it was often dubbed, the pro-Boer movement at home. The soldiers in Ladysmith had been either in South Africa prior to the war or had come to Natal as part of the 'Indian contingent', and, if aware of the pro-Boer movement at home had hardly been able to follow its activities, as they had been besieged for four months. In writing home after their relief, several of these soldiers requested the dispatch of a newspaper from Britain: Corporal Symonds, RE, indicated that he was 'looking anxiously for a letter and newspaper from home', and Corporal Roberts, Gordon Highlanders, asked his

---

24 'Letters from the Front', *Poole, Parkstone and East Dorset Herald*, 29 March 1900, p. 5.

parents to 'Send another paper, also Rudyard Kipling's latest, if you can.'[25] Although soldiers initially had access to Natal's newspapers [2],[26] several yearned to read the British press: as Private Walter Rhodes, King's Royal Rifles, asked of his brother in Manchester, 'You might send the 'Evening Chronicle' now and then when there is anything special in.'[27] So concern that the pro-Boers were providing the enemy with support and encouragement, and thereby stiffening his resolve, which would become a source of deep resentment for soldiers at the front as the conflict evolved into a protracted guerrilla war,[28] was not a key concern at this stage.

As personal feelings, aspersions about the enemy almost certainly reflected frustrations with the unexpected nature of the war, the need to offer excuses for costly reverses or bitterly contested engagements like Wagon Hill [110, 114], and the fact that many combatants had not come into any contact with the enemy. 'I have not come in contact with any Boers yet', wrote George McDowell, who served with the Army Medical Department in Ladysmith throughout the siege,

> but I saw all the prisoners coming in from Elandslaagte. If I could form an opinion of their character from the expression on their faces my opinion would not be very favourable. They have a hideous expression on their countenances.[29]

Lieutenant Walter Macgregor, who talked with these prisoners after Elandslaagte, formed a very different opinion and commended their bravery in that battle (despite the infamous misuse of the white flag) [14]. The British who were taken prisoner after Talana Hill and on Nicholson's Nek confirmed that they had been treated well, especially the officers as they were transported to Pretoria [11, 33–4].[30] The armistice of 25

---

25 'A Crewkernian in Besieged Ladysmith. Whiskey at £25 a Bottle', *Somerset County Gazette*, 7 April 1900, p. 2; 'Lively Epistle From A Gordon Highlander', *Manchester Evening News*, 12 April 1900, p. 5. *Northern Whig (Belfast)*, 25 April 1900, p. 6; 'Soldiers' Letters', *Cheltenham Chronicle*, 19 May 1900, p. 6.
26 'Letter from an Irish Trooper', *Northern Whig (Belfast)*, 25 April 1900, p. 6; 'Soldiers' Letters', *Cheltenham Chronicle*, 19 May 1900, p. 3.
27 'Losing Count of Time', *Manchester Evening Chronicle*, 19 May 1900, p. 3.
28 Spiers, *The Victorian Soldier in Africa* (Manchester: Manchester University Press, 2004), pp. 172–3; Spiers, *Scottish Soldier and Empire*, pp. 193–4.
29 'The Relief of Ladysmith. The Hour of Dundonald's Entry', *Northern Whig (Belfast)*, 27 April 1900, p. 6.
30 Ironically, the fact that these letters were subject to censorship fostered doubts about how well the Boers were treating their prisoners. Louis Creswicke, *South Africa and the Transvaal War*, 6 vols. (Edinburgh; T. C. & E. C. Jack, 1900), vol. 2, pp. 49–50.

February on Hart's Hill, a foretaste of the Christmas truce in the trenches on the Western Front, was another occasion when enemies met and talked amiably, sharing the wish that the war would soon be over [**198**]. Father Collins, though, provided the most remarkable account of his meeting with several Boers, including General Botha, on the summit of Spion Kop. Here the general maintained that he wished to fight the war 'in a Christian way', with a full exchange of wounded, and all the Boers expressed anguish over the carnage on the summit, praised the bravery of the British, and reiterated their desire that this war should end [**144**].

Once again these were clearly personal feelings, probably shared by a minority of the soldiers, and like those who commended the military aptitude of the Boers, and reckoned thereby that the war would take longer than expected [**209, 213**], soldiers could hold such views and still wish to pursue the war vigorously to a decisive end. Soldiers wanted to prevail irrespective of whether they respected or demonised their enemy or cast them in stereotypical terms: 'The Boers', wrote a Lancer with Buller's force,

> are awfully clever, though they are both deceitful and treacherous. They never show themselves, but keep in their trenches and 'pot' at our Infantry as they advance, but they don't stop there when they see the bayonets.[31]

Although many assumed that the succession of victories in late February served as harbingers of an early end to the conflict, a young bugler, Charles Snow, 2nd Battalion, Somerset Light Infantry, wrote perceptively on the cusp of victory in the battle for the Tugela Heights:

> This great war is going to last a lot longer than they thought. The strength of the Boers is not known, and never will be.[32]

---

31 'With the Ladysmith Relief Force', *Poole, Parkstone and East Dorset Herald*, 15 March 1900, p. 8.
32 'The Somersets in a Hailstorm of Bullets', *Somerset County Gazette*, 31 March 1900, p. 2.

Select Bibliography

This is only a select bibliography of the sources used. For supporting references from collections held in the National Army Museum and The National Archives, as well as references to material in journal articles, readers should consult the notes. The primary sources were culled from the following newspapers and the annotations from the secondary sources listed.

Newspapers

Aberdeen Journal
Armagh Guardian
Auckland Times and Herald
Ayr Advertiser or West Country and
    Galloway Journal
Ayr Observer and Galloway Chronicle
Blackburn Times
Bolton Evening News
Bristol Observer
Bristol Times and Mirror
Carlisle Journal
Cheltenham Chronicle
Coventry Herald
Crediton Chronicle and North Devon
    Gazette
Derbyshire Advertiser
Devon and Somerset Weekly News
Devon Weekly Times
Dorset County Chronicle and
    Somersetshire Gazette
Dover Express
Dover Telegraph
Essex County Standard, West Suffolk

Gazette and Eastern Counties
    Advertiser
Evening Swindon Advertiser
Evening News (London)
Fermanagh Times
Free Press (Aberdeen)
Glasgow Evening News
Glasgow Herald
Gloucester Journal
Gloucestershire Chronicle
Gloucestershire Echo
Hamilton Advertiser
Hampshire Independent
Hampshire Observer
Highland News
Inverness Courier
Irish Times
Kent Standard
Kinross-shire Advertiser
Leeds Mercury
Leicester Chronicle
Leicester Daily Mercury
Lichfield Mercury

Liverpool Courier
Liverpool Daily Post
Liverpool Mercury
Manchester Evening Chronicle
Manchester Evening News
Manchester Guardian
Mid Devon and Newton Times
Middlesex County Times
Midland Counties Express
Morning Leader
Nairnshire Telegraph
Newcastle Daily Chronicle
North British Daily Mail
North Devon Herald
North Down Herald and County Down
    Independent
North Wales Guardian
Northern Whig (Belfast)
Poole, Parkstone and East Dorset Herald

Rotherham Advertiser
Rugby Advertiser
Sheffield Daily Telegraph
Somerset County Gazette
Somerset Standard
Southern Times
Strathearn Herald
Stroud Journal
Sunderland Herald and Daily Post
Surrey Times and County Express
Tamworth Herald
The (Stockport) Advertiser
The Times
Totnes Times
Warrington Guardian
West Briton and Cornwall Advertiser
Western Morning News
Western Times
Yorkshire Post

Secondary Sources

Aggett, W. J. P., *The Bloody Eleventh: History of the Devonshire Regiment*, vol. 2, (Exeter: Devonshire and Dorset Regiment, 1994)

Amery, L. (ed.), *The Times History of the War in South Africa 1899–1902*, 7 vols. (London: Sampson Low, Marston and Co. Ltd, 1900–9)

Anglesey, The Marquess of, *A History of the British Cavalry 1816–1919*, vol. 4 (London: Leo Cooper, 1986)

Atkins, J. B., *The Relief of Ladysmith* (London: Methuen, 1900)

Blake, Colonel Y. J. F., *A West Pointer with the Boers* (Boston: Angel Guardian Press, 1903)

Brooks, R., *The Long Arm of Empire: Naval brigades from the Crimea to the Boxer Rebellion* (London: Constable, 1999)

Burleigh, B., *The Natal Campaign* (London: Chapman and Hall, 1900)

Burne, Lieutenant C. R. N., *With the Naval Brigade in Natal 1899–1900* (London: Edward Arnold, 1902)

Burnett, Major C., *The 18th Hussars in South Africa: The records of a cavalry regiment during the Boer War 1899–1902* (Winchester: Warren & Son, 1905)

Carver, Field Marshal Lord, *The National Army Museum Book of the Boer War* (London: Pan Books, 2000)

Chalmers, A., *Bombardment of Ladysmith Anticipated: The diary of a siege* (Weltevreden Park: Covos-Day, 2000)

Changuion, L., *Silence of the Guns: The History of the Long Toms of the Anglo-Boer War* (Pretoria: Protea Book House, 2001)

Childs, L., *Ladysmith: The siege* (Barnsley: Leo Cooper, 1999)

Chisholm, R., *Ladysmith* (London: Osprey Publishing Ltd, 1979)

Churchill, W. S. *London to Ladysmith via Pretoria* (London: Longmans Green, 1900)

— *My Early Life: A roving commission* (London: Odhams Press, 1920)

Coetzer, O., *The Anglo-Boer War: The road to infamy 1899-1900. Colenso, Spioenkop, Vaalkrantz, Pieters, Buller and Warren* (London: Arms and Armour, 1996)

Craw, Miss Bella, *A Diary of the Siege of Ladysmith: A day-to-day account of a young woman resident in the town* (Ladysmith: Ladysmith Historical Society, 1970)

Creswicke, L., *South Africa and the Transvaal War*, 6 vols. (Edinburgh; T. C. & E. C. Jack, 1900)

Cunliffe, M., *The Royal Irish Fusiliers 1793–1950* (London: Oxford University Press, 1952)

De Wet, C.R., *Three Years War (October 1899–June 1902)* (London: Archibald Constable and Co. Ltd, 1903)

Downham, Lieutenant Colonel J., *Red Roses on the Veldt: Lancashire regiments in the Boer War, 1899–1902* (Lancaster: Carnegie Publishing, 2000)

Driver, Nurse Kate, *Experience of a Siege: A nurse looks back on Ladysmith* (Ladysmith: Ladysmith Historical Society, 'Diary The Siege of Ladysmith', No. 6, revised edition 1994)

Dundonald, Lieutenant General The Earl of, *My Army Life* (London: Edward Arnold, 1926)

Durand, Sir M., *Field Marshal Sir George White* (Edinburgh: William Blackwood & Sons, 1915)

Evans, M. Marix, *Encyclopedia of the Boer War* (Santa Barbara, CA: ABC-CLIO, 2000)

Gandhi, M.K., *An Autobiography* (London: Penguin Books, 2001)

Gardyne, Lieutenant Colonel A. D. Greenhill, *The Life of a Regiment: A History of the Gordon Highlanders*, vol. 3 (London: The Medici Society, 1939)

Gillings, K. *Battles of KwaZulu-Natal* (Durban: Art Publishers, nd.)

Gooch, J. (ed.), *The Boer War: Direction, experience and image* (London: Frank Cass, 2000)

Gore, Lieutenant Colonel St John (ed.), *The Green Horse in Ladysmith* (London: Sampson Low, Marston & Co., 1901)

Griffith, K., *Thank God We kept the Flag Flying: The siege and relief of Ladysmith 1899–1900* (London and New York: Viking Press, 1974)

Hunter, A., *Kitchener's Sword-arm: The life and campaigns of General Sir Archibald Hunter* (Staplehurst: Spellmount, 1996)

Jackson, T., *The Boer War* (London and Basingstoke: Channel 4 Books, 1999)

Jeans, Surgeon T. T. (ed.), *Naval Brigades in the South African War* (London: Sampson Low, Marston & Co. Ltd., 1902)

Jeffery, K., *Field Marshal Sir Henry Wilson* (Oxford: Oxford University Press, 2008)

Knight, I. Colenso 1899: *The Boer War in Natal* (Oxford: Osprey, 1985)

Kruger, R., *Goodbye Dolly Gray: The history of the Boer War* (London: New English Library, 1964)

Lee, J., *A Soldier's Life: General Sir Ian Hamilton 1853–1947* (London: Pan Books, 2001)

Macdonald, D., *How We Kept The Flag Flying: The story of the siege of Ladysmith* (London: Ward Lock & Co., 1900)

McHugh, R.J., *The Siege of Ladysmith* (London: Chapman & Hall, 1900)

Marden, Major A.W. and Captain & Adjutant W.P.E. Newbigging, *Rough Diary of the Doings of the 1st Battn. Manchester Regt. During the South African War, 1899 to 1902* (Manchester: John Heywood, 1904)

Maurice, Major General Sir F.B. and M.H. Grant, *History of the War in South Africa 1899–1902*, 4 vols. (London: Hurst & Blackett, 1906–10)

Nevinson, H.W., *Ladysmith: The diary of a siege* (London: Methuen & Co., 1900)

Pakenham, T., *The Boer War* (London: Weidenfeld & Nicolson, 1979)

Park, Liuetenant Colonel C. W., *Letters from Ladysmith* (Ladysmith: Ladysmith Historical Society, 1972)

Pemberton, W. Baring, *Battles of the Boer War* (London: Pan Books, 1964)

Powell, G., *Buller: A scapegoat?* (London: Leo Cooper, 1994)

Pretorius, F., *The Anglo-Boer War 1899–1902* (Cape Town: Struik Publishers, 1998)

— *Historical Dictionary of the Anglo-Boer War* (Lanham, MA and Plymouth, UK: Scarecrow Press, 2009)

Price, R., *An Imperial War and the British Working Class: Working-class attitudes and reactions to the Boer War 1899–1902* (London: Routledge & Kegan Paul, 1972)

Prior, M., *Campaigns of a War Correspondent* (London: Edward Arnold, 1912)

Reitz, D., *Commando: A Boer journal of the Boer War* (London: Faber & Faber, 1929)

Romer, Major C.F. and A.E. Mainwaring, *The Second Battalion Royal Dublin Fusiliers in the South African War with a Description of the Operations in the Aden Hinterland* (London: A.L. Humphreys, 1908)

Sharp, G., *The Siege of Ladysmith* (Cape Town: Purnell, 1976)

Sibbald, R., *The War Correspondents: The Boer War* (Stroud: Alan Sutton, 1993)

Spiers, E.M., *The Late Victorian Army 1868–1902* (Manchester: Manchester University Press 1992)

— *The Victorian Soldier in Africa* (Manchester: Manchester University Press, 2004)

— *The Scottish Soldier and Empire, 1854–1902* (Edinburgh: Edinburgh University Press, 2006)

Steevens, G.W., *From Capetown to Ladysmith: An unfinished record of the South African War* (Edinburgh: William Blackwood & Sons, 1900)

Theron, B., *Pretoria at War 1899–1900* (Pretoria: Protea Book House, 2000)

Todd, P. and D. Fordham, *Private Tucker's Boer War Diary: The Transvaal War of 1899, 1900, 1901 & 1902 with the Natal Field Forces* (London: Elm Tree Books, 1980)

Treves, F., *Tale of a Field Hospital* (London: Cassell, 1900)

Viljoen, General Ben, *My Reminiscences of the Anglo-Boer War* (London: Hood, Douglas & Howard, 1903)

Warwick, P. (ed.), *The South African War: The Anglo-Boer War 1899–1902* (London: Longman, 1980),

Watkins-Pitchford, H., *Besieged in Ladysmith; A letter to his wife written during the siege* (Pietermaritzburg: Shuter & Shooter, 1964)

Watson, W., *The Siege Diary of William Watson Oct. 1899–Feb. 1900* (Ladysmith: Ladysmith Historical Society, 'Diary The Siege of Ladysmith', No. 7, 1989)

Wilson, H.W., *With the Flag to Pretoria: A history of the Boer War of 1899–1900*, 2 vols. (London: Harmsworth Brothers, 1900–1)

Woods, F. (ed.), *Winston S. Churchill: War correspondent 1895–1900* (London: Brassey's, 1992)

Index